JALLIANWALA BAGH, 1919

Celebrating
30 Years of Publishing
in India

JALLIANWALA BAGH, 1919

THE REAL STORY

KISHWAR DESAI

HarperCollins *Publishers* India

First published in 2018

This edition published in India by HarperCollins *Publishers* 2023
4th Floor, Tower A, Building No. 10, Phase II, DLF Cyber City,
Gurugram, Haryana –122002
www.harpercollins.co.in

2 4 6 8 10 9 7 5 3 1

Copyright © Kishwar Desai 2018, 2023

P-ISBN: 978-93-5629-475-2
E-ISBN: 978-93-5629-476-9

The views and opinions expressed in this book are the author's own and the facts are as reported by her, and the publishers are not in any way liable for the same.

Kishwar Desai asserts the moral right
to be identified as the author of this work.

All rights reserved. No part of this publication may be reproduced, stored in a retrieval system, or transmitted, in any form or by any means, electronic, mechanical, photocopying, recording or otherwise, without the prior permission of the publishers.

Typeset by Jojy Philip, New Delhi - 110015

Printed and bound at
Replika Press Pvt. Ltd.

This book is produced from independently certified FSC® paper to ensure responsible forest management.

For my grandmother, Leelavati 'Lily' Khanna, a young girl in April 1919, who lived at Dhab Khatikan, just a few lanes away from Jallianwala Bagh, close enough to hear the bullets being fired and the cries of the wounded and dying.

For all those, including my own relations, who were present at the Bagh when General Dyer launched his murderous attack… and for the silence they were forced to maintain during that reign of terror.

Contents

Introduction   ix

1. A State of War   1
   Baisakhi, 13 April 1919, Amritsar
2. A Gift of Fortune   41
3. Counting the Corpses   88
4. The Fancy Punishments   106
5. Fascist, Racist or Both?   184
6. 'You Cannot Kill a Tiger Gently'   210

Appendix I   239
Lala Lajpat Rai on 'Imperialism Run Amuck'

Appendix II   244
Rabindranath Tagore's Protest

Maps   246

Acknowledgements   257

About the Author   259

Introduction

Benevolent Imperialism is like a caged lion. However, you may play with it so long as it is caged or under the spell of a master-tamer; the moment it gets out of control it is bound to behave in conformity with its real nature. The atrocities perpetuated at Amritsar have proved that Imperialism run mad is more dangerous, more vindictive, more inhuman, than a frenzied uncontrollable mob.

—Lala Lajpat Rai, 5 June 1920[1]

Justice Rankin, cross-examining General Dyer about his shooting an unarmed crowd at Jallianwala Bagh: You thought it necessary to take action on the analogy of a state of war?

Dyer: Quite so. I looked upon these people who had rebelled as enemies of the Crown.

Sir C.L. Setalvad, cross-examining Dyer: Did it occur to you that you were really doing great disservice by driving discontent?

Dyer: No. I thought it was my duty to do it... and any man, any reasonable being with a sense of justice, would see that I was doing a merciful act, and that they ought to be thankful to me for doing it.

---

1. Lala Lajpat Rai, foreword to *An Imaginary Rebellion and How it Was Suppressed* by Pandit Pearay Mohan, vol. 1 (Lahore: Khosla Bros., 1920; Gyan Publishing House, 1999), p. 3. Citations refer to the Gyan edition.

Setalvad: But did this aspect (that the killings would make the people more 'rebellious' and 'discontented') of the matter strike you?
Dyer: Never. I thought it would do a jolly lot of good to the people.

(Extracts from the Hunter Committee Report on the Punjab Disorders. Evidence recorded on 19 November 1919, Lahore.)

One hundred years later, the Jallianwala Bagh massacre remains the most heartbreaking episode in the history of the Indian freedom struggle. Brigadier General Dyer deliberately murdered more than one thousand fellow British subjects—all Indians, including little children—and called it a 'merciful act'.

Not only did Dyer think the cold-blooded murders would 'do a jolly lot of good to the people', he even had widespread support among the British. Instead of condemning him, most of his compatriots commended him for saving the Empire as the massacre was thought essential to prevent another 1857-type mutiny. Prior to the killings at Jallianwala Bagh, there had been signs of increasing unrest in Punjab. These signs were being interpreted as sedition, even though the causes of the unrest were varied. Indeed, it is impossible to understand what happened on 13 April 1919, without an examination of the barbarism unleashed in Punjab under the regime of the then Lieutenant Governor Sir Michael O'Dwyer, to suppress the so-called rebellion. The 'rebellion' in retrospect was nothing more than the first signs of colonised people demanding equal rights. But it was constantly argued that Indians were incapable of self-rule and needed the British to govern them.

The scale of oppression in Punjab, and especially Amritsar, just before and after the Jallianwala Bagh killings was extreme. A deeply racist regime was in operation, no matter what kind of garb was put upon it, or the kind of defence made for it.

The murder of more than a thousand innocents at Jallianwala Bagh was not an isolated event. This was not the knee-jerk reaction of a deranged General. Dyer fired for ten minutes upon a peaceful crowd gathered to protest the Anarchical and Revolutionary Crimes Act, 1919 (usually referred to simply as the Rowlatt Act) and continued to fire upon them even as they tried to escape. This incident was squarely a part of a systemic failure of governance during which people were exploited and mistreated. When they, tormented beyond endurance, reacted occasionally with violence, they were sadistically suppressed, their rights snatched away by the Raj.

One wonders why the true events in the Punjab of that time have been given so little prominence in popular historical literature and cinema. The commonly held narrative runs as follows: people gathered at the Bagh on 13 April 1919 for an anti-Rowlatt Act meeting; many amongst them were outsiders who had come to Amritsar for the Baisakhi festival. Dyer decided they had broken the law, gathered his troops and fired upon them. Hundreds died during the firing, and many jumped into a well at the Bagh while trying to escape the bullets. The dead included women and children.

This basic narrative is correct but there are some fallacies. To begin with, the meeting was attended mainly by residents of Amritsar. Due to the restrictions prevalent at the time, it would have been difficult for large numbers of outsiders to enter the old walled city. Even at the time, it was estimated that no more than 25 per cent were from outside. No one jumped into the well—they fell in by accident while fleeing the shooting, as it did not have a rim around it. And it is very likely that the massacre was a carefully planned one, not spontaneous as has often been made out. In all likelihood, no women were present.

What I have tried to do in this book is to piece together what actually happened on 13 April 1919 as well as before and after, using mostly the words of the survivors and recorded statements describing those terrifying events. Also, as far as possible, I have used Indian sources and viewpoints because for far too long (with a few exceptions), this narrative has been told by Western historians.

This book is a homage to the people of Punjab who, one hundred years ago, were humiliated, tortured and killed under the pretext of martial law. The period ranged from two months in some districts to over four months in others.

During this reign of terror, people were whipped, bombed, incarcerated, forced to crawl, starved, beaten, caged—and even summarily executed. However, the combined atrocities led to a turning point in the freedom struggle; it brought all the anti-British forces together for the first time. Not only were Hindus and Muslims seen together, joining hands against the British, the impact of the Jallianwala Bagh massacre spread through Punjab—from Amritsar to Lahore to Gujranwala—and to other places across India.

The events before the massacre also demonstrate the emerging importance of Punjab in the freedom struggle. These were still early years and there was no collective effort against the British. In terms of political leadership, this narrative is dominated by a few leaders working in their individual capacities and not as leaders of the Congress Party, which was the dominant party at the time. It was Mohandas Karamchand Gandhi, then not yet a member of the Congress Party, who was responsible for organising the people by deploying the tool of protest he termed 'satyagraha', against the Rowlatt Act. The massacre on 19 April was part of a policy of oppression unleashed by O'Dwyer against the frequent 'hartals' or the Satyagraha Movement.

The question is, where did the widely accepted narrative of Jallianwala Bagh originate from, when the reality was so much more complex? How is it possible that so many of us are unaware that aeroplanes were called in to bombard Amritsar and Gujranwala (now in Pakistan) and machine guns were turned on protesters?

Hundreds of people, including schoolboys, were publicly whipped in Amritsar and Lahore for small transgressions such as walking two abreast on a pavement or not salaaming a British officer. In Kasur (now in Pakistan), people were held in open cages.

In fact, the civil administration of Punjab had already declared Amritsar a war zone, when the massacre took place at Jallianwala Bagh, and regarded the residents as their enemies. All of this paints the massacre in a completely different light.

This book begins at the point when Amritsar was declared a war zone around 11 April, because the reader must understand the claustrophobic conditions which the residents of Amritsar were living in at the time. If we obliterate the sacrifice of those who were at the Jallianwala Bagh (by assuming that they were there, accidentally, for the Baisakhi festival), we also continue to disregard the humiliations that the survivors had to endure. Some of those frightful conditions were already in place before the mass murder took place.

Knowing the context also helps us understand more clearly the heroism and courage of those who gathered that evening at Jallianwala Bagh. They knew that they could be killed at any moment—yet, they had faith that the British would respect their rights as citizens to attend a public meeting. That faith was to be forever lost.

Has this amnesia been deliberate, and did the people of Punjab simply forget in order to move on (as happened three decades later with the Partition)? Or was the attempt to rewrite history, by focussing on one event and just one individual, i.e. Dyer, a political move?

To some extent this might appear obvious. The supporters of Dyer (who was later forced to resign from the army) always suspected that he had been made a scapegoat by the British government. The Raj had wanted him to execute a powerful punishment so that the 'natives' would not rebel again. However, they subsequently withdrew their support of him, when the horror of his act became a blot on the 'fair' and 'just' British name. Everyone, from Viceroy Chelmsford, to the Secretary of State, Edwin Montagu, would claim that they knew very little of what Dyer actually did. Historians have filled reams of paper psychoanalysing Dyer in order to link some previous misdemeanour or mental disability to the massacre. The entirety of the blame was shifted onto him. A maverick and a black sheep, he became symbolic of the indiscretions of the Raj. By punishing him, the Raj washed its hands of the Punjab 'disorders'.

It would have suited the British perfectly to lay the blame at Dyer's door. They would not have wanted to reveal what is now obvious as I write this book: that the regime of Lieutenant Governor Sir O'Dwyer was racist and cruel, and apparently adept at manipulating 'Orientals'. Of course, he was no different from many others who were constantly resisting reforms, could not tolerate the induction of Indians into the administration and felt that only the British could rule India—and that, too, with force.

Ostensibly, the Raj defended the reprisals against Indian subjects between April and August 1919 by claiming that the unrest in Punjab was due to a larger conspiracy to overthrow the government, possibly hatched in Afghanistan, by the enemies of the British. This was not accepted by the Hunter Committee, which was set up to investigate the Punjab Disorders in 1919. I do not examine that hypothesis in the book as the events themselves are enough to prove that the trigger for the unrest lay elsewhere.

Many British and Indian historians may have made Dyer the main protagonist, the villain, of what happened in Amritsar. However, I agree with Mahatma Gandhi's view that Dyer was only symptomatic of what was happening in Punjab. He was not the only actor, as there were many others like him, who were encouraged by O'Dwyer. One such personage was the officer commanding Lahore, Lieutenant Colonel Frank Johnson, who imposed close to sixty-four bizarre and racist orders of martial law upon the unfortunate people of Lahore. A few instances of these orders are: people had to surrender all means of transport, had to salaam British officers in a particular manner, and school- and college-going children were expelled or forced to march in the hot sun, sometimes several times a day.

Martial law enabled many punishments, including the incarceration of hundreds of innocent people without charge, and, of course, the infamous 'crawling order' imposed by Dyer in Amritsar, in which respectable householders were expected to crawl through a 150 yard lane.

The orders did not apply to Europeans. These were primarily meant to frighten the population of Punjab and to teach them a lesson, because they had risen, and were guilty of sedition, against the King.

I also consider what happened in other states, which were similarly affected during the anti-Rowlatt Act protests. Indeed, we barely remember that violence had broken out in Delhi, Ahmedabad and Bombay—yet there was no incident of 'frightfulness' as at Jallianwala Bagh. (Churchill had used this word during the debates over Dyer's fate in the UK Parliament.)

The British violence in various Indian cities (after Gandhi's arrest) is referred to by many British authors, but only to justify it as the counter-violence used against protesters (who were largely unarmed). The crowd was unruly, they say, and provoked the police and the army.

The truth was that the world had changed dramatically by 1919. This was particularly evident in Punjab, where thousands of soldiers had returned after fighting for Britain and its allies' freedom at a huge personal cost. Instead of finding liberty at home, they faced bullets and repression. It was only natural that some of them should decide to strike back.

One of the saddest discoveries for me was coming across instance upon instance of how close-knit the Hindu and Muslim communities had become during the satyagraha called by Mahatma Gandhi and how the British made every effort to force them apart. The success of Gandhi's anti-Rowlatt Act protest was that it was a people's movement. Anyone could participate in it simply by refusing to work and going on strike or hartal. Gandhi had also encouraged the Khilafat Movement, which had been launched by a group of Indian Muslims to pressurise the British to not abolish the Ottoman Caliphate. This also provided an impetus for the two communities to come together. For the first time Muslims and Hindus drank from the same cup, attended meetings in mosques and temples equally, and showed their enthusiastic support for each other. The British found this unnerving.

In Lahore, where the Badshahi Mosque was used for joint community meetings, all get-togethers were banned. In Gujranwala, a dead calf was found near a temple and pork in a mosque. These were correctly interpreted as efforts by the police to drive a wedge between the two communities and break their united front. However, ultimately, fraternisation was dented, following large-scale arrests. Efforts were made to get witnesses from each community to indict members of the other. The savagery of martial law, the floggings, incarcerations and humiliations, finally wiped out the spirit of burgeoning bonhomie that Gandhi had awakened.

Going through the various reports of that period, there is little doubt that as the seeds of the Independence movement were sowed in the aftermath of the Jallianwala Bagh massacre, so might the seeds of Partition have been sown during the period of martial law.

The Jallianwala Bagh massacre and the events thereafter had a major influence on the freedom movement in India. The anti-Rowlatt Act agitation was one in which Gandhi had taken the lead, and the Congress Party was not really involved, though individual members like Dr Saifuddin Kitchlew took it upon themselves to organise rallies in Amritsar and later call for hartal. It was only once the details of the massacre and other atrocities being inflicted on the people began to be known that leaders of the Congress Party came together and joined the investigation for the truth. Pandit Madan Mohan Malaviya, at first a member of the Imperial Legislative Council, and Pandit Motilal Nehru, a member of the United Provinces Legislative Council, along with Gandhi, C.R. Das, Abbas Tayabji, M.R. Jayakar and K. Santanam (all of whom were barristers-at-law) formed the Punjab Sub-Committee, Indian National Congress (INC), which inquired into the 1919 Punjab Disorders. They interviewed witnesses and survivors in different parts of Punjab and it is their dedication that brings the voices of ordinary people to us across a hundred-year divide.

Their report also contained photographs, some of which are reproduced in this book. Especially poignant are the pictures of young victims who were wounded during the firing at Jallianwala Bagh, or the bombing at Gujranwala. It is impossible not to be moved when gazing at the photograph of an eleven-year-old who was charged for being an enemy of the King, or another who was shot dead for being present at a meeting. These are forgotten heroes whose lives ended before they had even begun.

The work of the INC Committee is also crucial because the Disorders Inquiry Committee (formed by the government and widely known as the Hunter Committee) paid little heed to Indian victims and witnesses. Many of the Indian leaders were in jail, and could not be called upon to testify. When they were released, Pandit Madan Mohan Malaviya sent a telegram stating that they should be interviewed, but the Committee rejected the request. Despite lengthy arguments by Pandit Madan Mohan Malaviya, the Hunter Committee was formed with fewer Indian members than British members. They went on to produce what was called the Majority Report and the Minority Report. The Majority Report followed what was the official version, while the conclusions of the Minority Report were at some variance. There was reportedly some strain between the white and non-white members of the committee.

The British Secretary of State, Edwin Montagu, must be credited with the formation of the Hunter Committee on 14 October 1919. Ironically, its revelations probably caused the end of his career and the end of the Liberal Party as the principal alternative party of the government in Britain. The President of the Committee was Lord Hunter, a former Solicitor General of Scotland. Among the other white members were Justice G.C. Rankin; W.F. Rice, Additional Secretary, Government of India, Home Department; Major General Sir George Barrow, Commander of the Peshawar Division; and Thomas Smith, Member of the Legislative Council of the Lieutenant Governor of the United Provinces. The non-white members were Pandit Jagat Narayan, Member of the Legislative Council of the Lieutenant Governor of the United Provinces; Sir Chimanlal Setalvad, Advocate of the High Court, Bombay; and Sardar Sahibzada Sultan Ahmed Khan, barrister-at-law, Member for Appeals, Gwalior State.

I have relied heavily on both the Majority and Minority Reports to provide the official versions; I have also relied upon them for descriptions of the cross-examination of Dyer, O'Dwyer and others who created such a tragic situation in Punjab. I have also quoted from some excellent books on the subject such as Nigel Collett's *The Butcher of Amritsar* and *The Rediscovery of India* by Meghnad Desai.[2] It is the constant mining for information by writers such as these that

---

2. Nigel Collett, *The Butcher of Amritsar: Brigadier General Reginald Dyer* (London: Hambledon and London, 2005); Meghnad Desai, *The Rediscovery of India* (Penguin Random House India Pvt. Ltd., 2009).

has facilitated a progressively deeper understanding of what happened a hundred years ago in Amritsar.

Throughout the writing of this book I could hear the cries of those hundreds, as they lay dying at Jallianwala Bagh, that sultry evening in April—deprived of water, medicine, help. These are voices I will carry with me forever, along with the sound of the whiplash across the back of young schoolboys as they begged for mercy. I will also carry the agony of the women who were trapped at home, without electricity or water, too afraid to step out to get help for their loved ones.

With the writing of this book, my world shifted dramatically. There is no doubt that history belongs primarily to the victor, but only as long as we allow it. The truth cannot remain hidden for all time.

Delhi   KISHWAR DESAI
April 2018

1

A State of War

Baisakhi, 13 April 1919, Amritsar

> The troops have orders to restore order in Amritsar, and to use all the force necessary. No gatherings of persons, no procession of any sort will be allowed. All the gatherings will be fired on. Any person leaving the city, or persons gathering in groups of more than four, will be fired on. Respectable persons should keep indoors until order is restored.
>
> Proclamation as heard by the people of Amritsar on 11 April 1919.
>
> —Report of the Commissioners Appointed by the Punjab Sub-Committee of the Indian National Congress.[1]

Two days before the festival of Baisakhi, the city of Amritsar had been declared a war zone by the British administration in Punjab. The mood was sombre. Fear was writ large on many faces. People felt trapped inside the city, as there was a guard at almost every exit. Rich or poor, it was impossible for them to leave without written permission, and in the strained circumstances, such permission was unlikely to be forthcoming.

---

1. Report of the Commissioners Appointed by the Punjab Sub-Committee of the Indian National Congress, Volume II, pp. 32, 54, statements 19, 5. Referred to as INC Report hereafter.

Since the satyagraha against the Rowlatt Acts was still ongoing, the resulting hartal meant that food and daily supplies were becoming scarce. News from the outside world barely trickled in and censorship disallowed any news from leaking out.

Even those who considered themselves close to the British rulers felt the sudden icing up of the relationship. The British were upset and they had to express their anger in every way possible. The feelings of the people of Amritsar were irrelevant. If at any time they had imagined that they could get political and social equality, now all they experienced was rejection. Indians were being clearly shown that they were a subject race. If they tried to resist or fight against the changed environment or assault a European, the full might of the British Empire would be brought to bear against them. The army had been called in and there were daily threats that the city would be bombed. The remains of buildings, still smouldering in the aftermath of the recent riots and shootings, bore the scars of a bloody battle.

On the morning of Baisakhi, Sunday, 13 April, the old walled city was unnaturally tense. Those who had come from neighbouring villages and towns expecting a colourful, festive celebration had to struggle through the twelve city gates. Guards posted at some of the entrances and exits checked their luggage for lathis or any other weapons. The violent incidents of 10 April continued to be talked about and there were apprehensions of impending reprisals—reinforced by the heavy presence of the army. Memories of turbulence were alive everywhere.

Just outside the Hall Gate of the old city was the railway bridge, where on 10 April, protesting residents of Amritsar had been wounded and killed. They had been trying to cross the Rubicon which divided the ordinary people of Amritsar from the Civil Lines and cantonment area. On the other side of the bridge was where the white sahibs, and more specifically, the British Deputy Commissioner, lived. The unarmed protestors sought desperately to meet him.

The old city, on this side of the bridge, with around 160,000 residents, was congested and criss-crossed by narrow lanes, including the area that contained the famed Golden Temple. This was in sharp contrast to the large well-planned bungalows, surrounded by broad roads and gardens, which lay on the other side of the bridge. The balance of power between the 'natives' and their rulers was maintained by this sharp distancing. Most British officers and their families lived in the cantonment area; however, some Europeans had set up thriving businesses and banks in the old city, recognising its strategic commercial importance.

Amritsar, at the turn of the twentieth century, was a prosperous trading centre for commodities and a textile manufacturing hub as well. It was close enough to the capital of Punjab—Lahore—and lay on the trade route between Afghanistan, Kashmir and Delhi, which explained its highly diverse population of Hindus, Muslims and, of course, Sikhs.

The presence of the Golden Temple drew pilgrims from all over—Baisakhi was one of the most significant Sikh festivals. This was the day when the Khalsa sect (or the sect of the Pure) had been created in 1699 by Guru Gobind Singh, and the Sikhs were given their distinct identity, including the tradition of maintaining long hair. The day was usually celebrated by the Sikhs with a visit to the Golden Temple. A cattle fair would be held at around the same time, and a joyous atmosphere would prevail throughout the city.

But this Baisakhi, following the troubles on 10 April, was already looking grim.

To prevent any further rebellion, soldiers bearing rifles had been placed all along the street, right down to the city centre near the half-burnt Town Hall, which had been attacked on 10 April; its jagged skeleton of charred wood gaped at passersby.

The central lane connecting Hall Gate to the Golden Temple also had debris strewn around. Apart from the Town

Hall, the facade of the Chartered Bank lay shattered and, at the other end, the Alliance Bank and the National Bank had been reduced to cinders, as were some other buildings in the area. People had to walk around the shattered remains. At least three British bank managers had been burnt and murdered in retaliation for the killings of Indians at the railway bridge on 10 April. One British soldier and a railway employee were beaten to death outside the Hall Gate.

The telegraph exchange building was attacked by the protestors and the telephone system of the city was cut off. In two other incidents, one British woman missionary was brutally assaulted, and a woman doctor had to hide from an angry crowd. In all, five Europeans and possibly about twenty Indians were murdered in the attacks and counter-attacks. As always, since the Europeans were precisely named in official reports and the Indians were neither counted nor mentioned by name or profession, it was difficult to ascertain the exact number of Indians who had died.

All the violence had taken place within a radius of about one mile, at a short distance from the Golden Temple.

The assault on a group of unarmed Indians on 10 April by the police and the army was seen as the catalyst for subsequent troubles. All that the group had wanted was to plead with Miles Irving, the Deputy Commissioner of Amritsar, for the release of their jailed leaders, Dr Saifuddin Kitchlew and Dr Satya Pal, both respected residents of the city. The two had been tricked into attending a 'meeting' at around 10 a.m. on 10 April at Irving's residence and had been whisked away to be jailed in Dharamshala.

Kitchlew (32), a lawyer, and Satya Pal (34), a doctor, had both been politically active for a while. They were inspired by Mohandas Karamchand Gandhi, at the time a 49-year-old lawyer and activist who had practised non-violent protest in South Africa before returning to India. He had begun the

Satyagraha Movement independently—he was not yet a leader with the Congress Party, which had been founded around 34 years earlier. The Congress Party leadership at the time was more interested in the idea of Home Rule.

Gandhi started his satyagraha or 'soul force' movement in a small way—by publishing proscribed literature and distributing it: the laws were to be broken but peacefully. He then decided to organise protests against the proposed Rowlatt Acts, which he and many others considered to be draconian. There were two bills, out of which the Criminal Law (Emergency Powers) Bill was considered the worse of the two. The protest was to be organised by Satyagraha Sabhas, for which all participants had to take the following oath:

> Being conscientiously of (the) opinion that the Bills known as the Indian Criminal Law (Amendment) Bill No. 1 of 1919, and No. 2 of 1919 are unjust, subversive of the principle of liberty and justice and destructive of the elementary rights of individuals on which safety of the community as a whole and the State itself is based, we solemnly affirm that, in the event of these Bills becoming law, we shall refuse civilly to obey these laws and such other laws as a committee, to be hereafter appointed, may think fit, and we further affirm that in the struggle we will faithfully follow (the) truth, and refrain from violence of life, person or property.[2]

The non-violent protests were to take the form of a hartal, that is, the general closing of shops, and suspension of all work, accompanied by fasting, public mourning and prayers, and other religious observances and public meetings.

Journalists like Benjamin Guy Horniman (who was based in Bombay, and was later externed to Britain for his frank coverage of the disturbances in Punjab and their severe repression)

---

2. Benjamin Guy Horniman, *Amritsar and Our Duty To India* (London: T. Fisher Unwin Ltd., 1920), p. 74.

reported an extraordinary response from the public to this call from Gandhi. (While the Indian National Congress was not officially part of this protest at the time, individual members were supporting it.) In Bombay, Horniman noted that ordinary people who had never taken part in politics felt encouraged to do so.

> In the city of Bombay...about a hundred thousand people opened the day by going to the sea shore and taking part in a purifying immersion in the sea. They then marched in processions to various temples and mosques, gathering numbers as they went, and held public prayers. No distinctions of creed were recognised. Hindus were admitted freely to the Mohammedan mosques and not only prayed but spoke to the congregations. Moslems were as freely admitted to the precincts of Hindu temples. This breaking down of religious barriers was unheard of before and almost incredible to those who had not seen it. It set the seal of approval of the whole population on the Hindu–Moslem entente, which the necessity for unity in the face of oppression of the whole people had brought about.[3]

Thus it was that at Amritsar, Kitchlew, a Muslim, and Satya Pal, a Hindu, took the satyagraha oath. The meetings organised by them to decry the Rowlatt Acts, and to propose satyagraha, were attended by all communities. Kitchlew, a good-looking and energetic Kashmiri, who had studied law at Cambridge and later at the Munster University in Berlin, was on the radar of the British. This was partly because Amritsar's Deputy Commissioner, Miles Irving, who had been posted there recently, in February, was nervous about the increasingly well-attended political meetings taking place in various parts of the city. He was particularly concerned that the well-spoken Kitchlew had a lot of influence in Amritsar, and felt he should

---

3. Op. cit., p. 77.

be prevented from organising any further meetings.[4]

Besides the efforts of Kitchlew and Satya Pal—who was a Lieutenant in the Indian Medical Service—the rallies proposed by Gandhi in Punjab in early April were also unwelcome for the British administration, particularly the Lieutenant Governor of Punjab, Sir Michael O'Dwyer.

O'Dwyer, who had been the Lieutenant Governor since 1913, was due to retire shortly. He did not want his reign to be disrupted. He was that rare breed, an Irishman without any sympathy for the Indian freedom struggle. Having begun his career in Lahore in 1885, he was to end it there over three decades later, at the top of his profession. He wanted to leave behind an unblemished record as a tough administrator. Over the years, he had ruthlessly uprooted all suspected ringleaders of rebellions and saw himself as someone who understood the 'Orientals' and their need to be ruled by force.

Raizada Bhagat Ram, a barrister based in Jalandhar, had met O'Dwyer sometime around 7 April. He noted that O'Dwyer had expressed his 'strong disapproval' of the ongoing hartal in different cities across Punjab, as also for Gandhi's satyagraha.

> After the meeting (of the Punjab Legislative Council) I met the Lieutenant-Governor in the drawing room. He asked me what sort of a hartal we had at Jullundur. I replied it was a complete hartal and there was no disturbance. Sir M O'Dwyer asked me what I attributed it to. I answered, 'To my mind it was due to the Soul-force of Mr Gandhi.' On this Sir Michael raised his fist and said, 'Raizada Sahib, remember there is another force greater than Gandhi's Soul-force.[5]

---

4. F.Z. Kitchlew, *Freedom Fighter: The Story of Dr. Saifuddin Kitchlew* (West Sussex: New Horizon, 1979), pp. 18–19.

5. INC Report (Bombay, 1920), p. 44, statement 650.

To Bhagat Ram this undoubtedly indicated that O'Dwyer would soon act against those organising the satyagraha.

O'Dwyer was not alone. Most British residents of Punjab found the hartals an enormous irritant. Not only did they unite the Hindu and Muslim communities against their common foe, the British, they were also well organised. In Amritsar the hartals had been very successful, and peaceful. A meeting on 30 March, at Jallianwala Bagh, had been attended by '30,000 to 35,000', so the numbers were growing. Kitchlew said right at the end of the speech, on that day: '... we will ever be prepared to sacrifice personal over national interests. The message of Mahatma Gandhi has been read to you. All countrymen should come prepared for resistance. This does not mean that this sacred town or country should be flooded with blood. The resistance should be a passive one. Be ready to act according to your conscience, though this may send you to jail, or bring an order of internment on you.'[6] He asked everyone to go in peace and not use harsh words.

Satya Pal had already been prohibited from speaking to the public on 29 March and now Kitchlew was served the same orders. The order dated 3 April said that: '...he shall until further orders (a) remain and reside within the municipal limits of Amritsar city (b) refrain from communicating either directly or indirectly with the press and (c) refrain from convening or attending or addressing in writing or otherwise any public meeting.'[7]

Despite this restriction on two important leaders, the meeting on 6 April was even larger. Presided over by another Muslim leader of the city, Dr Badrul Islam Khan, over 50,000 attended and a resolution was passed that the restrictions on Satya Pal and Kitchlew be lifted as 'the only fault found with

---

6. INC Report, p. 44, statement 650.
7. INC Report, p. 46.

them is that they informed all of us of the real object of the Rowlatt Act.'

Ram Naumi, a Hindu festival celebrating the birth of Lord Ram, fell on 9 April. 'The leaders (in Amritsar) had decided that there should be complete fraternisation between Hindus and Muhammadans on that occasion.' Ram Naumi was celebrated with enthusiasm, but it undoubtedly got a larger significance this time due to the Muslim participation. Several bands played on the day and Kitchlew and Satya Pal received a 'great ovation' from the procession as it went past. The Deputy Commissioner, despite his fears, was acknowledged gracefully as the bands struck up 'God Save the King' upon approaching him. While there was no incident, some of the participants in the procession wore the uniforms of Turkish soldiers and clapped—which was seen as a sign of disrespect by Irving, for it was obviously an allusion to the recent events in Turkey, which had upset the Muslims in India.[8]

Months later, Irving would express his unease at seeing the Hindu-Muslim unity despite the fact that the procession was peaceful. He thought that the motive was sinister.

He made this obvious in his answers to Sir C.H. Setalvad during the Hunter Committee gathering of evidence in Lahore on 13 November 1919.[9]

> Q: Then on April 9th were not the proceedings of the Ram Naumi day quite orderly in spite of the number of police being so very few in the city?
>
> A: It went off very well.
>
> Q: And this was the occasion when Hindus and Muhammadans fraternized between themselves?

---

8. Op. cit., p. 47.

9. Evidence Taken Before the Disorders Inquiry Committee, Volume III, Amritsar (Calcutta: Superintendent Government Printing, 1920), pp. 18–19. Referred to as Evidence, Amritsar hereafter.

A: Yes.

Q: Were you afraid of this? From a government point of view, from a political point of view?

A: It depends for what object they join. If for a good purpose I am all in favour of it.

Q: They give up their religious animosities and be friends? You are not against it?

A: No, certainly not.

Q: Therefore when you find that Hindus were drinking water which was touched by Muhammadans and that they were joining in the religious processions, was it not a matter of entire satisfaction to you?

A: It would give entire satisfaction if one did not fear that the underlying motive had a sinister purpose.

Q: You do not dislike their joint political action? You do not look with disfavour on Hindus and Muhammadans leaving their religious quarrels and taking up a common attitude and stand?

A: I have no objection. I was disquieted not by their unity but the fact they imported their unity into a religious ceremony.

Q: I do not think you believe in the principle of 'divide and rule'?

A: No.

Q: I think you are aware of the fact that since the time of the publication of the Montagu Chelmsford Reform Scheme, it has all along been alleged that one of the defects why Indians are not fit for responsible self-government is because of their religious differences and because Hindus and Muhammadans, the two important communities, do not see eye to eye with one another?... And therefore I think you will agree with me it is natural, in order to prove their fitness... the two communities try to accommodate one another and fraternize?

A: Except the remarkable thing that the Hindu ceremony had been converted into a political demonstration.

Gandhi was also expected to arrive in Punjab on 9 April, to take the peaceful protest against the Rowlatt Acts further. However, he was prevented from entering the state, and the arrest of Kitchlew and Satya Pal followed on 10 April. The Punjab government was obviously taking no chances, carefully targeting those who could lead an uprising against the Acts. There was also fear that the unity of the two communities would lead to an upset of the policy of divide and rule. According to Benjamin Horniman, 'Subsequent events in the Punjab served to strengthen this feeling of unity between the two great sections of the Indian people so greatly that never again will the ruling powers be able to look at the principle of Divide et Impera for their good.'[10]

The Punjab government did not want a successful agitation against the Rowlatt Acts—of which O'Dwyer was a supporter. The Acts would further enable men like him, who (as Secretary of State Edwin Montagu had said) would always 'try to govern by the iron hand'. O'Dwyer harboured deep antipathy towards the Indian educated classes who were now becoming politically engaged in urban centres like Amritsar. He much preferred the 'peasant behind the plough'. In one of his speeches, he said bluntly, 'Because half a dozen grasshoppers under a fern make the field ring with their importunate cries, while thousands of great cattle repose beneath the shadow of the British oak, chew the cud and are silent, pray do not imagine that those who make the noise are the only inhabitants of the field.'[11]

The responsibility for controlling Amritsar fell on the slight shoulders of Irving. He was the senior-most civilian officer in Amritsar, as the Lieutenant Governor, O'Dwyer, and the

---

10. Horniman, *Amritsar and Our Duty*, p. 78.

11. Alfred Draper, *The Amritsar Massacre: Twilight of the Raj* (Ashford Buchan & Enright, 1985), p. 33.

Commissioner, A.J. Kitchin, were both based in Lahore, 36 miles away. Irving had already sent a detailed letter on 8 April to Kitchin and O'Dwyer, expressing concern over the large, though peaceful meetings as well as organised hartals that were now frequently taking place. In his opinion, something big was about to happen.[12]

The success of the hartal on 6 April was worrying to the British, as everything in the city had shut down despite the fact that the strike had been announced less than 12 hours earlier. According to Irving, it was a 'triumph of organisation' and meant that there would be more and more severe tests until, as he said further in his almost prophetic letter: 'people will be ordered to go to jail by the thousands'.[13] Something had to be done urgently, as he was dismayed by the number of people showing up at the meetings. He referred to them with a touch of hysteria, as 'mobs'. Nothing had happened, not a stone had been thrown, everyone was following the Gandhian plan of satyagraha but for Irving, the situation was becoming a nightmare.

He strongly disliked the confidence of the leaders of the satyagraha. He felt he did not have the forces to deal with them and asked O'Dwyer for help from the army, to sort out 'who governs Amritsar'. The other annoyance—apart from the crowds gathering to hear political speeches—was the fact that on a hartal day nothing would function, and shops would be shut. For the British families living in Amritsar, this would have been frustrating as they were used to preferential treatment. Even public transport would have become a problem, not just for them, but for their staff and servants. Irving would have

---

12. Evidence Taken Before the Disorders Inquiry Committee, Volume VI (Calcutta, 1920), p. 3; Disorders Inquiry Committee (1919–1920) Report (Calcutta: Superintendent Government Printing, 1920), p. 28. The latter is referred to as Hunter Committee Report hereafter.

13. Evidence Taken Before the Disorders Inquiry Committee, Volume VI (Calcutta, 1920), p. 3; Hunter Committee Report, p. 28.

received a lot of complaints from his compatriots, who may have thought he was beginning to appear weak.

He therefore asked for an increase in forces, as well as machine guns and armoured vehicles, saying that they could not 'go indefinitely with the policy of keeping out of the way, and congratulating ourselves that the mob has not forced us to interfere. Every time we do this the confidence of the mob increases; yet with our present force we have no alternative. I think we shall have to stand up for our authority sooner or later by prohibiting some strike or procession which endangers the public peace. But for this a really strong force will have to be brought in and we shall have to be ready to try conclusions to the end to see who governs Amritsar.'[14] Obviously expecting a sudden attack, he asked for a movable column from Lahore to be available at '6 hours' notice'. This was an unusual request because no violence had been reported yet, even though the numbers at the gatherings continued to increase.

Irving had also noticed the rise of new leaders like Kitchlew and Satya Pal in Amritsar and felt he had no influence over them. Meanwhile, the older leadership with whom he had some links had ceased to have much influence.

What really upset Irving was that he had asked the Congress leadership in Amritsar to cancel the hartal to be held on 6 April and they had agreed. However, after a secret meeting at Satya Pal's home on 5 April, the hartal was declared anyway—with a small party going around with a drum, announcing it, at around 9 p.m. After 2 a.m. posters were pasted around the city as well. This sidelining of his request made Irving feel he had lost control. The only way forward was the arrest of the new leaders, i.e. Satya Pal and Kitchlew. O'Dwyer had already planned on deporting them and Irving received his orders at 7 p.m. on 9 April.

---

14. Evidence Taken Before the Disorders Inquiry Committee, Volume VI (Calcutta, 1920), p. 3; Hunter Committee Report, p. 28.

Irving immediately called a meeting of the British officials stationed at Amritsar—which included a few from the army and others from the police, whom he felt he could trust. Among these were Captain Massey, who was the Officer Commanding Station, Superintendent of Police Rehill, Civil Surgeon Lieutenant Colonel Henry Smith, and Deputy Superintendent of Police Plomer.[15]

It was decided that the two leaders (after their arrest) would be taken to Dharamshala by Rehill in a car. The officers at the meeting did not think that there would be a severe reaction—only that a 'noisy but not dangerous crowd' would go to the Deputy Commissioner's bungalow, or the kutchery to protest. Pickets would be set up to prevent them from reaching there. The other mistake made by Irving was that while he took steps to protect the 'official' Europeans, the non-official Europeans in Amritsar were neither protected nor told that there could be some trouble on 10 April.[16]

On 10 April, when word of the arrest of Kitchlew and Satya Pal spread, people started gathering as expected. Also as expected, a group wanted to walk to the residence of the Deputy Commissioner to request their release. At 11.30 a.m., it was reported that 'a large crowd formed in Hall Bazaar and made its way through Hall Gate and over Hall Bridge at the further side of which was a small picket of mounted troops.'[17] It must be noted that initially the unarmed group was peaceful—bareheaded and mostly unshod. Till this time they may have

---

15. Punjab Govt. Home Military Part B—January 1920—No. 265, quoted in Raja Ram, *The Jallianwala Bagh Massacre: A Premeditated Plan* (Chandigarh: Punjab University, 2002), p. 70.

16. Raja Ram, *Jallianwala Bagh*, p. 70.

17. Report of the Committee Appointed by the Government of India to Investigate the Disturbances in the Punjab, etc.: Presented to Parliament by Command of His Majesty (His Majesty's Stationery Office, 1920), p. 22. Referred to as Parliamentary Report hereafter.

been hopeful of a resolution or a dialogue with Irving as they walked by the National Bank, the Town Hall and the Christian Mission Hall, and remained non-violent even though they did encounter a few Europeans.

They were halted at the railway carriage overbridge by the military picket. Time and again, they tried to break through the pickets. Irving and Captain Massey arrived, with a fresh contingent, but the fracas continued, getting worse by the minute till 'two soldiers dismounted, took a safe position and fired...'[18] The soldiers were British, adding to the fury of the protestors. In the firing, three or four were killed, and possibly more were wounded. Again, though the killings are recorded in the Hunter Committee Report, there are no clear numbers or names of the Indians who were shot dead.

'At about 1 pm, Plomer appeared on the scene, with twenty-four foot police and seven sowars. The police marched towards the crowd with bayonets fixed and at the ready position. The crowd retreated, and by the time the infantry arrived, the footbridge and the carriage bridge were practically cleared of the crowd and taken over by the military, while the railway level crossing was taken over by the police picket.'[19]

Unable to proceed further, the crowd returned to Hall Bazaar, but the sight of the dead and wounded enraged others who had also gathered there. More and more people began to join in.

It must be remembered that the frequent meetings and discussions on the Rowlatt Acts had brought the ordinary people of Amritsar together and made them more aware of their rights. It was difficult for them to understand why they were

---

18. NAI-Home-Pol-Deposit–June 1919–No. 23: Report on the Rioting on 10 April 1919, as quoted in Raja Ram, *Jallianwala Bagh*, p. 73.

19. Raja Ram, *Jallianwala Bagh*, p. 73.

not being permitted to meet the Deputy Commissioner; there was also concern about what may have happened to Kitchlew and Satya Pal. If people were being prevented from crossing the railway bridge, perhaps something terrible was afoot. It is also possible that news of the arrest of Gandhi the previous day had come in (the telegraph wires and phone lines were still functioning, though they would be cut later in the day).

A larger crowd of around 30,000 began to spread through the bazaar, and some now went back to face the military picket—this time carrying sticks and pieces of wood. These would not be of much use against British guns, but the protestors were inflamed by the injustice of what had just taken place.

Many among the leaders were lawyers—which was a common feature in the early years of the freedom struggle. One among them, Maqbool Mahmood, a high court lawyer, volunteered to reason with the angry crowd along with Gurdial Singh Salaria, another member of the Bar, before the encounter took a turn for the worse. He remembered: 'Salaria and I shouted out to the Deputy Commissioner and the officers to get back and not to fire, as we still hoped to take the crowd back. A few of the crowd threw wood and stones at the soldiers. The soldiers at once opened a volley of fire without any warning or intimation. Bullets whistled to my right and left. The crowd dispersed, leaving 20 to 25 killed and wounded. After the firing stopped I went up to the soldiers and enquired if they had an ambulance car or any first aid arrangements at hand. I wanted to run to the hospital, which was close by for help. The soldiers would not allow me. Mr Seymour however let me go... The Deputy Commissioner himself was present when the fire was opened (sic). He knew that Salaria and I were members of the Bar and trying to get the people back to the city. It was by mere accident that our lives were saved. I still believe that if the authorities had a little more patience, we would have succeeded in taking the crowd back... I believe that some of the wounded might have been saved if timely medical assistance had been forthcoming. After the first few shots, the crowd rushed back, but the firing continued even after they began running away. Many of them were hit on the back. Most of the wounded were hit above the belt, on the face or on the head.'[20]

The picket had been reinforced with foot and mounted police, as well as infantry. What had begun as a peaceful protest led to many more deaths and injuries, as the British troops kept firing. 'The crowd made a rush, at the same time stoning the picket. The non-commissioned officer in charge was given the necessary order, the crowd was fired upon and between 20 to 30 casualties ensued.'[21] (Though later, in the Hunter Committee Report, it was claimed to be ten casualties.) Given the spontaneous nature of the uprising, the dead and wounded were residents of Amritsar, creating further tensions in the city. Eyewitnesses remembered bodies lying in the mosque at Hall Bazaar, enraging many. As the wounds were mostly on the upper part of the body, one can only conclude that the intent was to shoot to kill.

Seventy-three rounds were fired by the army, and several rounds by the police. Maqbool, who had tried to play a conciliatory role, then went to the Civil Hospital 'and brought Dhanpat Rai, a medico, to render first aid to the wounded. Stretchers were brought from the hospital but Plomer ordered the hospital staff to go back, shouting that the people must make their own arrangements.'[22]

The crowd had become increasingly agitated at witnessing the large number of casualties. It now retaliated by targeting symbols of British power. They burnt down buildings: part of the Town Hall, the National Bank and the Chartered Bank. The

---

20. INC Report, chap. 5, p. 50.
21. Parliamentary Report, p. 23.
22. Raja Ram, *Jallianwala Bagh*, p. 74.

Alliance Bank, though attacked, was not burnt, as the building belonged to an Indian. Three bank managers were beaten up and killed, but the Chartered Bank managers escaped, with help from their Indian clerks and some policemen, and hid in the Kotwali. The telegraph office was attacked and the telephone exchange destroyed. The Indian Christian Church and Religious Book Society's Depot and Hall were burnt. There was an attempt to burn the Church Missionary Society's Girls Normal School. The railways also came under attack, and one guard was killed, as was an electrician. A British female missionary was attacked, and another British woman, a doctor, escaped. The latter, Mrs Easdon, had watched the mayhem from the rooftop of the Zenana Hospital (which was under her charge) and had allegedly said the natives deserved to be shot. This further angered the crowd, which went hunting for her twice; she was hidden inside a closet till the danger passed.[23]

In total, five Europeans died in the attack on the banks and elsewhere.

(Note: In all the reports, the name and occupation of each of the five Europeans who died are known. But, as mentioned, it is difficult to find the name or occupation of any Indian casualty—especially if they were from among the protestors. Therefore, there is little information about the estimated twenty who died, and many more who were wounded. Nor do we know the exact details of how they died. The unarmed protestors are continuously referred to as a 'mob' by the British government, and it is assumed that their intentions are violent. Yet, only the British police and army were armed.)

This was probably the worst confrontation between the British government and its Indian subjects in recent times, and it left both sides suspicious and alarmed. No action was taken over the killing and wounding of more than twenty Indians,

---

23. Hunter Committee Report, pp. 38–40.

but arrests were made for the murder of the five Europeans and harassment of the two European women. The tenuous relationship that had been carefully nurtured by the British through clever appeasement, inclusion and distribution of favours now seemed strained. Punjab had provided the most soldiers to fight for the Allies in the First World War, yet when they came back, inspired by the speeches of Woodrow Wilson and the idea of liberty, their own government was ready to shoot them dead. While many continued to collaborate with their colonial masters, the agitation against the Rowlatt Acts showed there was a growing resistance, a search for a more liberal order.

The killing of unarmed Indians exposed the dichotomy within the colonial structure. From the British point of view, the Rowlatt Acts were more necessary than ever. Not just in Punjab but all over the country, since they permitted arrests for acts of sedition. Any gathering of people that proposed the shutting down of the city could be considered just that. After the events of 10 April in Amritsar, suppression of rebellion was paramount for the Punjab government—which till this point had been represented by the local civil administration reporting to O'Dwyer, the Lieutenant Governor based in Lahore.

O'Dwyer, like Irving, smelt a larger conspiracy in the recent events. The hartals had been very successful, not just in Amritsar, but also in Lahore, Gujranwala and elsewhere. Delhi, Bombay and even Ahmedabad had seen the spread of the anti-Rowlatt Act movement. In many places such as Bihar, Orissa, the Central Provinces and right up to Burma, the hartals remained peaceful.

Perhaps O'Dwyer and his officers were concerned that this satyagraha, if it spread to the army, could lead to a repeat of the Mutiny of 1857. It could also be argued that as the World War had ended only in November 1918, its memories were fresh in everyone's mind. There was concern about the demobilised soldiers, as this was a group that could be easily organised, or turn rebellious. Even though some suspected an effort to destabilise the British regime in India, the fact remains that in Amritsar most of the violence of 10 April was restricted to a small area.[24] It erupted only after some protestors had been killed. No guns, bombs or ammunition of any variety were used by the protestors. However, they were stung into burning, looting and killing—after the British troops fired and killed their compatriots.

Instead of releasing the two political prisoners, Kitchlew and Satya Pal, which might have calmed down the tense atmosphere, in a complete overreaction, more troops were brought into Amritsar. The walled city and its surroundings were militarised over the next two days. The British were preparing for war, and by 11 April they had declared war on the people of Amritsar.

Between 1 and 2 p.m. a party of 1-9th Gurkhas, unarmed but 260 strong, had arrived at the railway station on their way to Peshawar under Captain Crompton. They were detained in Amritsar. One hundred of them were armed from the Fort and pickets were strengthened. The railway station itself was now safe, and the Rego bridge could be strongly guarded while the (British) women and children were being got to the Fort.

Late that night, after 10 p.m., 300 troops—125 British, and 175 Baluchis—arrived from Lahore under Major MacDonald, who took over command from Captain Massey. Early on 11 April, 300 more troops arrived from Jullundur—100 British and 200 Indian.[25]

Irving very likely had overstated the case, because when A.J. Kitchin, Commissioner of the Division, and D. Donald, Deputy Inspector General, drove down from Lahore on 10 April, arriving at the railway station at 5 p.m., to check the

---

24. Parliamentary Report. See 'Map of Amritsar City' in the appendix of this book.
25. Hunter Committee Report, p. 41.

situation, they were not stopped or harassed in any way. This was evidence that the violence, which had spread through the city, was not part of a conspiracy to attack Europeans, but had been a spontaneous display of anger because protesters had been brutally killed and the wounded left to their own resources.

In fact, when Kitchin and Donald arrived, the city was quiet. The residents of Amritsar had gone home. But late at night, when the appointed Officer Commanding, Major MacDonald, arrived with his men from Lahore, 'the Commissioner told him verbally that the situation was beyond civil control, and that he, as Senior Military Officer, was to take such steps as the military situation demanded.'[26] Throughout the time Kitchin was in Amritsar or even upon his return to Lahore, he kept looking for a military solution. It is possible that O'Dwyer had sent him down with an agenda: to extract revenge for the murder of the five Europeans.

Nothing further had happened, and the city was peaceful, but the civil authorities were still fearful for the security of the remaining Europeans. They wanted the army to take over and perhaps take some punitive measures. Irving, and now his superior, Kitchin, also wanted to mete out severe punishments. They would either take action themselves or get someone else to control the rebels.

In a telegram dated 10 April 1919, 11.30 p.m., sent by hand to the Private Secretary, Punjab, Kitchin made it clear that he had another, rather more violent plan in mind. Even though everything was quiet, he noted that the European casualties were five and the city's casualties about thirty. He added: 'Reported that processions are to form in the morning to bury and burn corpses. We intend to prohibit and break up such processions with military force. I have informed Officer Commanding that he is in charge and can use military force… Expect trouble in the morning…'

---

26. Hunter Committee Report, p. 41.

The accompanying notes reconfirm this: 'Processions in the morning for burial of native victims. These will be forbidden and broken up. Further rioting expected in consequence.'

At 6.45 a.m. on 11 April, Kitchin received a telephonic message from the Private Secretary, Lahore, stating: 'Lieutenant Governor approves your proposed action. Will send aeroplanes and armoured cars this morning.'

These were ominous words. There was obviously a plan to fire upon the funeral processions with machine guns from inside armoured cars, and perhaps drop bombs as well. But the fact remained that while MacDonald had been told he could use military force, he did not do so.[27] In the Government House War Diaries, and in the notes that Kitchin sent on 11 April, it is apparent that there was no outbreak of violence, and that the city remained peaceful. The only issues were that Kitchin wanted to dominate the city, and the residents wanted the funerals to be conducted with the proper ceremonies.

The note sent by Kitchin on 11 April to Lahore, at 11.30 a.m., stated: 'I have now expressed to Officer Commanding that we should occupy as much as possible of the city this afternoon. He has agreed. It is essential to persuade the city that Amritsar is ours.' At 2.30 p.m., he reiterated that the city was quiet, but at 3 p.m., his telephonic message insisted on the necessity for a march of British troops through the city.[28]

A telephonic message was sent at 2.30 p.m., from Kitchin to the Private Secretary, Punjab, Lahore: 'Funerals of victims of yesterday are going on. The crowd has been told that funeral party must disperse by 2 o'clock: 15 minutes after that time they will be treated as rioters and dispersed by force. There has not been any trouble today. The troops have not yet

---

27. V.N. Datta, *New Light on the Punjab Disturbances in 1919* (Simla: Institute of Advanced Study, 1975), p. 376.

28. Datta, *New Light*, p. 376.

entered the city. We expect to send a force into the city by this evening.'

In another telephonic message at 3 p.m., he notes: 'Burial party quite orderly and returned to the city half an hour before time given them. British troops are going through the city now in company with civil officer and will break up any gatherings they may meet.

'It is reported that the city is quiet and the shops will soon re-open. A message has come from the different heads of Dharamshalas that all is well.'

It was apparent that after the terrible events of 10 April, the residents of Amritsar had swallowed their pain and decided to normalise the situation as much as possible.

In the same note, Kitchin also went on to reiterate that the situation continued to be peaceful: 'So far as known only eight corpses (Indian) have been produced. There has been no firing today. The present situation is that Officer Commanding Troops is anxious to give crowds time to bury their dead and to disperse, before entering the city. Emissaries are said to have gone out into villages, but there is no news of response. Trains are running quietly and an attempt is being made to restore telegraph communication. I am anxious not to reduce British force until we know that the Indian troops are sound. Of the Gurkhas here—250—only 100 have rifles, the others being armed with kukris. There has been no general looting. Damage is confined to Government buildings and to missions and to banks. A wounded English lady was got out last night in the burka (sic).'

Despite reporting peace and quiet in Amritsar, Kitchin had initially, on the morning of 11 April, openly displayed his suspicion of Amritsar residents when they had come to request if they could take out funeral processions. He may have done this in order to implement his plan of firing and dropping bombs upon the funeral processions. This is corroborated in the evidence gathered by the Hunter Committee. The Commissioner said he viewed those seeking permission for burials and funerals as 'representing rioters' and said they maintained a 'defiant' attitude. In reality, those arranging the funerals were mostly young lawyers who turned up on behalf of the bereaved families, who were both grieving and worried about what would happen if they appeared before the administration. (In the next few months, there would be constant suspicion of the legal profession as lawyers were at the forefront of the anti-Rowlatt Act protests and gatherings.)

Kitchin stated in the Government House War Diaries, on 11 April: 'This morning I issued order prohibiting processions and mobs on pain of being fired at. Two pleaders conveyed the orders to the city and a deputation came back asking leave to bury their dead.' This statement is important as it shows that though the residents of Amritsar were complying with orders and ready to obey whatever new laws were being created, the British officers were giving permissions for the funerals very reluctantly—they simply did not want a crowd to gather.

The families of the dead and wounded would have been distraught and worried; they were not allowed to openly grieve for their dead for as long as they wanted. On the other hand, many of those who were wounded may have been unwilling to come forward since they were likely to be arrested. Thus the number of those who died or were severely maimed from the firing could have been higher than reported. (This was to be the case in Jallianwala Bagh as well.)

It was to prevent further clashes or trouble that Irving had summoned two young lawyers, Yasin and Maqbool Mahmood to meet him at the railway station on the morning of 11 April. He explained to them that the city was under military control and that only four people would be allowed for the burial or cremation of a corpse. After being told it was a religious ceremony, Irving and Kitchin increased the number to eight.

The order was then read out by Maqbool to a large crowd inside the Hall Gate. They all gathered around to listen to the first of many strange proclamations:

> 'The troops have orders to restore order in Amritsar, and to use all the force necessary. No gatherings of persons, no procession of any sort will be allowed. All the gatherings will be fired on. Any person leaving the city, or persons gathering in groups of more than four, will be fired on. Respectable persons should keep indoors until order is restored. The dead may be carried out for the burial or the burning, by parties of not more than eight, at intervals not less that fifteen minutes, by the Ghee Mandi, Lohgarh, Khazana and Chatiwind Gate.'[29]

As is apparent from this strained dialogue between the people and the officers, frustration was rising on both sides. Irving was trying to appear as though he was still in command but the crowd of mourners wanted to conduct the funerals with proper solemnity, not under threat of being shot. In the face of increasing numbers coming out onto the street, and Major MacDonald's reluctance to open fire without cause, the situation would have deeply upset the administration, goading them into issuing further threats.

The mourners sent emissaries to request for more people to accompany the funeral processions. These were the first deaths since the Satyagraha Movement began in Punjab, and those killed would be considered martyrs. However, the British—including Smith and Reverend Mackenzie—felt that even tougher measures were required, and giving in was not the solution. They were still enraged over the five Europeans who had been killed the previous day, and any pandering to the crowd could be considered a sign of weakness.

---

29. INC Report, Volume II, pp. 32, 54, statements 19, 5.

Gerard Wathen, the principal of the Khalsa College, was of the opinion that officials 'should not take such a harsh view of the situation and should behave more calmly and soberly'. Irving shouted, 'No more talking. We have seen our dead bodies charred. Our temper is changed.'[30] However, he succumbed finally and allowed processions, provided they were not of more than 2,000 people. So the numbers increased from 4 to 8 to 2,000.

The following conditions were finally laid out for the funerals:

1. The processions would only go out of the Sultanwind and the Chatiwind Gates.
2. Everything was to be over by 2 p.m.
3. At 2 p.m. there would be a warning by bugle.
4. After 15 minutes past 2 p.m., they would fire.
5. No lathis were allowed.[31]

Wathen was also asked to spread the word through his students that a state of war had broken out.[32]

The tensions between the British and the Indians continued to escalate.

Kitchin told the Hunter Committee that he had issued a proclamation on the morning of 11 April, which was handed over to those who had come to meet him since there was no time to make it known through any other manner. It was obvious that he was disappointed by the relatively mild reactions of Irving and MacDonald. Something more needed to be done to make the people of Amritsar realise their enormous folly—as in the statements he recorded and conveyed back to Lahore, he stated they were unrepentant.

---

30. Raja Ram, *Jallianwala Bagh*, p. 79.
31. INC Report, p. 55; Raja Ram, *Jallianwala Bagh*, p. 80.
32. Parliamentary Report, p. 27.

He also said, 'I asked the Principal of the Khalsa College who was thereabouts to send his own students to tell the people that we considered that a state of war had broken out and they must settle down. I understand he had sent a number of students to tell the people in the city that our patience was nearly exhausted. There was no intention of firing until the people had been adequately and sufficiently warned. I had expected some penitence after the murders and the lootings of the previous day, but there was no indication of anything of the kind.'[33]

Gerard Wathen's wife noted that 'On 8 am, on Friday— Gerard heard that the commissioner was coming over and the troops were to march through the city, firing on everyone they saw. He saw what a frightful blunder this would be, as of course hundreds of innocent people were out to look at the damage. He tore off to the station and for an hour argued with the authorities and at last got them to see that they must give warning, now that the actual mob had dispersed.' There were also plans for bombardment from aircraft.[34]

However, MacDonald had made it clear that the proclamation (which was more or less the same as the one that Dyer was to issue the next day) needed to be widely known. Even with a limited circulation, he managed to ensure there were no further killings, and gave people time to return home.

In a telephonic message sent at 2.30 p.m., on 11 April, to Lahore, Kitchin did indicate that things were going quite differently to the plan of the previous night, which had been approved by O'Dwyer. While they were prepared to shoot and

---

33. Evidence, Amritsar, p. 158.

34. The Wathen Papers, quoted in Nigel Collet, *The Butcher of Amritsar: Brigadier General Reginald Dyer* (London: Hambledon & London, 2005), p. 237.

bomb people, the funerals had taken place without further incident. The British also buried their dead, quietly.

Kitchin said on 11 April that MacDonald did not want 'wholesale slaughter' so he allowed time for the crowds to disperse: 'Officer Commanding Troops was unwilling to start shooting till the crowds had time to learn the orders. They were given permission by Officer Commanding to bury their dead outside the city, provided they did not exceed 2000 men and did not carry arms and that they dispersed at 2 p.m. We just heard that the bodies are to be buried inside the city. Officer Commanding Troops has said that he will allow crowds to disperse. He does not want wholesale slaughter, which would be the result of earlier interference.'[35]

MacDonald had noted in his message to Officer Commanding, 16th Division, Lahore (sent between 1 p.m. and 2 p.m.) that two aeroplanes had flown over the city at 7 a.m. (as promised by O'Dwyer in his message sent at 6.45 a.m.) and an 'armoured train with two British Officers and 34 men arrived from Lahore at 09.00 hours. Party of one British Officer and 20 gunners arrived at 10.30 p.m.' But MacDonald did not use the option of bombing or shooting. If Kitchin or O'Dwyer were hoping for some more deaths due to the lack of penitence—it did not happen. Not on 11 April.[36]

Kitchin may well have preferred that MacDonald start firing at the funeral procession because it was obvious that those who died had participated or been present at the protests on 10 April. It was, therefore, easy to presume that some of those in the funeral procession might themselves be the arsonists and rioters who burnt the buildings and killed the five Europeans. By permitting the funeral processions, in fact, the British got a chance to identify the 'culprits'. It was, sadly, almost like an

---

35. Datta, *New Light*, p. 377.
36. Datta, *New Light*, p. 377.

identity parade, which those conducting the funerals did not realise.

The city had a well-established system of spies and the Criminal Investigation Department was often used to identify offenders. Undoubtedly, the crowds of people now appearing on the streets would have been easy targets. The arrests were not made immediately, but later at night, once the troops had gone into the city, and more reinforcements had arrived.[37] In his longer report dated 11 April 1919, sent between 1 p.m. and 2 p.m. and received at 2.25 p.m. from Officer Commanding, Amritsar to General Officer Commanding, 16th Division, Lahore, Major MacDonald said that on 10 April, following the firing and the resulting riots in the morning, more reinforcements of troops were requisitioned for Amritsar, even though the situation afterwards remained peaceful. 'On my arrival I found all quiet and immediately proceeded to patrol City with my detachment from Lahore and brought in the remains of the three Bank managers murdered and also released four other civilians held up in the City. Night remained quiet. At 05.15 hours troop special under command of Major Clarke arrived from Jullundur with one British Officer and 100 ranks London, two British officers and 130 ranks 151st, and one British officer and 100 ranks 59th, together with Medical Officer and staff. Parties from these latter details were sent out on arrival to relieve pickets and remainder posted at exits to city.'

Importantly, when MacDonald went to rescue the officers of the Chartered Bank and two other Europeans who had taken shelter inside the Kotwali at Town Hall, '... instead of the party having to fight its way through the streets, as the Commissioner anticipated, the streets were found deserted.'[38] Yet, a siege

---

37. Datta, *New Light*, p. 378.

38. Hunter Committee Report, p. 41.

mentality had taken hold. All European women and children had been transported to the Gobindgarh Fort, where they were kept in 'extreme discomfort'. Some European missionaries as well as Indian Christians had also been similarly taken to what was considered a safer zone, even though there were no attacks from the Indian side. However, the fear of further attacks from the Indian 'mob' continued to be felt—and a nervous Irving, did little to placate these fears.

Perhaps having been posted recently to the city, Irving had scarcely any idea of local politics and both Kitchin and O'Dwyer were more impressed with the advice of Smith, the Civil Surgeon in Amritsar, who throughout these disorders, and later, would demonstrate his own preference for a more brutal repression. The idea of deporting Kitchlew and Satya Pal was also supported by him.

O'Dwyer would tell the Hunter Committee: 'I may add that a day or two before the deportation, Colonel Smith, the Civil Surgeon, who has a unique knowledge of Amritsar and great influence there, come (came) to see me at Lahore. I asked him if he thought the deportation would be likely to lead to any disturbance. His reply was that it would not, that the Khatris and Kashmiris (Hindus and Muslims) would not offer any open resistance.'[39]

Despite the fact that he had been proven wrong, Smith continued to advise the Punjab administration—advocating increasingly harsh measures. So far, no one seemed to have considered the fact that all the rioters of 10 April had been unarmed civilians protesting the arrest of their leaders, and that the number of deaths on the Indian side was much, much higher. It is also likely that there were a large number of wounded as over 70 rounds were fired into the crowd.

Smith was among those Europeans who was attacked by the crowd on 10 April as he 'took his ambulance into

---

39. Datta, *New Light*, p. 167. Marginal note on proof by the witness.

the city to rescue Europeans from the schools and hospitals, but was stoned, and eventually had to desist.'[40] The safety of European women and children was another factor that drove the administration to their extreme reaction. The sight of around 130 women and children sheltering in the Gobindgarh Fort under unsanitary conditions has been described in an anonymous eyewitness account, 'By An Englishwoman', in *Blackwood* magazine (April 1920): 'surrounded by the miseries of dirt, heat, and overcrowding. There was no sanitation... no privacy. Sixteen people shared one small room for the first three days.' The lack of facilities, including fans and proper bedding, in a space infested with sandflies and mosquitoes made these women, who were used to servants waiting on them hand and foot, even more miserable. The 'Englishwoman' notes that it was the plight of the babies and children, without fresh food or milk, which made the situation very serious. One child developed typhoid. The proliferation of rumours kept everyone's nerves on edge—as did the news about those Europeans who had been attacked on 10 April.

Not a word, however, was recorded or spoken by the officials or indeed, anyone else in a position of authority, about the trauma experienced by Indian women and children in the city of Amritsar, whose relations had died and who were now—just like the women and children in the Fort—being held hostage in a hostile environment. Their situation was worse because they were vulnerable within their own homes—not guarded or protected as the Europeans were by armed Gurkhas. While the European women and children would be evacuated to a hill station after around two weeks, those residents of Amritsar who survived the repression and killings would be trapped in the city to undergo torturous humiliation for the next three months.

Clearly, as more and more battalions and brigades came into Amritsar and took over the administration of the city,

---

40. Collett, *Butcher of Amritsar*, p. 234.

attacks on the people of Amritsar were set to escalate. Baisakhi was further drained of colour as the water supply was cut off by the civil administration. Later it was said that the water supply had been cut because hydrants had been broken by the 'mob' on 10 April, and there were rumours that the water was poisoned, 'so it was shut off by the Municipal Engineer'.[41] During discussions over the Indemnity Bill, J.P. Thompson, Chief Secretary to the Government of Punjab, said in response to a question from Pandit Madan Mohan Malaviya, regarding the cutting off of electricity and water: 'On the 10th of April two out of the three feeders which gave energy to the city were damaged by the mob around 1 p.m. Later on at 2.30 p.m. the mob entered the power-house and stopped the whole plant. At 7 p.m. the one remaining feeder was started. On 11th the mob prevented a mistri from mending the two damaged feeders. That evening the power was cut off (in) the city altogether by order of the General Officer Commanding, and remained off till the 19th. In regard to the water supply, I mentioned the story that the supply had been poisoned. But the water was turned on again early on the 11th after having been cut off on the evening of the 10th, and it was again cut off later on the 11th and remained off till the 14th. Those were the facts and that is the explanation.'[42] However, we know that the city was quiet on the evening of 10 April, and 11 April as well. There were no mobs on 11 April. There were obviously other reasons for depriving people of water and electricity—as Malaviya was to comment sarcastically during the debate, the electricity could not have been poisoned.

People would have found it difficult in these circumstances to not just adhere to cleanliness at home but also perform the

---

41. Collett, *Butcher of Amritsar*, p. 234.

42. Pandit Pearay Mohan, *An Imaginary Rebellion and How It Was Suppressed* (Lahore: Khosla Bros., 1920; Gyan Publishing House, 1999), p. 944. Citations refer to the Gyan edition.

rituals associated with the funerals, which were conducted on 11 April. It would have been impossible for them to bathe the corpses, which were the legacy of the events of 10 April. How were the blood-soaked streets and clothes washed? How was the area cleaned up? We can only imagine the plight of those who were without electricity for around ten days and without water supply for more than four days. (Some witnesses claimed this period was actually longer.)

Meanwhile, all third-class bookings at Amritsar railway station were stopped, so that no 'innocent' persons coming to Amritsar on Baisakhi were affected. This meant no one could leave. Those residents who returned to Amritsar at this time found a city under seige, with soldiers everywhere, smouldering buildings, and fellow citizens urging them not to stay.

Lala Girdhari Lal, Deputy Chairman of the Punjab Chamber of Commerce and Managing Director of the Amritsar Flour and General Mills Company, reached Amritsar on 11 April 1919 at about 11.30 a.m., but could not find any conveyance, or anyone to help him with his luggage. He recollected: 'From and on the canal bridge near Amritsar, I saw batches of policemen guarding the railway line. When the train steamed into the station here, the whole place looked like a regular military post, with soldiers and guns scattered all over. No coolie or conveyance of any kind was to be had. Sardar Bikram Singh met me and advised me to either go back where I had come from, or not to enter the city in any case. Being extremely nervous it appeared to me he did not talk to me for long...

'At the footbridge there was a guard of some European soldiers, who would not let anyone enter the city without searching all things thoroughly. Sticks of all kind were taken away from everyone. After a thorough overhauling of all my things I was allowed to proceed further. No one was permitted to go over the carriage bridge. This continued for days, till the

15th April probably. At every step outside the city, one could see nothing but only military or police at short distances with rifles and bayonets... The first thing that struck me, immediately on entering the city, was the stoppage of water supply completely... Later in the evening, I found the electric connection all over the city proper also cut off. To the best of my memory, the inconvenience also lasted at least up to 18th or 19th April, if not later. While proceeding to the Golden Temple, I saw marks of violence. Telegraph wires were cut, some buildings were burnt.'[43]

What Lal noticed was a familiar sight in some other cities as well, where the Satyagraha Movement broke into violence, as the news spread that on 9 April Gandhi had been arrested. These disorders were particularly noted in Delhi, Bombay and Ahmedabad, where protestors had joined Gandhi in demonstrating against the Rowlatt Acts. However, it was when Gandhi was stopped from entering Punjab that serious clashes took place in some places, including Ahmedabad and Amritsar.

In comparison to Amritsar, in Ahmedabad the protestors were far more organised (as we will see in a later chapter). Even though this led to the lynching of at least one European, the agitation was swiftly brought under control. Amritsar would stand out from the rest of the country as each day brought new oppression and concerns, with the city completely cut off through severe restrictions. Geographically, most of the residents lived inside the walled city and could be isolated quite easily from the surrounding areas.

It would soon become apparent that much of the cruelty imposed on Amritsar would also be imposed elsewhere in Punjab as the regime under O'Dwyer decided to institute some rather uniquely barbaric ways to deal with the protests against the Rowlatt Acts, and any suspected rebels.

The truth was that there were many reasons for the people of Punjab to be unhappy. Perhaps one of the reasons why they

---

43. INC Report, p. 52, statement 1.

were drawn to the meetings and helped organise the hartals was the hope that there could be a better and less repressive future.

The four years of the First World War had taken away many of their young and able-bodied men, and yet the conscription had not ended. This was one of the most worrying factors in Punjab, which was primarily an agricultural state. With 7.5 per cent of the country's population, Punjab provided 60 per cent of the troops.

Who would plough the fields, tend to the aged, support the family? Yes, the blandishments of land and money might still be offered but recruitment was now being done forcefully and there were quotas for each tehsil. If young men were not provided for the British fighting machine, there would be heavy fines. These also led to embarrassments and daily humiliations for those who resisted.[44]

There were other issues as well, such as the forced contributions towards the war loan, heavy taxes and spiralling prices, which meant that Gandhi's appeal against the Rowlatt Acts had united those hoping for a more democratic setup. As mentioned earlier, a large number of Indian soldiers who had fought for the British—and for liberty in Europe—had come back victorious, to find shockingly repressive measures being enacted at home, especially in Punjab. It is possible that some of these former soldiers might have expressed their own anger through disruption of the railway network and cutting of telegraph lines. Strategies used to break the communication system of the enemy during the World War were being used against the British. It was not a declaration of war but an attempt to bring the country to a halt—a total 'hartal'—and to force the British to withdraw the Rowlatt Acts. However, these tactics were consciously perceived to be part of a much more sinister design by the British.

---

44. Horniman, *Amritsar and Our Duty*, pp. 23–4.

How widespread were these attempts at disruption? In the disorders of 1919, according to the Hunter Committee Report, seven Europeans were murdered and around 54 attacks took place on the communications network in Punjab, from 10 April to 21 April—but then nothing further happened till 29 August.[45] Though there was arson and disruption of the railways, none of this pointed towards a grand conspiracy. In fact the disorders appear to have been sporadic in nature.

In his letter of 8 April to Kitchin and O'Dwyer, Irving admitted that ample grounds existed for a revolution in Punjab: 'As regards the local material for revolution, the soil is prepared for discontent by a number of causes. The poor are hit by high prices, the rich by a severe income tax assessment and the Excess Profit Act. Muhammadans are irritated about the fate of Turkey. From one cause or another the people are restless and discontented and ripe for revolution.'[46]

Ironically, the so-called 'rebels' (including Gandhi) were not actually asking for the exit of their colonial masters—just a withdrawal of the Rowlatt Acts. Many who joined the Satyagraha Movement may admittedly not have read them but what they heard at the rallies made them intensely worried. *No Vakil, No Dalil, No Appeal!*—was how the Acts were described by opponents. If anyone was arrested under the Acts—he or she could be held without recourse to a lawyer or a trial, or even an appeal. (The Acts are discussed in detail in a later chapter.)

Meanwhile, because of the restrictions on travel and the disruption of the communication system, news of the shooting on the unarmed crowd did not travel far beyond Amritsar. The media did not report the confrontation on 10 April at all. It is unlikely that Gandhi or his cohorts knew anything of

---

45. Parliamentary Report, p. 55.

46. Evidence Taken Before the Disorders Inquiry Committee, Volume VI (Calcutta, 1920), p. 3.

the situation in Punjab, particularly within the walled city of Amritsar, as it was unfolding.

The residents of Amritsar found themselves in an increasingly perilous, helpless situation. The attitude of their administrative masters had greatly changed by 11 April. 'The very men towards whom they were in the habit of showing courtesy now repelled them. Lala Dholan Das, a reputed resident of Amritsar was one such man, but when he went at the request of the authorities to see them, he found them in an angry mood.'[47] He remembered that 'All were in (an) excited temper (sic).'

So much so that Seymour (the Magistrate) is reported to have said that for every one European life, one thousand Indians would be sacrificed. Someone suggested bombarding of the town (Amritsar). As aeroplanes had flown overhead in the morning, the news of the proposed bombardment spread rapidly.

Das believed that he had averted the bombardment of Amritsar. He informed the officers that if, in any way, any part of the Golden Temple was touched or damaged, there would be no end of trouble, as the temple was held sacred all over Punjab.[48]

But the idea persisted.

Mohammad Sadiq, who also met the British authorities on 11 April to arrange for the disposal of the bodies of the murdered Indians, said: 'The impression I got from the talk I had with them was that, as Europeans had been murdered, their blood could not remain unavenged, and if there be the least resistance or disobedience of any breach of the peace, sufficient amount of force would be used, and if necessary, the city would be bombarded.'[49]

---

47. INC Report, p. 63.

48. INC Report, pp. 57–8, statement 1.

49. INC Report, p. 58, statement 19.

The threats continued on 11 and 12 April, causing worry and concern. Because of the 'war-like' environment, increasing militarisation, the cutting off of the water supply, the talk about bombardment and the reluctance of the civil authorities to give any kind of reassurance, the fear within the walled city spiraled higher, and so did, probably, people's frustration at being treated like criminals. The increasing number of soldiers on the streets meant that women and children remained indoors and few men ventured out unless there was urgent work. The city would have been deserted due to the ongoing 'hartal' and it is likely that food supplies were affected too.

Amritsar was becoming increasingly isolated from the rest of the world.

Dr Balmokand, Sub Assistant Surgeon, recollected a conversation with Smith, the Civil Surgeon, who said 'that General Dyer was coming and he would bombard the city. He drew diagrams and showed us how the city would be shelled and how it would be razed to the ground in half an hour. I said I lived in the city, and what was to become of me if there was bombardment. He replied that I had better leave the city and live in the hospital if I wanted to save myself.'[50]

This conversation, which took place before General Dyer came to Amritsar, indicated that there was already a plan to bring him in to take extreme measures. For the British, the death of twenty Indians was not a high enough price, nor were the restrictions that had been placed on the residents of Amritsar. Could there have been, already, a plan discussed with Dyer, which Smith knew about? The question does arise whether Smith had discussed bringing Dyer to Amritsar when he had met O'Dwyer, as mentioned earlier. (Dyer, however, denied any knowledge of plans to bomb Amritsar while giving evidence before the Hunter Committee.)

Oddly, even though the people of Amritsar were being

---

50. INC Report, p. 58, statement 20.

systematically terrorised, and even though there was no further violence, Irving was extremely concerned that British control over the old city had been lost.

More troops went out and picketed the city all around, according to the ironically named 'Government House War Diaries'. Around 100 troops with rifles went into the city as far as the Kotwali, leaving strong pickets on the side streets. From this point the Kotwali and all its approaches were held by troops.[51] This is important to note as the city was being fortified and prepared for another battle. By the morning, Dyer, who was based in Jullundur, had sent 100 British and 200 Indian troops to Amritsar.[52] This could have been in preparation for his arrival, later in the day.

The authorities continued to worry that Hindu–Muslim unity remained unshaken.[53] 'The dead were taken from Khair-ud-din's Mosque out by the Sultanwind Gate; large processions both of Hindus and Mohammadans seem to have followed in the city but not further.' Near the Sultanwind Gate, on 12 April, there were shouts of 'Hindu-Mussalman ki jai.'[54] At another city (Lahore), Hindus and Muslims were seen drinking from the same water pot. This was shocking enough for the British to report it, and similar reports were coming in from other parts of the country, including Bombay.[55]

While Kitchin was in Amritsar, he also noted in his report, sent at 11.30 a.m. on 11 April 1919, that: 'All is quiet outside. Hindus and Mussalmans have combined, the Mussalmans being the more violent.'[56]

---

51. Parliamentary Report, p. 28.
52. Datta, *New Light*, p. 377.
53. Parliamentary Report, pp. 27–28; others.
54. Parliamentary Report, p. 28; others.
55. Horniman, *Amritsar and Our Duty*, p. 77–8.
56. Datta, *New Light*, p. 377.

Yet, even before Kitchin went back to Lahore, on 11 April at 10.40 a.m., his wife had already reported that her husband had wired at 9 a.m. to say the situation was calmer and that he hoped to return the same evening to Lahore.[57] Similar reports that the area was quiet came in from the Station Master and Kitchin himself, who said that the funeral processions were orderly. However, as mentioned before, he was disappointed with MacDonald. He made sure his disappointment was directly communicated to O'Dwyer. They obviously required someone who could take a hard line.

That would explain why the more pacific MacDonald might not have been in charge by the evening of 11 April. The first indication of this, in a day of rapid developments, was another ominous telegram dated 11 April 1919, which was sent at 9.30 p.m. from the Officer Commanding, Amritsar, to Aviation, Lahore:

> Return aeroplane which went back this evening if possible. Send bombs and machine guns by first available train.[58]

Brigadier General Reginald Edward Harry Dyer CB, who commanded the Jullundur brigade, had arrived in Amritsar by 9 p.m. to take over from MacDonald.

---

57. Datta, *New Light*, p. 375.
58. Datta, *New Light*, p. 378.

2

A Gift of Fortune

> But this unexpected gift of fortune, this unhoped for defiance, this concentration of the rebels in an open space—it gave him an opportunity as he could not have devised. It separated the guilty from the innocent, it placed them where he would have wished them to be—within reach of his sword. The enemy had committed such another mistake as prompted Cromwell to exclaim at Dunbar, 'The Lord hath delivered them into my hands'.
>
> —*The Life of General Dyer* by Ian Colvin[1]

Reginald Dyer was not a very well-known entity when he arrived in Amritsar, though there are indications that a few people, such as Lieutenant Colonel Smith, had heard about him. Before he hit immortality as a mass murderer, he had a fairly humdrum career. He was the son of a brewer and had grown up in Simla, studying at Bishop Cotton School. He was able to speak Hindustani fluently, and this would have definitely helped him in his career, as he could communicate

---

1. Ian Colvin, *The Life of General Dyer* (London: William Blackwood & Sons Ltd., 1929), p. 172.

easily with his troops. He was said to have been quite popular with them. However, he came from the 'tradesman' class and this was a drawback in the army, which had its own caste system. The highlight of his career so far had been a stint at the Sarhad (at the far end of Baluchistan) where he tried to play at being Lawrence of Arabia and aimed to annex properties for the British, through a series of misadventures. Finally, after practically wrecking the force there, he was recalled. By the time he reached Jullundur, he was in his 50s and quite unwell, but he managed to hide his illnesses as he needed the commission. He suffered from arteriosclerosis (hardening of the arteries), which is often quoted as one of the reasons for his behaviour at Jallianwala Bagh. There are also accounts of blinding headaches for which the only cure was alcohol, served by his trusted aide, Brigade Major F.C. Briggs. Perhaps he came to Jallianwala Bagh still looking for a moment of glory by which to prove himself to his peers, who had already done far better than him.

But Dyer was not the only 'Officer Commanding' sent to Amritsar. When examining the tragic circumstances surrounding the killings at Jallianwala Bagh, there is an underlying sense that the army officers being sent to Amritsar had been given free rein. It is possible that O'Dwyer, sitting miles away in Lahore, was attempting to keep a lid on Amritsar, while attending his own farewell parties and preparing for a glorious departure. The steel frame of the British bureaucracy showed signs of rot as there was little connect between the events unfolding in Amritsar—which was quiet now—and the repressive commands flowing back from Kitchin and O'Dwyer. It is also doubtful whether others further up the ladder like Viceroy Chelmsford, Secretary of State Edwin Montagu, or Prime Minister Lloyd George had all the facts before them.

Whatever the circumstances, the fact is that three commanding officers were simultaneously present in Amritsar on 11 April.

As M.H.L. Morgan was to write in his recollections of the

period, *The Truth About Amritsar: By An Eyewitness*: 'MacDonald had been less than forty eight hours in Amritsar when I was summoned to the Divisional office. I was shown a letter from Kitchin, the Commissioner, to General Benyon, saying "Major MacDonald has done nothing to quell the rebellion. Please send an officer who is not afraid to act." General Benyon decided that I was the officer. I was ordered to proceed as soon as possible to Amritsar...'[2]

Morgan was told that 'Amritsar is in the hands of rebels. It is your duty to get it back.'

Yet there had been no rebellion after the clash on 10 April morning. Only funerals had taken place on 11 April, while rumours flew thick and fast. The city was quiet, if not calm. Where were the rebels?

General Beynon, who had asked Morgan to go, added cautiously while giving his evidence to the Hunter Committee: 'Owing to the importance of the Command at Amritsar, I deemed it advisable to send a more senior officer, and accordingly Major Morgan, DSO, Commanding 1-124th Baluchis, proceeded to Amritsar on the night of the 11th April to take over command there.'

He added: 'Arrival of Brigadier General Dyer, CB, at Amritsar...General Dyer had however arrived at Amritsar at 21.00 hours and assumed personal command in addition to establishing his Brigade Headquarters there.'

Nowhere does he mention that he had asked General Dyer to come to Amritsar.

In the confusion between the civil administration and the army, it later appeared that Dyer, who had been posted in Jullundur, might have indeed come of his own volition.[3]

---

2. M.H.L. Morgan, 'The Truth about Amritsar: By an Eye Witness', 72/22/1 T, in the Imperial War Museum.

3. Nick Lloyd, *The Amritsar Massacre: The Untold Story of One Fateful Day* (London: I.B. Tauris Co. Ltd., 2011), p. 86.

Never one to tolerate 'insolence', he had arrived in the city to teach the people of Amritsar a 'moral lesson', as he later put it. This would have been entirely in character; he was known to have extended his brief in the past, particularly when he was asked to go to the Afghan border. A few times, he had even used his fists to settle scores—the tough facade hid a quick temper.[4]

He also had a fairly inflated belief in himself. He had asked to be promoted to General while at the Sarhad and had been given a temporary rank as Brigadier General. Even when he was given command of the 45th Infantry Brigade in Jullundur, it remained a temporary rank. Thus the Army List, May 1919, states his rank as 'Colonel (temporary Brigadier-General) R.E.H Dyer, C.B., Brigade Commander Jullundur Brigade (45th Infantry Brigade).' Despite all the bluff and bravado, he remained a Colonel till the end.[5]

He claimed (even though there is no evidence of it in his report of 25 August to the 16th Division) that at around 2 p.m., on 11 April, he had received a telegram from the 16th Division to go to Amritsar and take charge. As there is no trace of the telegram or any summons to him, it is possible that he just decided to go. While giving evidence in Lahore, he added that there was a roundabout way of communication as many of the telegraph and phone lines were down.

Irving had by now given up his authority, and despite the quiet atmosphere, and the funerals being completed peacefully, he still maintained the city was 'impertinently hostile'. He did not actually enter the walled city after 10 April, and later remarked, 'it was freely said that it might be the Raj of the Sarkar outside, but inside it was Hindu-Musalmanon

---

4. Nigel Collett, *The Butcher of Amritsar: Brigadier General Reginald Dyer* (Hambledon and London, 2005), pp. 141, 152, 214.

5. Collett, *Butcher of Amritsar*, p. 476.

ki hakumat.'6

This was not quite correct, as the streets were largely deserted on 11 and 12 April, apart from the funeral processions. But a few people had come out to see the destruction of the buildings. When he was questioned by the Hunter Committee about not going into the city after 10 April, Irving said, 'Neither cared, nor were allowed by the Military authorities. None of us were such fools as to put our heads into a hornet's nest.' Obviously the death of the five Europeans made him imagine others were equally at risk.

Clearly, the civil administration preferred a military occupation. But the question then arose, which was never really answered—was it legal?

O'Dwyer was asked during the Hunter Committee hearings whether, upon arrival in Amritsar and having consulted the Deputy Commissioner on the spot, Kitchin came to the conclusion that he should hand over charge to the military.7

O'Dwyer answered 'yes'. When further pressed if this was legal—or whether the authority was handed over under a specific law, O'Dwyer replied, 'I do not know of any specific law, but I should think that if the civil authority were powerless and if the military authority alone could cope with the situation, an officer would be failing in his duty if he did not transfer the authority and ask the military to take charge.' When again asked whether there was a law or rule under which it could be done, he said there was no rule or law under which the commissioner could on his own accord hand over his authority to a military officer. 'I take it that it was necessary in the emergency: it was an act taken for the benefit of the public. That is the only way I can explain it. I am not a legal authority on constitutional

---

6. Evidence, Amritsar, pp. 6–7.

7. V.N. Datta, *New Light on the Punjab Disturbances in 1919* (Simla: Indian Institute of Advanced Study, 1975), pp. 226-7.

law. Anything that is not expressly prohibited may be taken as allowed.'

Perhaps because there was no clear cut process, and both Kitchin and O'Dwyer were simply trying out various options for a tough executioner, when Major Morgan—who had been 'officially' sent by Beynon—arrived in Amritsar, he found that Dyer was already in situ. As the chain of authority had broken down, it was Dyer who asked Morgan to stay on.

In the Hunter Committee Report, O'Dwyer appeared unable to explain exactly how Dyer took charge from Major MacDonald, who was still in command in Amritsar. Meanwhile, Morgan was not even mentioned in the cross-examination.

> Q: Then when General Dyer arrived he was handed over charge by Mr Miles Irving. That again complicated the position. The authority had already been handed over to Major MacDonald by Mr Kitchin?
>
> O'Dwyer: Did he say so? I did not know it. Perhaps when the General arrived he wanted some definite authorisation.
>
> Q: That authority had already been absolutely handed over to Major MacDonald?

Still unable to confirm that General Dyer had simply taken over without anyone asking him to do so, O'Dwyer said, 'I suggest that such authority as had not been transferred still vested in the Deputy Commissioner.' (Implying that, despite Kitchin having handed over authority to MacDonald, Irving still had some remaining authority which could be handed over to Dyer. It was a peculiar reply.)

> Q: Could it be divided? Was there a division of authority?
>
> O'Dwyer: It was only my suggestion. The situation was one that could not be controlled by the civil authority; the military had to take charge to re-establish order.

Q: On the 11th I presume that there was no civil authority. Then Mr Miles Irving hands over the same authority handed over (to Major Macdonald) by Mr Kitchin the previous day to General Dyer.

O'Dwyer, still hunting for an answer for the fact that there was no actual record of the transfer of authority from MacDonald to Dyer, replied:

> 'It was perhaps understood that the transfer of authority in the first instance was a temporary one, and now that a new commander had arrived, it was necessary to make a fresh transfer. Perhaps that was in their minds…it might have been done to regularise the whole thing, Mr Kitchin probably had not given anything in writing.'

Q: Then again you think that if he thought the situation demanded the handing over of authority to the military authorities, he was justified in doing it?

O'Dwyer: I think he was justified; in fact the situation required it.

Q: But there is no specific instruction about it?

O'Dwyer: I have had no access to books.

Q: Your contention is that what is not generally prohibited is allowed.

O'Dwyer: Yes.

Even though no direct message came from Lahore (at least, there is none on record), it could be that Dyer, quite presumptuously, took over the command. A telephonic message was sent on 11 April at 10.30 a.m. (by railway telephone) from the Private Secretary, Lahore, to the Commissioner, Amritsar:

> Please instruct Officer Commanding Troops, Amritsar, to report situation to General Officer Commanding, Jullundur, and repeat to General Officer Commanding, Lahore Cantonments.

While the Officer Commanding had been asked to report the situation to Dyer, he might have taken it as a signal that he had been asked to go to Amritsar. However, some authors, both British and Indian, claim that there was a premeditated plan to send Dyer to Amritsar. They say that O'Dwyer had spoken to Dyer prior to the massacre, and that is how it was planned.

O'Dwyer had always maintained that a senior official in the Viceroy's office had told him 'they should make an example.' This is on record. But according to Terence Blackburn:

> O'Dwyer noted the instruction carefully in his diary. He then called a meeting with the top British military and civil officials at Government House in Lahore, to decide on a course of action. The meeting was unofficial and no notes were taken. At the meeting, Brigadier General Dyer was verbally instructed '*to teach Indians the lesson that revolution was a dangerous game*' and to avenge the deaths of the five English civilians.[8]

Could this be true? There is no reference to it in Dyer's own accounts—unless a decision was also taken that he should not speak about it. On the other hand, if he had received instructions from O'Dwyer it would explain Dyer's own sudden appearance on the scene despite the fact that Morgan had already been sent to take over from MacDonald. It would also explain why no one asked any questions about who had asked him to come; certainly, O'Dwyer, when questioned by the Hunter Committee, had no answers. It would also explain how Smith already knew on 11 April that Dyer was coming to the city.

However, Dyer's own statement on 25 August 1919 (from Brigadier General REH Dyer, CB, Commanding 45th Brigade, to the General Staff, 16th Division) puts a slightly different spin

---

8. Terence Blackburn, *A Miscellany of Mutinies and Massacres in India* (New Delhi: APH Publishing Corporation, 2007), p. 172.

on events, making it difficult to prove if a telegram was sent to summon him to Amritsar. He wrote, 'All communication between Amritsar and Jullundur were interrupted at 4.0 P.M. on the 10th, but at 8.0 p.m. we got a wire through to Amritsar by the Railway telegraph, in a roundabout way, telling Amritsar that troops were coming. At about 2.0 P.M. on the 11th April I received a telegram from the 16th Division (Lahore) telling me to proceed to Amritsar and take charge of the situation if the situation at Jullundur permitted it.' He met the Commissioner at Jullundur and left as soon as he could, arriving in Amritsar at nine in the night. He held his first meeting inside a railway carriage at the Amritsar railway station which had become a temporary headquarter for the civil and military authorities.[9]

Almost immediately upon arrival, Dyer took charge of the situation. There were 1,185 troops in Amritsar by then and all were reporting to him. He co-opted Morgan to work with him.

At just past midnight, Dyer went into the city with around 50 troops, along with Irving and Massey. Ashraf Khan, the Indian Inspector of Police for the city, had a conference with them about the arrangements for 12 April. Khan fed the fears of the others by claiming that villagers were gathering from surrounding areas to drive out the British, creating a 'danda fauj'. As Indians had no weapons, sticks were commonly used. And while this literally meant 'army with sticks' to make it appear more ferocious perhaps, it was commonly known as 'bludgeon army' or 'danda fauj'.

At around 2 a.m., Dyer ordered that the electricity be cut off. (This has already been mentioned in detail before but no reason was given for the action.) We can only assume he needed to show the population of Amritsar that he had arrived and things would be different from now on.

---

9. Evidence, Amritsar, p. 202.

The next morning, Dyer shifted camp from the railway station to the much grander milieu of Ram Bagh, where the nineteenth-century summer palace of Maharaja Ranjit Singh was located. He set about placing pickets to ensure that people could not enter the city without being checked. Commissioner Kitchin and Deputy Inspector General Donald had again driven down from Lahore and heard rumours about an attack from the Manjha area on Amritsar. Though nothing happened en route, Kitchin was perhaps still hoping for revenge for the killings of the five Europeans. He stated: 'I was advised on the road that the trouble would go further unless Amritsar riots were stopped at once.'[10]

He complained that (despite the severe reprisals of 10 April) the people of Amritsar did not show their 'good disposition towards us...We could get no information, and they would give us no assistance.' According to him, it was only after martial law was imposed de facto with the arrival of Dyer that the attitude of the people changed and they became more cooperative. Now the British wanted an example to be made, which would terrorise the people in Punjab in general. As the news of Gandhi's arrest as well as the detention of Kitchlew and Satya Pal spread, uprisings were taking place all over. And it was only after the killings at Jallianwala Bagh that Kitchin felt 'the troubles were over'.

As he said during his cross-examination by C.H. Setalvad:

> Q: So I take your view to be that it was necessary to do something on a grand scale to strike terror into the minds of the people, was that the idea?
>
> A: Well, with some modifications of epithets, yes...the military situation was so serious that an example was necessary?

---

10. Evidence, Amritsar, p. 221.

Q: The military situation, not in Amritsar itself, but in the surrounding parts?

A: In the surrounding parts and in the Punjab generally.[11]

Well briefed by the time of enquiry about all the various disorders taking place, Dyer would quote some of these, including the purported rising in Manjha, in his own defence later. O'Dwyer did not need to be present to urge Dyer to take strong steps as everyone was encouraging him to act against an invisible (and possibly make-believe) threat of rebellion.

Amritsar was peaceful, even according to the official messages that were being sent to Lahore, for instance: 'Troops have gone into the city to occupy and make arrests. General Dyer from Jullundur commanding. No news yet. Village peaceful. Headquarters now Rambagh. Message can be sent from station.'

Because of the aircraft hovering over Amritsar on 12 April, Dyer was able to find out that a crowd was gathering at Sultanwind Gate and headed there. He was out on the streets with 120 British and 310 Indian troops along with two armoured cars.

Dyer was a showman who felt that the very sight of military power would immobilise the enemy. He had tried this bluff before when he was posted at the Sarhad—where he would apparently position his forces in such a way that they appeared more sizable than they actually were.

Malik Fateh Khan, the Naib Tehsildar, remembered the procession which had City Inspector Ashraf Khan and his Sub Inspector Obeidulla mounted on horses at the head. Then came the occupants of the bamboo cart, followed by the contingent of white troops, and two cars: Dyer and Irving seated in the first and Rehill and Plomer in the second. The Indian troops brought up the rear. A similar procession without the Naib Tehsildar in the bamboo cart was taken out on 12 April.

---

11. Evidence, Amritsar, pp. 164–5.

In his evidence, the Naib Tehsildar said the hartal was on, and Europeans were not being served in any of the markets. As he was working for the government, he too found it difficult to get provisions. He said the city was in bad shape as everywhere people said that Amritsar belonged to Hindus and Muslims.

While the grouping at Sultanwind Gate turned out to be another funeral procession, Dyer was not pleased. He said: 'the bearing of inhabitants was most insolent and many spat on the ground as the troops passed.' The slogans they raised on Hindu-Muslim unity would have annoyed him even more. He later reported that it was difficult to disperse them, and that he had considered shooting them. This was despite the fact that the large crowds were coming back possibly after a prayer meeting for those who had died on 10 April.

Indeed, people returning from the burial grounds did encounter soldiers kneeling on the ground, facing the crowd, ready to shoot.

It was obvious that the presence of Dyer and his troops did not intimidate the crowd, which was still upset over the loss of their loved ones and not inclined to welcome a long line of marching soldiers accompanied by cars. This was the first large-scale display of military might that the disgruntled residents of Amritsar were exposed to.

One among the crowd, Somdatt, later said that the Deputy Commissioner held a gun to his head and asked him to surrender.[12] Somdatt was also accused of being 'Ratto'. 'Ratto' and 'Bugga' were two of the 'ringleaders' (according to the information with the British) who had led the riots on 10 April. They faced immediate arrest.

Interestingly, both Mahashe Rattan Chand (Ratto) and Chaudhri Bugga Mall (Bugga) were much more than what the British administration files would have us believe. They

---

12. K.D. Malaviya, *Open Rebellion In The Punjab: With Special Reference to Amritsar* (Allahabad: Abhyudaya Press), p. 32.

are examples of how respectable men were deemed terrorists because they organised political meetings or led processions. Ratto came from an orthodox family. He supplied piece goods for Marwari firms but was known more for his physical prowess. He and Bugga set up akharas, or wrestling academies, where they taught exercise and wrestling to young men. Having developed an interest in politics, they were influenced by some of the leaders in Lahore, such as Lala Duni Chand, who was a barrister. In turn, they persuaded Kitchlew and Satya Pal to hold the next Congress session at Amritsar in 1919 and had attended the one in Delhi. According to the *Tribune* (13 April 1961):

> Both Mahashe Rattan Chand and Chaudhuri Bugga Mal underwrote the entire bill of a Congress session, which was estimated at Rs 50,000. A sort of guarantee had to be given to the AICC headquarters.
>
> As evidence of their capacity to organise such a big gathering, both these leaders had arranged the Punjab Political Conference at Amritsar in 1918.

Obviously well appreciated in Amritsar, they encouraged Hindus and Muslims to come together as they were convinced that India could never be a free country without this communal harmony. They had helped to organise the Ram Naumi celebrations on 9 April 1919 in which Hindus and Muslims had displayed a remarkable unity.

As it happened, Bugga was arrested on 12 April (when Dyer went into the city later in the day, hunting for the 'criminals') as was Ratto a few days later. Under martial law, their property was confiscated and they were both sentenced to death. When the appeal for their death sentence was rejected, it was Pandit Madan Mohan Malaviya who spoke for them at the Imperial Legislative Council—his intervention extended to several hours—and forced the sentences to be commuted to life imprisonment. They were sent to the Andamans, kept in solitary confinement and tortured until Bugga's health was broken. He was shifted to Alipore Jail in Bengal, then to Lahore and Multan. The two leaders were finally released in 1936—and received a huge welcome when they returned after 17 years to Amritsar.[13]

Despite their importance to the political narrative unfolding in Punjab, these 'heroes' of Amritsar were treated as no better than 'thugs' or 'hooligans', mainly because they had been key figures in the organisation of the hartals, were in touch with other political leaders and so were considered dangerous.

On 12 April, Dyer warned the crowds on the street that they they would now be dealt with under military law, through a proclamation which was issued by his Brigade Major, F.C. Briggs on his behalf:

> The inhabitants of Amritsar are hereby warned that if they will cause damage to any property or will commit any acts of violence in the environs of Amritsar, it will be taken for granted that such acts are due to incitement in Amritsar city, and offenders will be punished according to Military Law.
>
> All meetings and gatherings are hereby prohibited and will be dispersed at once under Martial Law.

The proclamation was given to the police, but there is no clarity even in the Hunter Committee evidence whether it was published or displayed.[14]

Even though there was no official declaration of martial law (it would not be pronounced till 15 April), the Brigadier General issued the proclamation announcing the commencement of 'Military Law' with the full compliance of

---

13. *Tribune*, 13 April 1961, quoted in Raja Ram, Appendix B: 'Forgotten Heroes' in *The Jallianwala Bagh Massacre: A Premeditated Plan* (Chandigarh: Punjab University, 2002).

14. Evidence, Amritsar, p. 219; Hunter Committee Report, p. 43.

the Deputy Commissioner, Irving. As far as shooting the 'mob' was concerned, it would not have been easy, as the inner city was quite compact. The narrow streets made it difficult for a substantial crowd to gather, and at best he could only shoot a few. That would not have created the large-scale remorse that O'Dwyer and Kitchin were looking for.

However, while in the city, Dyer arrested a few people. 'Small parties of troops were sent with police to make arrests in connection with the crimes of the 10th and several important arrests were made.' But again, there is little information regarding the names of all those arrested.[15] Dina Nath, another important leader and organiser of political meetings was arrested around this time.

In the telephonic message dated 12 April 1919, which he sent to Lahore, Dyer tried to establish his credentials:

> I marched in force through city yesterday. In combination with arrests made this apparently had a very good effect. Am going to occupy important parts in city today and issue proclamation.

Dyer was never one to fall short on praise for his own efforts. Apparently seven arrests were made in all. This was the official figure, but from then on, hundreds were randomly arrested and taken to the Kotwali, to be forced to confess to having taken part in the riots, or to give false evidence or be tortured.

The records of the 1/25th London Battalion, which had been brought from Jullundur to Amritsar, provide a slightly more colourful description and one can sense the awe in which the men held Dyer:

> At 10 a.m. on the 12th, General Dyer, with his usual vigour, hurried the majority of the Force down to one of the furthest

---

15. Hunter Committee Report, p. 42.

city gates (the Sultanwind Gate), where he and the Police Commissioner, in breaking up a prohibited, and therefore seditious, meeting, which jeered and spat at them, caused a number of arrests to be made.

It is obvious that these unfortunate men were arrested, not for acts of so-called sedition, but for simply slighting the white sahibs. As mentioned before, the troops misunderstood the reason for the gathering—which was a funeral procession. It is also possible that some among the distraught might have wanted to show their disregard for the troops.

What is surprising is that Dyer seemed to have misunderstood too. He had, after all, been born and brought up in India and knew the language well. Yet, that day in Amritsar, in 1919, at the age of 55, the mockery from the civilians stung deep: his subsequent actions were meant to prove to everyone his tough military acumen, thus far overlooked.

Other arrests were also made near the Kotwali. The London Battalion witnessed the deep humiliation of civilians, which was to set the tone for the next few months of military-led barbarity in Punjab: 'The prisoners were immediately handcuffed and marched back with the column to the Ram Bagh Gardens, where they were chained, under a strong Gurkha guard, round a tree in the centre of the camp.'

The troops were told to remain on full alert. 'As a result, for many days not so much as a boot-lace was untied, even had any individual found sufficient free time to commence the operation.'

According to Dyer, he wanted to punish the citizens of Amritsar for the 'crimes' they had committed on 10 April. This is regardless of the fact that he had arrived on the evening of 11 April—which had been a quiet day—and he (nor anyone else) had any idea who precisely had killed the five Europeans, or indulged in arson and looting. It is possible that many of those responsible were either dead or wounded or had escaped from Amritsar, but that seems to have been a minor consideration. He was guided entirely by the information given to him by the local Criminal Investigation Department (CID) or the network of spies that the British relied on.

Possibly unaware of the 'proclamation' of the morning (which was not yet printed or posted in public), on the evening of 12 April, a meeting was called at the Hindu Sabha School, at Dhab Khatikan, which proposed a gathering the next day at Jallianwala Bagh.[16] According to the Congress Report on the Punjab disturbances, Hans Raj, a young man who later turned approver in the 'Amritsar Conspiracy Case', called the meeting 'on the 13th April at Jallianwala Bag under the chairmanship of Lala Kanhya Lal'. Kanhya Lal (75) was a pleader, and a popular one. He later denied having asked for a meeting. It was suggested that his name was used to 'draw a large crowd'. There were murmurs that Hans Raj was in the pay of the British. The fact that he turned approver later does lend some credibility to this suspicion.

However, at the meeting, it was decided that the hartal would continue till their two leaders, Kitchlew and Satya Pal, were released. This would have meant further trouble for the residents of Amritsar, but they were determined to defy the authorities. Gurbaksh Rai, a homeopathic doctor made a forceful speech in which he said that the 'government had threatened them. They (the people) should not mind the government but obey the orders of their leader, Gandhi ji.' He seconded the proposal regarding the suspension of business.[17] These meetings were noted in the Amritsar police diaries and the CID reports, showing that despite the precautions taken by the organisers of the meeting, it had been infiltrated

---

16. INC Report, p. 52.

17. Extracts from the Amritsar Police Diary and CID Reports, quoted in Raja Ram, *Jallianwala Bagh*, p. 81.

by informants. Or in it was a trap, as many were to suspect later.

In fact, there are varying reports about who called for the meeting at Jallianwala Bagh the next day. But many of those attending saw it as a special way of remembering their leaders, and a means of somehow carrying on with the protests against the Rowlatt Acts. It was a remarkably courageous move, given that the atmosphere was so vitiated and arrests had been made over the events of 10 April. Various resolutions were also drafted in which the proposed gathering the next day was referred to as 'this grand meeting', which meant that a large crowd was assured for 13 April. It is also obvious from the tone of the resolutions that the meeting was meant to be entirely peaceful. Its purpose was to reassure those whose family members had been arrested that they had the support of the inhabitants of Amritsar and that the anti-Rowlatt Act agitation would continue.

The resolutions that were framed for debate the next day survived in the evidence of a witness, Lala Rup Lal Puri. It was clear that those attending were against the 'despotic conduct of the Government' which might, in fact, prove 'deleterious to the British Government'.

Copies of all resolutions passed during the meeting at Jallianwala Bagh were to be sent to the Secretary of State, the Viceroy, the Lieutenant Governor of the Punjab, and the Deputy Commissioner of Amritsar, and a copy of the Resolution No. 4 was to be sent to the families of both the respective deported leaders. 'The Resolution No. 4 was specifically about those who had been arrested and interned—and was to request the government for immediate release.'[18]

---

18. Transcript of the Sir Michael O'Dwyer versus Sir C. Sankaran Nair trial, May 1924 and evidence of Lala Rup Lal Puri taken by the commission in Punjab, quoted in Collett, *Butcher of Amritsar*, p. 247.

If this was to be a large meeting, and the resolutions were already framed, the CID and other spies of the government would have definitely known about it. If these resolutions were drafted on 12 April, and copies were prepared to be handed out to all the authorities, then Dyer, Irving, Kitchin, and most importantly O'Dwyer, would have known and had time to plan for it. However, at that time, very few survivors of the massacre were to admit that they were present at the Bagh and what the purpose of the meeting was, for fear of arrest. It was only when the Congress Sub-Committee started gathering evidence almost six months later, that the truth began to slowly emerge. This evidence from witnesses at the Bagh was not part of the Hunter Committee report, and so was left out of the official narrative.

In his evidence before the Hunter Committee, O'Dwyer said, 'I do not think that any one who was there is likely to come forward and tell you he went to that meeting with a specified object. That was the difficulty I found. When I went to Amritsar no one would come forward and say he had been at the Jallianwala Bagh because they all evidently looked at it in this way that probably if they said they were at the Jallianwala Bagh they might get run in for defiance of authority. It might have been that they had a guilty conscience; it might have been that the authorities would think they had a guilty conscience in the matter.'[19]

It was also a huge problem getting information about the dead and wounded, as family members and friends of the victims were worried about large-scale arrests.

As O'Dwyer said in his evidence: 'When I asked in Amritsar a week later (after the massacre), the information given to me was that there were a good number of people wounded but they were hidden away and would not come forward because they were afraid of being prosecuted. It was difficult to ascertain anything owing to the unwillingness of

---

19. Datta, *New Light*, p. 231.

the people who had been in the Jallianwala Bagh and had got away from there, whether safe and sound or whether wounded to come forward. I did not go into the thing in greater detail, I had so many other things in my mind, but that was the general impression conveyed to me.'[20]

The fear among the people would have been very real. Records show that at least 200 people—if not more—were arrested from Amritsar in the 'National Bank Loot Case' and tried under martial law.[21] This was only one case against the residents of Amritsar and, despite the lack of evidence, people were arrested, tried and even jailed. Under martial law (which was already de facto in place) anything was possible. Naturally, when the massacre took place at Jallianwala Bagh, it was impossible for anyone to speak up—it would have led immediately to imprisonment. Dyer's own report about the massacre was not sought till August 1919.[22]

As there was no attempt immediately after the event to find out (in an empathetic fashion) who called the meeting, and what its purpose was, much of the surviving evidence and witnesses fell through the cracks of unrecorded history. The other problem was that, over the next few months, witnesses were forced to give false testimony or incriminate others. There would soon be thousands of these cases, and it would be difficult to ascertain the truth, for years. Thus many would claim that they had only been at the Bagh to attend the Baisakhi festival. This claim allowed them to be released—if they were believed. This led later to the myth that the crowd was largely comprised of those who had come to attend the Baisakhi festival.

---

20. Datta, *New Light*, p. 231.

21. Datta, Appendix 23: 'Statement Showing the Sentences Passed by the Martial Law Commissions Together with the Orders of the Government' in *New Light*, p. 643.

22. Evidence, Amritsar, p. 201.

The people of Amritsar were already overwhelmed by the huge presence of the mobilising army, the cutting off of water and electricity and the arrests made in the past few days. In the frightening atmosphere created by the British Army, where none could enter or exit the city without permission, and where troops lined the city, it was a courageous act for a crowd to gather at Jallianwala Bagh, or indeed anywhere at all. They would only have gathered if they thought they could find a way to save their families and loved ones. That if they held their heads high and displayed dignity and a peaceful purpose, they would be safe. They were continuing their peaceful protest as requested by their jailed leaders and, in particular, Gandhi.

Perhaps they still vested some faith in the British administration: there was good reason for thinking they were secure as there had been no incidents after 10 April. Holding a political meeting at Jallianwala Bagh was not uncommon. Meetings had been held as recently as 29 March, 30 March, 6 April; and each time the crowd had grown larger and larger—reaching up to 50,000.

What was strange was that no steps were taken to stop the 'forbidden' meeting. Physically blocking people or putting up notices at the entrance would have been very easy. One hundred soldiers stood guard on the main street from Hall Gate, leading up to Town Hall and Jallianwala Bagh. Around 75 policemen were at the Kotwali, next to the Town Hall, less than a six-minute walk from Jallianwala Bagh. Clearly, the only way the traumatised population of Amritsar would have taken such a huge risk was if they believed that it would be a peaceful meeting held under the guidance of a sage leader, Kanhya Lal. This must have been why so many of them took their children along as well.

The Bagh was a barren piece of land, surrounded by houses, and was often used for gatherings and even the occasional function. It was an irregular quadrangle. There were just three trees, a well on one side, and a small shrine on the other. There was no place to hide. The land was used as a playground for children, or for cattle to graze upon. It had one narrow entrance. This was also the main exit. The only other way out of the Bagh was to leap over one side of the wall that was lower—around five feet—than the other sides. There were also a few very narrow openings to squeeze through. It was close to the Golden Temple, so people would come in to rest after they had made their obeisance.

Since 13 April was a Sunday, many of the shops were closed in any case and the hartal was still on. With the constant presence of the army on the streets, few people would have been out in the morning. However, at 9.30 a.m., Dyer decided to make two proclamations—neither of which was likely to have been heard. The Naib Tehsildar who was making the proclamations said he had halted at around 19 places where anywhere between 100 to 500 people had gathered. Most of them, he said, were jeering, and it was doubtful if anyone grasped the importance of his words. He also mentioned that there were announcements of the Jallianwala Bagh meeting taking place simultaneously, or at least discussions about it.

There are also reports of people staying indoors when Dyer's entourage passed by. In any case, the terms of the proclamations were unclear, perhaps deliberately so. They were read out to the beat of a drum by the Naib Tehsildar.

The first proclamation said:

> The inhabitants of Amritsar are hereby warned that if any property is destroyed or other outrages committed in the vicinity of Amritsar it will be taken that incitement to perform these acts originates from Amritsar City, and such measures will be taken by me to punish the inhabitants of Amritsar according to Military law.
>
> All meetings and gatherings are hereby prohibited and I mean to take action in accordance with Military Laws to forthwith disperse all such assemblies.

It was signed 'R.E. Dyer, Brigadier General, Commanding Jullundur Brigade'.

This was a printed proclamation, as was the first part of the second one. But the final and most crucial part of the second proclamation, which spoke of dispersal by 'force of arms', was only read out.[23]

The first part said:

> It is hereby proclaimed to all whom it may concern, that no person residing in the city is permitted or allowed to leave the city in his own private or hired conveyance, or on foot without a pass from one of the following officers
>
> The Deputy Commissioner
> The Superintendent of Police—Mr Rehill
> The Deputy Superintendent of Police—Mr Plomer
> The Assistant Commissioner—Mr Beckett
> Mr Connor, Magistrate
> Mr Seymour, Magistrate
> Ara Muhammad Hussain, Magistrate
> The Police Officer-in-charge of the City Kotwali
> This will be a special form and pass

The next part of the proclamation, which was only read out, said:

> No person residing in the Amritsar city is permitted to leave his house after 8 p.m.
>
> Any persons found in the streets after 8 p.m. are liable to be shot.
>
> No procession of any kind is permitted to parade the streets in the city, or any part of the city, or outside of it, at any time. Any such processions or any gathering of four men would be looked upon and treated as an unlawful assembly and dispersed by force of arms, if necessary.

A note by Irving clarified, 'I have put in the words "if necessary" in the draft which I was asked to edit in legal language so as

---

23. Op. cit., pp. 67–9.

to bring it into line with "liable to be shot" in paragraph 2. 14-4-19'[24]

But did the addition of these words really have any preventive impact or was it only to protect Dyer and Irving?

This second (ambiguous) statement was read out in Urdu and Punjabi and it is the addition of the last two words that indicated that some kind of warning would be given before shooting. The additional information that people would be shot if they were out after 8 p.m., also made it confusing for most. Many who heard it may have thought that people would only be shot after 8 p.m. if they were still on the streets. In any case, the proclamation was made at 19 places, none of which were close to Jallianwala Bagh or even the Golden Temple—the most crowded part of the city and an area where even visitors were likely to throng to. This fact was discussed during the recording of the statement of the Government of Punjab at the Hunter Committee hearings in December 1919.

During the cross-examination, the Naib Tehsildar also clarified that the last and most crucial part of the proclamation was not printed and thus not handed out:

> A: The printed one was as follows:—'The people of Amritsar are hereby warned that if there is any damage to property or life in the city of Amritsar or at any places outlying it'...
>
> Q: Was that the notification that was printed?
>
> A: Yes, this was printed.
>
> Q: The one about meetings was not printed?
>
> A: It was part of this.
>
> Q: The other about going out at night after 8 pm, was it printed or not?
>
> A: That was not printed.[25]

---

24. Datta, *New Light*, p. 380.

25. Evidence, Amritsar, pp. 67–9.

The printed notices were only distributed by the Naib Tehsildar to those who were attending the meetings, and as he was being heckled throughout, it is doubtful if anyone was really interested in reading them. Khan remembered the crowd mocking his words in disbelief and speaking about their own meeting to be held later, at 4 p.m.[26]

Not reading out the proclamation near the Golden Temple was another serious mistake. Copies of it were not pasted at the entrance to Jallianwala Bagh, nor were the Kotwali policemen told that they must prevent a crowd from gathering at Jallianwala Bagh in the evening. This could have been done simply by placing a guard at the single corridor which led in and out of the Bagh.

Not only were insufficient announcements made and the notices not printed in toto, the process of making the proclamation across the city came to an abrupt end when the afternoon sun blazed overhead.

DSP Plomer laconically provided the reason for which the promulgation was insufficiently advertised, in his evidence to the Hunter Committee. He thought that 8,000 to 10,000 people had heard the proclamation by 3 o'clock:

> Q: You thought that was sufficient notice for a town like Amritsar to give of an important proclamation?
>
> A: I did not think anything. When it was too hot to walk in the city I took the nearest route out.
>
> Q: You did not suggest to the General that a longer time might be given?
>
> A: No. When we got to the Majid Mandir the General remarked that it was getting too hot for the troops so took the route to Lohgar Gate.[27]

---

26. Evidence, Amritsar, pp. 67–9.

27. Evidence, Amritsar, p. 40.

Q: And then this proclamation was stopped?

A: Yes.

During the recording of evidence by the Hunter Committee, O'Dwyer was asked about the 'certain precautions' that had been laid down which officials would have to comply with, as enormous powers had been vested in them. From his answers, it became clear that Dyer had neither gone to the area around Jallianwala Bagh, nor made any proclamation there:

> Q: You told the committee that Jallianwala Bagh was the place where meetings were frequently held, good meetings, bad meetings and all sorts of meetings?
>
> O' Dwyer: Yes, that was my information. I was speaking only of inflammatory meetings. I had heard of no other meetings there.

(Later O'Dwyer added that there had been a suggestion that this could have been a prayer meeting.)

> Q: And this must have been known to the civil authorities in Amritsar. Well, when he started on his tour through certain parts of Amritsar City on the 13th of April to prohibit meetings, as you say, why should he have not gone of all places to Jallianwala Bagh to proclaim this notice?
>
> O'Dwyer: I fancy that if he had gone to Jallianwala Bagh, he would have found it empty. It is only used when a great gathering assembles there.
>
> Q: But this is the place, as you have stated, frequently used for the purpose of meetings. If it was his object to prohibit meetings it was an ordinary precaution that certain amount of publicity should have been given to the prohibition notice at that particular place and especially by pasting the notice there which was circulated in the town of Amritsar?
>
> O'Dwyer: I do not suppose General Dyer knew of the existence of the Jallianwala Bagh.

Q: I see there were with him Mr Miles Irving and Mr Plomer who has been all his life in Amritsar. He would have consulted them as to what places he should have this notice circulated in?

O'Dwyer: The Deputy Commissioner says in his report that they went through the city and the proclamation was read.

Q: On that point I very closely questioned the gentleman who read the notice and so on, but it was certainly not done, and General Dyer himself in his evidence said that he did not have it pasted on the Jallianwala Bagh?

O'Dwyer: Yes.

Q: Then further he says in his report that at 12.40 while he was still in the city he got news that a meeting was going to be held at Jallianwala Bagh at 4.30 pm?

O'Dwyer: Yes, the Deputy Commissioner says it had been advertised.

As became clear during the questioning, Dyer was more interested in how to dispose his troops and he 'took absolutely no step to send any notices there (Jallianwala Bagh) or to send anyone there to tell them they ought not to be there.'[28]

And lastly, the term 'unlawful assembly' in a public space was also confusing. Jallianwala Bagh was not a public space—it was 'private property owned in common by several people' and its narrow approach kept it discreetly away from the public sphere. If people met there, it could be construed as a private assembly—so long as the people arrived separately and not together in groups of four. Further, as noted earlier, other assemblies had been held there: the police were aware of it, and had not stopped anyone.

---

28. Datta, *New Light*, p. 229.

In his report to O'Dwyer, dated 14 April 1919, sent at 1 a.m., Irving admitted that, regarding the proposed meeting at Jallianwala Bagh, 'the *General said he would attend it with 100 men.*' This was told to Irving at around 12.40 p.m. on 13 April.²⁹

'On 13th April, 1919 (yesterday) I accompanied the Brigadier-General Commanding into the city where two proclamations were read forbidding all public meetings... these were read by the beat of drum and explained. We went through the city and the proclamation was read in a number of places. It was not only read in legal phraseology but explained by a professional public orator.'

Irving's statement was somewhat of an exaggeration, as already mentioned.

He further said: '*A meeting had been advertised for 4.30 pm that day and the General said he would attend it with 100 men.* I did not think that the meeting would be held, or if held would disperse. So I asked the General to excuse me as I wanted to go to the Fort.'

It is inexplicable that Irving decided not to attend even though Amritsar was under the joint control of military and civil authorities. Nor did he do anything to ensure that the people of Amritsar (under his care) were aware of the dangers of going to that meeting, by pasting posters and so on.

For the residents of Amritsar who wanted to attend, the fact that a respected local elder and barrister, Kanhya Lal, was going to address the assembly meant they could expect to receive some 'sound advice'.

Kanhya Lal himself said in his evidence to the Congress Committee: 'I heard that some men (who have not been traced up to this time to my knowledge) had on the 13th April, proclaimed that a lecture would be given at Jallianwala Bagh

---

29. Datta, *New Light*, p. 379.

by me. This led or induced the public to think that I should have given them some sound advice on the situation then existing.'[30]

A boy with a tin can had also gone around announcing that Kanhya Lal would preside over the 4.30 p.m. meeting at Jallianwala Bagh. He too could not be traced later. Neither could Hans Raj, the person said to have called the meeting, be questioned about the meeting, as he became a government witness in the 'Amritsar Conspiracy Case'. He did not give evidence before the Hunter Committee as he had left for Mesopotamia by then.

Some historians suspect that Hans Raj was used to gather a crowd because Dyer wanted a large number of people to be 'punished'.

That the meeting was going to be held at 4.30 p.m. was confirmed at 1 p.m. to Dyer, who remained at Ram Bagh till at least 4 p.m., and later said, 'I went there as soon as I could. I had to think the matter out. I had to organise my forces and make up my mind as to where I might put my pickets. I thought I had done enough to make the crowd not meet. If they were going to meet I had to consider the military situation and make up my mind what to do, which took me a certain amount of time.'[31]

The 'military situation' meant he must have asked for a map of the area and studied how he could attack the enemy—with maximum impact. He was proud of his technical skills.

Something of what was going through his mind is in his biography, *The Life of General Dyer*, written by Ian Colvin, in close association with Dyer's wife, Anne, in 1929. Puzzled about how to attack the 'rebels', he had exulted over the 'gift of fortune' when the 'rebels' decided to congregate in an open

---

30. INC Report, pp. 52–3, statement 29.
31. Evidence, Amritsar, pp. 114–39.

space. He wanted to take 'immediate action' on the Amritsar 'mob' which had tasted blood and 'began to feel themselves masters of the situation'. He realised that he needed to bring a sizeable crowd together, but how could he do it?[32]

> In the narrow streets, among the high houses and mazy lanes and courtyards of the city the rebels had the advantage of position. They could harass him and avoid his blow. Street fighting he knew to be a bloody, perilous, inconclusive business, in which, besides, the innocent were likely to suffer more than the guilty. Moreover, if the rebels chose their ground cunningly, and made their stand in the neighbourhood of the Golden Temple, there was the added risk of kindling the fanaticism of the Sikhs. Thus he was in this desperate situation: he could not wait and he could not fight.

The fact that the rebels themselves chose to go to an open space, where they could be corralled in was an unexpected 'gift of fortune': something he could only have hoped for and not devised. As his admirer Ian Colvin said, now the enemy was within easy reach of his sword. *'The enemy had committed such another mistake as prompted Cromwell to exclaim at Dunbar. "The Lord hath delivered them into my hands."'*[33]

For Dyer, this was not a murderous attack on defenceless, innocent people. For him the people assembled were all guilty; it was a state of war, in which he wanted to teach them a 'moral' lesson. He assumed all of those present at Jallianwala Bagh to be guilty without any idea of who they were.

Dyer's planning was impeccable. He ensured that he conscripted soldiers who were sufficiently removed from Punjab so they were able to shoot without compunction. He deliberately

---

32. Colvin, *Life of General Dyer*, p. 172.
33. Parliamentary Report, pp. 112–15.

took no British troops, because he wanted no blame to fall on them. He took none of the other commanders—what would have happened if they resisted his orders?

He was thus accompanied by twenty-five Gurkhas and twenty-five Baluchis armed with rifles. These were fierce fighters and the Gurkhas, especially, were incredibly loyal. They had no connections with Punjab, they did not even know the language. Aware that if the crowd rushed towards him, there might be hand-to-hand combat, he took forty Gurkhas armed only with khukris. He was prepared for a bloodbath. Knowing fully well that they would not fit into the entrance, he took two armoured cars. This was more for effect and, if things got out of hand, for escape. He also placed pickets all along the routes to the Bagh so people could be shot even if they escaped.

As the Hunter Committee admitted in its report to the British Parliament in 1920, 'It appears that General Dyer, as soon as he heard about the contemplated meeting, made up his mind to go there with troops and fire' because they had 'defied his authority' by assembling. The fact that they may have been unaware of his prohibitory orders was not important for him. He wanted to create a 'wide impression'.

He said, 'If they disobeyed my orders it showed that there was complete defiance of law, that there was something much more serious behind it than I imagined, that therefore these were rebels, and I must not treat them with gloves on. They had come to fight if they defied me, and I was going to teach them a lesson.'[34]

In his defence, British historians have said that he took a very small force and that he was surprised by the crowd that he found, forcing him to react the way he did. This is contrary to the facts. He had carefully calculated how he would spread the force available to him all around the city and an aircraft flying

---

34. Parliamentary Report, pp. 112–15.

over the meeting had already conveyed to him the strength of the crowd.[35]

Among the British troops, he had the following allocated already:

Duty	Men
Station pickets	37
Bridge guard	11
Detachment Tarn Taran	22
Armed train to Pathankote	26
Armoured train	17
Fort Govindgarh	80
Cantonments	190
	389

And Indian troops

Duty	Men
Detachment, Dhariwal	26
Detachment, Tarn Taran	34
Train escorts	80
Repairing line escort	10
Construction train	10
Blockhouse on railway from Amritsar to Atari	40
Amritsar pickets	132
Kotwali (reinforcing police)	50
	382[36]

---

35. Parliamentary Report, pp. 112–15; Evidence, Amritsar, pp. 114–39.
36. Colvin, *Life of Dyer*, p. 173.

He stationed around fifty men to protect his Ram Bagh base, and also dropped off five pickets of forty each en route to Jallianwala Bagh. It was thus that he was left with 'fifty rifles, forty armed Gurkhas and two armoured cars.' But he also had another fifty stationed at the Kotwali, which was not very far from Jallianwala Bagh.

Of course, the people assembling at the Bagh had no inkling of his plan, while he knew about their meeting. The CID, based in the Kotwali, were keeping a close eye on the assembly, as they had been asked to do. They too did not request people to leave, or stop them from going to the Bagh, following the morning proclamation by Dyer. This would have added to the confidence of the gathering at Jallianwala Bagh, as the police would have watched them assemble and done nothing about it. Some members of the CID and a few police constables were even seen at the gathering—as was normal.

It is also interesting to note that despite the large presence of the army and the discomfort and deprivations they had been subjected to, the people of Amritsar still had faith in the system, in each other and, to a large extent, the British. They were defiant, but also sombre—after the deaths on 10 April, they could not imagine that a peaceful gathering, so close to the Golden Temple, on the festive day of Baisakhi could become a bloodbath. The events of 10 April were seen as an aberration. The two days of calm that followed had given them false hope, leading them to believe that things had calmed down and they could carry on with their satyagraha.

The afternoon meeting began quietly as the Bagh filled up. One by one, the speakers got onto the makeshift stage. Most were well-known personalities from Amritsar. Many of them interacted with the British on a daily basis—as traders, doctors, lawyers—and came from well-established families. They had no reason to suspect their white masters; why would local officials like Irving and Rehill or Plomer attack a peaceful crowd of people they knew? They had not accounted for the fact that an outsider would arrive with a clear agenda to punish them.

The fact that the organisers of the meeting were able to erect a stage is also peculiar. If the activity was illegal, or if someone had properly understood the morning proclamation, it should have set off alarm bells. Some villagers had come with their families to attend the Baisakhi fair or ask for blessings at the Golden Temple. Jallianwala Bagh, being an open area, was a good place to catch a bit of rest before heading back to their villages. Of those killed, around 20 per cent were from outside Amritsar. Very few women (the popular narrative holds that there were women present) attended the meeting—among the dead, only two bodies of women were recovered. None of the eyewitnesses spoke of any women being present at the meeting.[37]

At this point in time, most of the 'respectable' women of Amritsar would not be seen in public, and many observed purdah. Sarojini Naidu, in her angry speech in London in June 1920, protested the atrocities against the 'veiled women of Punjab' during the tragic occurrences in 1919. She said that 'women whose face had never been seen by a stranger... or touched by the curious sun or the moon were dragged into the market place' by the minions of the British government. On 13 April, most of these women in purdah would have been at home. It was Sunday, and the markets were all closed due to the hartal. They had no reason to step out.[38]

But many of the young boys had headed to the Bagh, where they were easily trapped and killed. Their parents were unlikely to have stopped them because it was an ordinary occurence—they would often attend the various public functions held there,

---

37. Raja Ram, *Jallianwala Bagh*, pp. 128–51; INC Report.
38. Sarojini Naidu, *Words of Freedom: Ideas of a Nation*. Speech given in London, 3 June 1920. Accessed online.

or play with their friends. One such parent lived just 100 yards away.

It was 4 p.m. when Dr Mani Ram, a 38-year-old dental surgeon, reached the Bagh.[39] A crowd of about two thousand had already gathered and someone was speaking from the raised platform. He too walked in to listen.

The first indication that something was amiss was when an aircraft flew overhead at around 4.30 p.m. This was extremely unusual. 'It did not hover over the meeting but turned back after taking a glimpse,' said Rup Lal Puri, who was among the speakers on the makeshift stage, along with Dr Gurbaksh Rai.[40]

Rup Lal Puri was the son of Lala Nand Lal Khatri, a merchant from Amritsar. All the men on stage were residents of Amritsar and most of them belonged to the educated elite—except Hans Raj, who had called the meeting.

'I suggested that Dr Kitchlew's photo be placed on the presidential chair. He was highly respected by the people,' Rup Lal Puri said later.[41]

Dr Saifuddin Kitchlew was remembered fondly by those present. On looking at his photograph, people would have been reminded of the unfair treatment meted out to him.

The crowd, squatting on the ground, was listening to the speakers intently, while the children played in the Bagh. Mani Ram began looking around for his young son, but it was difficult to spot him in such a large crowd.[42] Just as he was wondering how to find him, he heard what he thought were gun shots and saw people drop to the ground beside him. It

---

39. INC Report; Evidence, Amritsar, p. 103.

40. Transcripts of the Sir Michael O'Dwyer vs. Sir Sankaran Nair trial and the evidence published, quoted in Nigel Collett, 'The Jallianwala Bagh Revisited II', *United Service Institution of India*, no. 565, http://usiofindia.org/Article/?pub=Journal&pubno=565&ano=430.

41. Collett, 'The Jallianwala Bagh Revisited II'.

42. Collett, 'The Jallianwala Bagh Revisited II'.

is important to note from his evidence that those attending the meeting had not even seen Dyer's arrival or heard his order to shoot. Obviously he gave no warning, or a chance to escape.

A shocked Mani Ram found people around him dying from bullet wounds. In the brief lull in which the guns were reloaded, he ran and leapt over a low part of the wall, and returned to the safety of the stables next door. Transfixed by the horrific sight of a line of soldiers firing on the unarmed crowd, he remained in the stables. By now everyone was running for the very few, narrow openings. The main one was blocked by the soldiers kneeling in front of it, steadily firing to the command of the British officer whom they did not know or recognise. This, of course, was Dyer. He had a few other officers with him.

Meanwhile, Rup Lal Puri, from his vantage point, had seen two constables enter the Bagh shortly after the aeroplane flew away.[43] He also noted that the crowd before him was unarmed—barring a few who carried sticks. As he had been attending political meetings frequently, he was more familiar than Mani Ram with the ways of the police. He too remembered that no warning or order to disperse had been given before the shooting began.

According to eyewitness accounts, a few minutes after the two constables left, the Gurkha sepoys, accompanied by Deputy Superintendent of Police Plomer, General Dyer, and a number of policemen, arrived. Dyer ordered the sepoys to fire. The sepoys were in line when the firing began. They were standing on a raised platform, which was higher than the dais of the meeting. The first volley passed over the seated crowd and struck the wall opposite. The sepoys were ordered to kneel down and fire.

---

43. Collett, 'The Jallianwala Bagh Revisited II'.

'I then jumped down from the dais onto the floor and ran. I was hit on my back. I saw a large number of people killed and wounded,' Rup Lal Puri recalled.[44]

As many of the people attending the meeting were sitting or squatting on the ground, they would have found it difficult to get up and escape. Many died on the spot. They took bullets in their back, and on their legs and even soles of their feet, as they lay flat to escape the bullets, or ran to the walls and tried to climb over or push their way through the few narrow exits on the side—which became impossible as bodies began to pile up.

Meanwhile, Mani Ram still could not spot his 12-year-old son, Madan Mohan, in the melee. People were screaming and running for an escape route wherever they could find it. He went back into the Bagh to look for his son, once the shooting stopped.

'I saw a dreadful sight. The wounded were crying and lying in heaps of blood. There were two cows which had been killed as a result of the firing. The dead and wounded were on one another and I had to look for my son among them. Some of the wounded were crying for water. There was no one to give them water. I was unable to find my son there,' he said. It was only when he returned later in the evening, accompanied by his wife, with some water for the wounded who lay untreated in the open, that he found his son.

He was lying dead under a pile of bodies.[45]

Dyer later testified as follows:

Q: When you got into the Bagh, what did you do?
Dyer: I opened fire.

Q: At once?

---

44. Collett, 'The Jallianwala Bagh Revisited II'.
45. Collett, 'The Jallianwala Bagh Revisited II'.

Dyer: Immediately. I had thought about the matter and doubt it took me more than 30 seconds to make up my mind as to what my duty was.

Q: As regards the crowd, what was it doing?

Dyer: Well they were holding a meeting. There was a man in the centre of the place on something raised. His hands were moving about. He was evidently addressing. He was absolutely in the centre of the square, as far as I could judge. I should say some 50 or 60 yards from where my troops were drawn up.[46]

Lord Hunter asked: 'On the assumption that there was that risk of people being in the crowd who were not aware of the proclamation, did it not occur to you that it was a proper measure to ask the crowd to disperse before you took that step of actually firing?

A: No, at that time I did not. I merely felt that my orders had not been obeyed, that Martial Law was flouted, and that it was my duty to fire immediately by rifle.

Q: Before you dispersed the crowd, had the crowd taken any action at all?

A: No sir, they had run away, a few of them.

Q: Did they start to run away?

A: Yes. When I began to fire, the big mob at the centre began to run almost towards the right.

Q: Martial Law had not been proclaimed. Before you took that step which was a serious step, did you not consider as to the propriety of consulting the Deputy Commissioner who was the civil authority responsible for the order of the city?

A: There was no Deputy Commissioner to consult at the time. I did not think it wise to ask anybody further. I had to make up my mind immediately as to what my action should

---

46. Evidence, Amritsar, pp. 114–29.

be. I considered it from the military point of view that I ought to fire immediately, that if I did not do so, I should fail in my duty...

Q: In firing, was it your object to disperse?

A: No sir. I was going to fire till they dispersed.

Q: Did the crowd at once start to disperse as soon as you fired?

A: Immediately.

Q: Did you continue firing?

A: Yes.

Q: And after the crowd indicated that it was going to disperse, why did you not stop?

A: I thought it was my duty to go on until it dispersed. If I fired a little, I should be wrong in firing at all.

He also said that: '... there were no women and children in the meeting, and its appearance confirmed the reports I had received as to its character.'

This was only partially correct—there were, actually, a large number of young boys and even babes in arms—and one witness appearing before the Congress Sub-Committee remembered seeing the bodies of up to 500 young boys strewn on the ground.

Dyer deployed his men in two firing parties on either side of the main entrance, Gurkhas to the right and Baluchis to the left. The soldiers fired 1,650 rounds, or 33 rounds per man.

One of the organisers of the meeting (it could have been Hans Raj) had shouted out that the British would not fire, and even if they did, blanks would be used. Plomer later claimed that Pandit Durga Dass, the editor of *Waqt*, may have given the false reassurance that the bullets would be blanks.[47] The reason appears to be that on 6 April 1919, the *Aftab* newspaper

---

47. Colvin, *Life of General Dyer*, pp. 176–9.

had claimed that in the riots of 30 March in Delhi's Chandni Chowk, the Gurkhas had 'fired blank cartridges in the air'. This remark was untrue and appears now to be inexplicable. Did this article form the basis for the belief that the bullets now being fired were blank or *'phokian'*, perhaps encouraging people to remain seated and causing many more casualties? Or was the crowd told that fake bullets would be fired in order to ensure they remained seated and increase the number of casualties? Interestingly, Hans Raj escaped unscathed and hid under the platform, according to some accounts. It was a platform he had erected, possibly with this very escape in mind.

The Hunter Committee described Dyer's actions thus:

> He put 25 Baluchis and 25 Gurkhas on the raised ground at the entrance, and without giving any warning or asking the people to disperse, immediately opened fire at the people, who were at a distance of 100 to 150 yards. The people, as soon as the first shots were fired, began to run away through the few exits the place has got, but General Dyer continued firing till the ammunition ran short.

Why did Dyer continue to fire for ten minutes? Over a period of time, the explanations he gave would change. But as Rupert Furneaux says, his first claim was that the crowd came surging 'to rush' him.[48] 'To Sir Michael O' Dwyer he said he thought the crowd was trying to get behind him, and to General Beynon he explained he thought they were gathering for a rush, two slightly different explanations which suggest that Dyer's memory was confused.'

In his own initial report, he said his force was small, and 'to hesitate might induce attack'. Which meant that he actually did not face an attack, but was concerned that any hesitation might lead to one.

---

48. Rupert Furneaux, *Massacre at Amritsar* (George Allen & Unwin, 1963), p. 174.

Other officers present did not remember anyone 'gathering for a rush'.

'The men did not hesitate to fire, and I saw no man firing high,' said Captain Briggs later.[49] They all fired directly into the crowd.

The result was the bloody massacre of an unarmed crowd. Even if some in the crowd rushed towards him, it was not an attack—it was a desperate attempt to escape through the sole exit, which he and his troops had completely blocked.

Hundreds of people present that day had experiences similar to that of Mani Ram.

> Few outsiders who were present could have left the city even after the firing stopped. Leaving the city was immensely difficult as they required passes from one among the long list of civilian authorities that Dyer had named, and, at this point, they were mostly unavailable. Many of those outsiders who had attended, including the wounded, or even local residents who survived, hid in Amritsar with anyone who gave them shelter.

And so Jallianwala Bagh and Amritsar became enormous traps out of which people could not escape. It was a textbook military exercise on how to encircle the enemy.

Thirty-three-year-old Pratap Singh waited till the firing squad had left, before getting up. He 'saw bodies on all sides'.

> 'The bodies were so thick about the passage, that I could not find my way. I had my son with me and men were rushing over the dead bodies. I took my son (Kripa Singh, nine year old) also over the dead bodies. In my opinion there must have been nearly 2000 dead in the garden. Nearly all my clothes were left behind. I never saw any lathis (sticks) the whole time I was there, neither among those sitting nor on the ground

---

49. Colvin, *Life of General Dyer*, p. 178.

afterwards... as I was creeping near the dead bodies, I slipped and fell and lost hold of my son. The people behind, now began trampling all over me, and I had many blows and wounds on my chest. All my breath was taken out of me and I thought I was dying. When the rush was over, I revived and got out from amongst the dead bodies and ran into the lane. I had no dhoti, only a shirt and a coat... I could not speak. I was stunned and went into some house. I don't know whose it was. Just then I heard someone saying, "They are coming again, they are coming again." I rushed out and fled down through another lane. On the road I was so thirsty that I could not run or stand anymore. I took some water from an old woman... and asked her for a loin cloth. Then I began crying, "Has anyone seen my child?" but no one had seen him. I ran home and found my son had not reached there. My relations went in all directions to find him. After half an hour the boy came back himself. After that for some twenty to twenty five days I was very ill in bed and could not sit up.'[50]

Most of the survivors wanted to keep their presence at the Bagh a secret. Even if badly injured or mentally stressed, like Pratap Singh, they did not go to a hospital. Several died on the streets, outside the Bagh. They succumbed to bullet wounds from the shooting inside, or after being shot at by the pickets that Dyer had placed around the city. All this meant that the final numbers of dead or wounded would never be known. There are some eyewitness who remembered people crawling out of the Bagh, seriously wounded, even days later.

Lala Gian Chand, a 27-year-old working in a shop in Kakra Jarnail Singh, said in his evidence to the Congress Committee: 'After the firing was over, I saw about five or six hundred persons of all ages, including the dead and the wounded, lying about in the street, outside the Bagh. I reached my house with

---

50. INC Report, Evidence, p. 111–12; Raja Ram, *Jallianwala Bagh*, pp. 95–6.

the greatest difficulty, and there I learnt that my two nephews were not in the house. I then went back to look for them in the garden, I found my nephew's body riddled with bullets. His skull was broken. There was one shot under his nose on the upper lips, two on the left side, one on the left (side of the) neck, and three on the thigh and some two three on the head.'[51]

Many spoke of the large number of children who had been killed or wounded. Mian Sikander Ali went to the Bagh at 7.15 p.m. and discovered the dead body of his son under a pile of corpses near the wall, east of the well. He also found his cousin Ismail dead. Both had been shot in the head and the legs, probably while trying to scale the wall. He remembered: 'There were a number of children among the dead. I saw an aged man lying prostrate on the ground with a two year old baby in his arms. Both appeared to be lifeless. The number of dead and wounded lying in the garden, was about two thousand.' He recollected that there was no one to help as they removed the corpses.[52]

Sardar Partap Singh's son, Sundar Singh, had attended the meeting—but Partap Singh himself did not go. As he ran to the Bagh after hearing the sound of firing, he saw many wounded people lying on the streets. He hid from the soldiers who were coming out of the Bagh, and then jumped over the wall. 'Dead bodies were lying on all sides near the enclosure walls. When I entered, a dying man asked for water. There is a drain which carries water from the canal to Darbar Sahib. It is called Hansli. The drain is covered, but there is a pit connected with it which is about four feet square. When I tried to take water from the pit, I saw many dead bodies floating in it. Some living men had also hidden themselves in it and they asked me, "Are they (soldiers) gone?" When I told them they had gone, they

---

51. Op. cit., pp. 40-1.

52. INC Report, Evidence, Volume II, p. 118.

came out of it and ran away... There were about 800 or 1000 wounded or dead lying near the walls of the Bagh, besides others who ran away wounded and died either in their own houses or in the surrounding lanes. I remained there from fifteen to twenty minutes but could not find my son. I heard the wailing of those shot and who were crying for water. Then I ran back home and heard that my son was safe. I asked three-four men to accompany me to the Jallianwala Bagh and gave water to some of the wounded.'[53]

A bookseller from the area, Partap Singh, said, 'I did not hear any proclamation on the 13th forbidding people to attend public meetings nor did I hear that any such proclamation had been made in the bazaar.'[54]

The final tally would be closer to one thousand dead and hundreds more wounded (the official figures were much lower). Not all died on the spot. Many died slowly from bullet wounds and others died at home over a period of time.

The victims received no help from the authorities. Some assistance from the neighbourhood might have been available between 6 p.m. and 8 p.m., but as orders had already been given in the morning by General Dyer, no one could stir outdoors after 8 p.m. It was difficult for women to remove the injured and dead by themselves. Some just sat by their husbands and sons and fathers, watching them die. Many of the wounded were left to cry in pain the whole night—several simply bled to death.

Among the dead was Rup Lal Puri's 18-year-old son, a student at the Hindu Sabha High School. He had been shot thrice.

Lala Girdhari Lal, who had returned to Amritsar just a day earlier, was in his home overlooking the Bagh that evening. He remembered:

---

53. INC Report, Evidence, Volume II, pp. 94–5.
54. INC Report, Evidence, Volume II, pp. 94–5.

I saw hundreds of persons killed on the spot. The worst part of the whole thing was that firing was directed towards the gates through which the people were running out.

There were small outlets, four or five in all, and bullets actually rained over the people in all these gates and many got trampled under the feet of the rising crowds and thus lost their lives. Blood was pouring in profusion. Even those who lay flat on the ground were shot... No arrangements were made by the authorities to look after the dead or wounded...

The dead bodies were of grown up people and young boys also. Some had their heads cut open, others had their eyes shot, and nose, chest, arms or legs shattered. I think there must have been over 1000 dead bodies in the garden then...

Many amongst the wounded, who managed to run from the garden, succumbed to injuries on the way and lay dead on the streets. It was like this that the people of Amritsar held their Baisakhi fair.[55]

Inside the Bagh, the firing had gone on for 10 minutes without respite.

Dyer said, 'My work that morning in personally conducting the proclamation must be looked upon as one transaction with what had now come to pass. There was no reason to further parley with the mob, evidently they were there to defy the arm of the law.'[56]

He added, 'I fired and continued to fire until the crowd dispersed, and I consider this is the least amount of firing which would produce the necessary moral and widespread effect it was my duty to produce if I was to justify my action. If more troops had been at hand the casualties would have been greater in proportion. It was no longer a question of merely dispersing the crowd, but one producing a sufficient moral effect from a

---

55. INC Report, pp. 56–7.
56. Evidence, Amritsar, pp. 114–39.

military point of view not only on those who were present but more specially throughout Punjab. There could be no question of undue severity.'⁵⁷

He also said that he wanted to disperse the crowd and went on firing because: 'If I fired a little, I should be wrong to fire at all.' Had he stopped, 'they would have all come back and laughed at him and he would have made a fool of himself.'⁵⁸

Even though the crowd was unarmed and were merely trying to find an escape route, he thought 'they were trying to assault me and my force suddenly. All these pointed that this is a widespread movement which was not confined to Amritsar alone and that the situation was a wide military situation which was not confined to Amritsar.'⁵⁹

He did not attend to the wounded, either. He explained that the hospitals were open and medical officers were available. 'The wounded only had to apply for help. But they did not do this because they themselves would be in custody for being in the assembly. I was ready to help them if they applied.'⁶⁰

Despite all the evidence provided, the Hunter Committee said in its final report: 'It has not been proved to us that any wounded people were in fact exposed to unnecessary suffering from want of medical treatment.'

However, the evidence provided by all those who went to the Bagh later, looking for their loved ones, disproved this testimony. Those among the wounded who could not get away lay in the open for nearly two days, dying slowly. There was no attempt to do a proper body count till August 1919, by which time it was too late and many would have been left out of the final tally. Those who went to the Civil Hospital for treatment

---

57. Evidence, Amritsar, pp. 114–39.
58. Evidence, Amritsar, pp. 114–39.
59. Evidence, Amritsar, pp. 114–39.
60. Evidence, Amritsar, pp. 114–39.

were called 'rabid dogs' by Lieutenant Colonel Smith and turned away. He said they should go to Gandhi, Kitchlew or Satya Pal for medical help. What happened to many of them is unknown.

As per the Report of the Commissioners appointed by the Punjab Sub-Committee of the Indian National Congress, mainly authored by Gandhi: 'Let it further be remembered, the fire was directed even into and from the Hansli, the narrow lane to the right, on the plan. We observed bullet marks on a balcony opposite the lane; and evidence has been laid before us to show that soldiers were posted at points outside the Bagh to guard approaches, and men were shot whilst they were effecting their escape through these approaches. There can be no doubt that General Dyer's plan was to kill the largest number, and if the number was 1000 and not more, the fault was not his.'[61]

How the hours following the massacre passed in Amritsar is the stuff of nightmares.

---

61. INC Report, p. 57.

3

Counting the Corpses

Sir Michael O'Dwyer's point of view was and still is the same as that of General Dyer. In his view it did not matter if the people assembled at Jallianwala Bagh were different people from those who had committed murder and arson on the 10th. The very fact that they had assembled was enough to treat them as people who had done murder and arson.

—Report of the Committee Appointed by the Government of India toInvestigate the Disturbances in the Punjab, etc.[1]

Ratan Devi, who lived close to Jallianwala Bagh, heard the shots and later went with two other women to look for her husband.[2] She found his corpse among heaps of dead bodies. She asked some people she recognised, who were also at the Bagh looking for their relatives, to help her get a charpoy to take her husband's body back home, but as it was 8 p.m. and curfew had been announced, no one came forward. She even asked people from adjacent homes to help. It was 10 p.m. by

---

1. Parliamentary Report, p. 114.
2. INC Report, Volume II, Lahore, pp. 116–17.

then, and though some were willing, they were also scared of being shot. So she went back to her husband's side and sat there all night.

> Accidentally, I found a bamboo stick which I kept in my hand, to keep off the dogs. I saw three men writhing in agony, a buffalo struggling in great pain; and a boy, about twelve years old, in agony entreated me not to leave the place. I told him that I could not go anywhere leaving the dead body of my husband. I asked him if he wanted any wrap, and if he was feeling cold, I could spread it over him. But he asked for water, and water could not be procured in that place.
>
> I heard the clock ticking at regular intervals of one hour. At two o'clock, a Jat, belonging to Sultan village, who was lying entangled in a wall, asked me to go near him and to raise his leg. I got up and, taking hold of his clothes, drenched in blood, raised his leg up… I passed my whole night there. It is impossible for me to describe what I felt. Heaps of dead bodies lay there, some on their backs and some with their faces upturned. A number of them were poor innocent children. I shall never forget that night. I was all alone… in that solitary jungle… amidst hundreds of corpses. I passed my night crying and watching. I cannot say more. What I experienced that night is known only to me and to God.

Many like Lala Atmaram, who lived near the Bagh, heard the cries and moans of the dying and wounded through the night. Their agony must have resonated through the neighbourhood, with its close-built houses. He also saw people with lanterns moving about all night, probably searching for their loved ones.

By the morning vultures had started wheeling around in the sky overhead, waiting for a chance to swoop down on the dead and dying. In the heat, the bodies soon began to decay.

Lala Nathu Ram, a 35-year-old contractor, remembered how difficult it was to keep his turban on his head as the vultures flew close, snapping at flesh while he searched desperately for his son and brother.³

Later it was said that 120 corpses were recovered from the well (of which there is no mention in the Hunter Committee Report). This fact, that bodies were pulled out from the well, does not appear specifically in any of the official evidence. According to one account by Raja Ram, people had not jumped in, but fell into the well as they fled the bullets: 'Many people also ran in the direction of the well... and blinded by terror and unable to check their momentum some fell into the well, which unfortunately had no protection wall around it in those days.'⁴

But had all the corpses been retrieved? When a few members, including Pandit Malaviya of the Indian National Congress visited Amritsar, some doubts were raised whether the authorities had done their job. At the end of June 1919, Motilal Nehru wrote to his son Jawaharlal that he 'had seen badly decomposed bodies floating in the Jallianwala Bagh well.' It is possible that some bodies still remained, though when divers were sent in by the administration, they said they had found only some cloth and an earthen pot. The Congress members said that the stench of death remained in the air till June. Many bodies had apparently been recovered from the Hansli and the canal running through the Bagh in April—though there is no official record of it.

During debates at the Imperial Legislative Council in September 1919, the Chief Secretary to the Government of Punjab, J.P. Thompson, dismissed the discovery of a corpse still floating in the well in June (as had been notified by Pandit Malaviya) saying:

> As regards the corpse which the Pandit says he saw in the well, really the incident is hardly worth dealing with. But

---

3. INC Report, Volume II, pp. 99–100.

4. Raja Ram, *The Jallianwala Bagh Massacre: A Premeditated Plan* (Chandigarh: Punjab University, 2002), p. 88.

one thing is certain, and that is, that if there was a corpse down the well when the Pandit visited the place at the end of June, it was not the corpse of anybody who had been killed on the 13th of April. It is established by expert evidence that after 2 1/2 months in the hot weather a corpse would be a mere collection of bones at the bottom of the well—so that as evidence of anything that had been there from the time when the firing took place on April the 13th, there is nothing in it at all. But it does seem to me that when the Pandit wrote to the Municipal Committee saying that there were 'still' one or more corpses down the well, it was perfectly obvious that what he was doing was trying to create horror or pity in the minds of his hearers in connection with the incident at Jallianwala Bagh.

Even if the corpses had rotted in the water and the heat, and their bones had sunk to the bottom of the well, the smell would have been all-pervasive. It would have also affected the well water and the hygiene of the area—something that Thompson did not venture to address, instead dismissing Malaviya's concern as one of creating 'horror or pity'. The British government could only be aggressive in its approach as they had no answers for much that had taken place. How difficult would it have been to arrange for an earthen pot and a pile of clothing to dismiss Pandit Malaviya's allegation?

Undeniably, ordinary life would have been severely impacted after the massacre, as blood would have flowed down the streets and mixed with the well water, apart from the flesh and bones of those who died inside the well, and the canal (the hansli) whose waters flowed to the Golden Temple. How was the water itself cleaned up? Could this have been the reason why the water supply was cut off for such a long time? There is no official account anywhere of how the area was finally scoured clear of blood and bodies, either. Was the blood allowed to dry into the mud and any residual skin pecked clean by vultures? Nor are there any accounts of this in the Congress report as by the time the Committee began its work of recording testimonies, it was more focussed on the actual happenings in the Bagh and the callous treatment of the victims. The disposal of the bodies, apart from the hundreds of joint funerals and burials, was never really discussed.

Without water, how were these hundreds of bodies collected, washed and taken to funeral pyres? All the official records were maintained by the British, and no official visited the Bagh till nearly four days later, so there are no clear answers available.

By July, when the writer K.D. Malaviya visited Amritsar, he found that the Bagh had been sealed with planks 'and rendered impassable for any intending visitors'. (These barriers, he said, were erected the day after a visit by Malaviya and Motilal Nehru, which was possibly when they noticed the corpse.)[5]

Where were the doctors or the hospitals to deal with a calamity of this magnitude? From the evidence, it appears that most people took their wounded home and cared for them without letting the authorities know.

But there were also those who desperately needed a doctor. The difficulty was that the injured did not want to go to the Civil Hospital for fear that Smith, who was in charge, would turn them away. Dr Balmokand, who treated up to 50 of the injured himself—as did other Indian doctors—remembered that Smith was furious. He not only chastised Balmokand for having been at Jallianwala Bagh, he even insisted that he should go to the railway dispensary and stay there, or be whipped. A frightened Balmokand stayed at the railway dispensary for one whole week.

Smith said that the official figure for casualties at Jallianwala Bagh had been 'set' at 1800.[6] Given the circumstances, and

---

5. K.D. Malaviya, *Open Rebellion in the Punjab: With Special Reference to Amritsar* (Allahabad: Abhyudaya Press, 1919), pp. 3–4.

6. Nigel Collett, 'The Jallianwala Bagh Revisited II', *United Service Institution of India*, no. 565. Accessed at http://usiofindia.org/Article/?pub=Journal&pubno=565&ano=430.

the lack of information or help from the British, the numbers could have risen to 2,000 or higher, assuming that hundreds of wounded men and boys were refused medical aid.

Approximately 100 of the wounded were brought to the home of 26-year-old Assistant Surgeon Dr Ishar Dass Bhatia, at Karman Deohri, Amritsar, on 13 April. He treated them but many died at his house.[7] There is no way to know if these numbers entered the final tally.

Most of the wounded had been shot in the back or the back of their legs or arms, or even the soles of their feet. Dr Kidar Nath Bhandari, Senior Assistant Surgeon, who had treated the wounded on 10 April, did so again on 13 April. He visited some of the injured at home.[8]

Had it not been for individual doctors who took the risk of being arrested or accused of sedition, it is possible the overall casualty list would have been much, much higher.

Ram Saran Singh (30), who managed to escape from the Bagh, returned the next day to hunt for his brother-in-law, and found dead bodies spread all over, even outside the Bagh—in the lanes as well as near the entrance of the Bagh. Possibly some among the wounded had been trying to get home but died on the way. He could not find his brother-in-law, though he saw a lot of young boys who had been killed.[9]

He recollected the difficulties people faced as hundreds of bodies had to be cremated:

> Early in the morning on the 14th, I again went to the garden with three or four other persons. I saw people removing the dead bodies even then. I found my relative's dead body in the canal amongst the other corpses. He had three bullets. One on the forehead, and another on the side, and the third

---

7. INC Report, Volume II, Evidence, pp. 38–9.

8. INC Report, Volume II, Evidence, pp. 38–9.

9. INC Report, Volume II (Lahore, 1920), pp. 42–5.

in the back. I brought my relative's body to his house in the Nimak Mandi, and removed it from there to the cremation ground at Chattiwind Gate. The place was full of dead bodies burning, and we had to cremate my relation out in the open; and there were many others being cremated likewise. There was no one to record the number of deaths.[10]

Meanwhile, on 13 April, after unleashing this holocaust, Dyer had returned to his camp by 6 p.m. He then marched through the city again at 10 p.m. 'to make sure that his order as to the inhabitants not being out after 20 hours (13th) was obeyed; he found the city absolutely quiet and not a soul to be seen.'[11] The sound of marching boots and the pickets still in place all over the city would have ensured that people stayed indoors. The irony was that in many homes only the women and girl children would have been at home, or the elderly. How could they have stepped out to rescue their husbands, brothers or sons in the middle of the night?

What could have been more cruel than this? To force people to stay at home while their loved ones lay dying a few streets away? Many men and women, nonetheless, defied the law and crept down with lanterns, hunting among the bodies, as people lay screaming in pain, waiting for death to arrive.

Few would have slept that night. There was no electricity and no water—the drains were full of blood as were the streets. The cries of the dying rent the air. Dyer may not have seen a 'soul' on the street but the city was awake and in agony.

According to the 'War Diary' that was maintained at the time by Captain Briggs for his General, permission was granted on 14 April for the inhabitants to bury or burn their dead.[12]

---

10. INC Report, Volume II (Lahore, 1920), pp. 69–70.

11. Parliamentary Report, p. 116.

12. Evidence, Amritsar, p. 218.

Unlike 11 April, there was no large gathering of people. Those who were fortunate enough to have found the bodies of their family members in the mangled heaps would have wanted to hold the funerals quickly, as the bodies would have rotted through the night (April is a warm month); and as already noted, the vultures were circling.

'It does not appear that any steps were taken by the Punjab Government for a long time to ascertain the real facts about so serious an occurrence and to find the correct number of casualties. Sir Michael O'Dwyer when asked about it, says in his evidence that, on the 15th April he had an interview of about a quarter of an hour with General Dyer and that afterwards the Punjab Government were awaiting General Dyer's report.

'As Dyer was moving about in Punjab, and later sent off to the Afghan war, he did not make his report till the end of August, 1919, and that was made in response to a communication from the Adjutant General dated the 19th July, 1919, evidently asking for a special report. The Punjab Government do not appear to have taken any steps till the end of June to ascertain the casualties'.[13] Mr Thompson, the Chief Secretary, said that it was at the end of July that 'we told the Deputy Commissioner to make inquiries'.[14]

Notices were issued to the public on 8 August to give information regarding 'those who had met their death at Jallianwala Bagh'. This was four months after the massacre.

On the other hand, the action taken by Dyer was approved of, not just by the army, but by the civil authorities as well. Despite the magnitude of what had happened, no one dwelt upon it. Irving left the report entirely to Dyer and, till the

---

13. Parliamentary Report, pp. 116–17.

14. Parliamentary Report, pp. 116–17.

Hunter Committee was set up, no one was the wiser. It would have been fairly easy to do this as the Secretary of State for India, Montagu, was based in London. Viceroy Chelmsford was in Simla and Lieutenant Governor O'Dwyer was in Lahore. The latter made little effort to find out any more than he had been told about the events at Amritsar, as he would reveal during his cross-examination at the Hunter Committee hearings.

Basically, there was relief in the British camp, as it was believed that after this incident, not a single European would be harmed, and any talk of a mutiny in the armed forces (of which there was very little evidence so far) had also been averted.

However, Kitchin remained worried about the loyalty of the Indian troops. Just as he had (wrongly) anticipated fighting in the streets of Amritsar on 11 and 12 April, Kitchin seemed to imagine enemies of the Empire everywhere. He had already stated in a message, at 11 a.m. on 11 April, while he was in Amritsar: 'Troops arrived from Jullundur 5 a.m. (100 British, 200 Indian). The latter are somewhat under suspicion and have been split up into smaller parties.'[15]

Was this suspicion of the Indian troops just fear or based on facts? It appears to be the former, since there is no evidence, even in this difficult time, of a mutiny in the army.

By splitting them into smaller groups, it may have been easier to spot sedition, but by forcing them into increasingly repressive behaviour against their own countrymen and women, the British were knowingly brutalising them—and unknowingly alienating them.

This was another aspect of the divide and rule policy clearly discernable at Amritsar. The policies were meant not just to create rifts between the different communities but to deepen the divide between civilians on the one hand and the army and

---

15. V.N. Datta, *New Light On the Punjab Disturbances in 1919* (Simla: Indian Institute of Advanced Study, 1975), p. 377.

the police on the other. There would be even more reason now to fear that the disgruntled elements in the army, or the soldiers returning from World War I, might be aroused to strike. While the British were approving of Dyer's actions, they continued to be nervous—which is why there was no option but to seek a further continuation of martial law.

Thus, while there were no actual signs of a mutiny, there was continuing unease in the enforcement agencies over recent happenings, despite their hope that the Jallianwala Bagh massacre would end any further rebellion.

The ban on news continued—but the official information was certainly being carried through those telegraph lines, which were still functioning, or through word of mouth. The news about the massacre would have spread rapidly in the local areas, but it only reached Lahore close to midnight, and O'Dwyer learnt of it in the early hours of 14 April. Why did it take so long? And why did the aeroplanes assiduously hovering over Amritsar and reporting on everything, suddenly vanish from the skies? It appeared almost as if, having started the cruel game, O'Dwyer did not want to know about the results till it was all, very firmly, over.

Even though there was physical movement between Amritsar and Lahore by road, and the army was in control, the communication on the night of 13 April about the events of the day reached Lahore via a 'mutilated message' to the Deputy Inspector General of the CID at about 11 or 11.15 p.m. Mr Thompson, the Chief Secretary, received a peculiarly worded message on the telephone.

> 11.30 pm. Chief Secretary reports code message received from the Deputy Commissioner, Amritsar, much mutilated. But sense seems to be that seven arrests were made today and a prohibited meeting dispersed at which 200 were killed. Communicated to Colonel Casson who had no report from the General Officer Commanding Amritsar. But said there

were rumours in Cantonments that there had been heavy casualties in Amritsar today.[16]

Typically, the General Officer Commanding Amritsar, Dyer, had not given a report as yet. The emphasis in the coded message was on the arrests and dispersal of the meeting, instead of the large number killed. The latter information was dismissed as 'rumours'. The message could have certainly contained more detail.

Because in reality, Irving (who sent the message to Thompson) had accompanied Dyer on his late night walk through Amritsar to check if the curfew orders were being obeyed.[17] Even if they avoided going near Jallianwala Bagh, it would have been impossible not to hear the cries of pain, and see the streets lined with blood and bodies. The selective use of information meant that Irving, who was still technically in charge (martial law would not be officially imposed through an order till 15 April), could downplay the heavy casualties.

However, he did state in a separate report to O'Dwyer dated 14 April at 1 a.m. that 'I much regret that I was not present (at Jallianwala Bagh) but when out previously with the military the greatest forbearance had been shown in making people disperse. I had absolutely no idea of the action taken.'

Irving's note to O'Dwyer arrived with Wathen, the principal of the Khalsa College, who was very disturbed by the events. He obviously expected that there would be a terrible backlash and so he had driven down to Lahore, clutching a loaded revolver all the way.

O'Dwyer was asleep, having just come down from Simla. He was woken up by Wathen, who handed him the very brief report from Irving and gave him his own account as well, stating

---

16. Datta, *New Light*, p. 379.

17. Datta, *New Light*, pp. 379–80.

(mistakenly) that British troops had been used at Jallianwala Bagh. He also said that men had been 'shot down like rabbits as they ran'. Thompson and Kitchin were roused and came in, still in their pyjamas. At around 4 a.m, O'Dwyer asked for further details from Dyer's superior, General Beynon. The latter had still not heard from Dyer. All they knew was that around 200 had died in Amritsar and that the firing went on for 10 minutes. Beynon would send an aeroplane the next morning to learn more. Wathen added to the confusion by saying that the region of Manjha was up in arms.[18]

O'Dwyer approved of the action even though he knew that Dyer had fired 'without warning'.[19] He also took refuge in the fact that the army was in charge. He later said, 'I approved of General Dyer's action in dispersing by force the rebellious gathering and thus preventing further rebellious acts. It was not for me to say he had gone too far when I was told by his superior officer that he fully approved General Dyer's action. Speaking perhaps with a more intimate knowledge of the then situation than anyone else, I have no hesitation in saying that General Dyer's action that day was the decisive factor in crushing the rebellion, the seriousness of which is only now being generally realised.'[20]

'Crushing the rebellion'—even if the rebellion was non-existent—was evidently very important to the Punjab regime, especially O'Dwyer. The fact that the dead and injured belonged to an unarmed group of peaceful protestors was consistently ignored.

But how many had been crushed?

The numbers of the dead kept changing. It all depended

---

18. Nigel Collett, *The Butcher of Amritsar: Brigadier General Reginald Dyer* (Hambledon & London, 2005), p. 265.

19. Parliamentary Report, pp. 111–14; Datta, *New Light*, p. 78.

20. Parliamentary Report, p. 31.

on whose word the government or the people were prepared to believe.

On 10 September, almost five months later, in a discussion at the Imperial Legislative Council, the number of those dead was given as 301. On 12 September, Pandit Malaviya said it was 1,000.

According to a list compiled by the government along with the Allahabad Seva Samiti, 379 were killed, out of which 87 were unknown, perhaps villagers who had come to Amritsar for the fair.[21] However, while giving his evidence before the Hunter Committee, J.P. Thompson admitted that while the government had stated that 291 had been killed, the original estimate by the Seva Samiti was almost 531.

At this point, Major General Sir George Barrow interrupted Thompson's cross-examination by Setalvad. He said, 'I know how many shots were fired. If every bullet hit someone, the figure given by Mr Thompson will be about accurate according to experience. One in five would get killed.'[22] If 1,650 bullets were fired, as claimed by Dyer, the dead would have numbered a little over 300.

Later reports would show that the dead numbered many times more than the official figure of 379 and the numbers of those wounded, though said to be three times more than the dead, were actually much higher.[23] It wasn't just bullet wounds that killed people—many died when they were crushed in the stampede or when they fell into the well—and the wounds were not caused only by bullets. For the young children who could not escape in time, even a fracture or a small wound would have been fatal as they bled through the night.

It was evident that the Punjab government was doing its

---

21. Parliamentary Report, p. 29.

22. Parliamentary Report, p. 29.

23. Parliamentary Report, p. 29.

best to make the numbers appear as low as possible, and they could offer ignorance as an excuse. It is undoubtedly strange that when every act of rebellion was noted meticulously in the minute-to-minute War Diaries, there was silence over these hundreds of deaths, until August, which is when they began to take stock of how many had died or were wounded.

The government had also bought into Dyer's view that the assembled crowd was guilty of breaking his prohibitory order. They were all criminals and had to be shown extreme disregard, and no sympathy at all.

Dyer said, in a submitted statement to the General Staff, 16th (Indian) Division, dated Dalhousie, 25 August 1919: 'I had the choice of carrying out a very distasteful and horrible duty or of neglecting to do my duty, of suppressing disorder or of becoming responsible for all future bloodshed.'[24]

He was asked by Setalvad whether it was because the crowd was attending a meeting prohibited by Dyer that gave the drastic measure a punitive effect.

He answered: 'I want to punish the naughty boy; it would be difficult to say what would be the effect of punishment on a boy who is not naughty.' He admitted that it had a better effect when the meeting was prohibited rather than not.[25]

When further pressed about how he could hold all those people at the Bagh responsible for the disorders (the riots which took place following the arrests of Gandhi, Kitchlew and Satya Pal), he said: 'They were there to show their sympathy with the people who committed murder and rebellion, and their hostility to the Government which was repressing it.' He inferred all of this because they had gathered at Jallianwala Bagh after 'what had happened in Amritsar for three days, and taking that the prohibition (order had been) issued in the morning.'

---

24. Evidence, Amritsar, p. 203.

25. Evidence, Amritsar, p. 131.

On 15 April, martial law was formally declared in Amritsar and other places in Punjab. The punishments subsequently meted out under martial law were harsh and whimsical. No distinction was made between the guilty and the innocent. All of Amritsar, particularly, was guilty since they had protested against the arrest of their leaders and because five Europeans had been killed in the ensuing melee.

Once again, the attempt was to denigrate and enmesh the population of Punjab in a web of fear so they would never rebel again. It was hoped, through the severe humiliations inflicted on them, that their spirit would be broken.

The Jallianwala Bagh massacre was hailed as high strategy and Brigadier General Reginald Dyer, who showed little empathy for the victims, was feted for having averted another 1857-type mutiny. The press reports, which were to come out much later—and very few reported the conditions that prevailed in Punjab in April, May and June—revealed only how a rebellion had been halted.

From then on, an atmosphere of fear prevailed. Even those who were severely wounded would not come forward for treatment because they feared reprisals. This fact came out during the recording of witnesses in 1919 by the Congress Sub-Committee and in 1921 (not that it made any difference to admirers of Dyer) when compensation was offered to those who were wounded and others who had lost family members at Jallianwala Bagh.

For instance, Hakim Singh, a clerk at the Khalsa College, was wounded in the left leg and the knee bone of his right leg was dislocated. He finally came forward for a very paltry compensation in 1921. Being an employee of the college, he did not reveal for two years that he had been at Jallianwala Bagh. It is possible that Wathen, the principal, may have known about his injury and advised him to stay quiet, rather than face arrest.

Similarly, Hans Raj, son of Kapur Singh from Amritsar, did not give his name for compensation, even though he was wounded at Jallianwala Bagh on the upper part of his right thigh.[26]

> **ORDER RESTORED AGAIN IN INDIA**
>
> LONDON, April 17.—Order has been restored at Lahore, Amritsar and Ahmedabad in India, following revolutionary disturbances, the governor general of India reported from Simla today.

Mohan Lal, son of Bhagat Ram, from tahsil Tarn Taran, also received two bullets in his left leg. He too did not reveal his presence at the Bagh, until two years later.

Very few of the victims received any professional medical care. For instance, Mohammed Din, son of Fazl Din, a weaver from Amritsar, was shot thrice—in the right thigh, in the left arm, and on the right side of the abdomen. He remained ill for one and half years, after which he died at home.

---

26. Details from applications for compensation from persons wounded in the Disturbances of 1919, Punjab Archives.

While fear of punishment kept many of the wounded at home, no one from the administration reached out to them, either. Unless it was to arrest them or force them to confess to a larger conspiracy.

It was not until November 1919 that news of the shocking events of 13 April began to be known in greater detail as the public hearings of the Hunter Committee started and the Congress Sub-Committee also began recording evidence. But the reporting in the British media and some of the English language press in India remained largely in favour of Dyer. So, it was not till 1920, when the British Parliament was forced to take cognisance of the brutal killings, that the truth was finally known to the world. Even then, much of it remained concealed as some of the evidence was thought to be too volatile to be revealed at the time.

UNREST IN INDIA
HOW A RISING WAS QUELLED.

BULLETS POURED INTO A CROWD.

A TEN-MINUTE MASSACRE.

(By Electric Telegraph.—Copyright.)
(Aust.-N.Z. Cable Association.)
London, Dec. 12.

Evidence before the Commission of Enquiry at Lahore into the Amritzar risings in April is causing a sensation among the public. It appears that a general rising was threatened in the Punjab, recalling the Indian mutiny. General Dyer, commanding the loyalist troops, ordered indiscriminate shooting, with the result that 500 natives were killed and 1500 wounded.

The Punjab outrages included the cutting of telegraphic wires, burning three bank officials, the murder of a railway guard, burning the town hall and public offices at Amritsar.

General Dyer in his evidence stated that when he found his orders had been disobeyed he had to do something strong. "I shot well and strongly 1650 rounds, lasting 10 minutes.

The crowd had disobeyed the law. No middle course was possible, so I fired until I ran out of ammunition."

Asked if the idea was to strike terror, General Dyer replied: "I did not intend frightfulness, but had to give them a lesson and thought from a military point of view, shooting would give the widest impression in the Punjab. The Lieut.-Governor wired approval of the action. Miss Sherwood, a missionary, while cycling had been beaten with shoes and sticks and left for dead. General Dyer said: "We look upon women as sacred, therefore I ordered the street to be picketed from 6 in the morning until 8 in the evening. No Indian was allowed to pass in except by crawling on his hands and knees." He merely wanted to keep the place sacred.

It was clear by then that the massacre was far worse than originally claimed and it was felt that there would be a demoralising effect on the army if the fear of an impending 'mutiny' was made public. The third reason for concealment was, of course, the possible impact of full disclosure on the national movement in India. The sheer horror of what had happened would encourage the anti-British forces to come together and so it was important to keep the details hidden as far as possible.

There was a constant effort by the Punjab government to link the happenings of Amritsar to a larger conspiracy but ultimately, none could be proven. The massacre was nothing more than an attempt to enslave people under martial law and to rip away their dignity. It was done to ensure that they 'respected' the British and reinforce the belief that they were themselves an inferior race. They should be so punished that never again would they dare to organise a revolt or kill a white European.

4

The Fancy Punishments

The Amritsar business cleared the air, and if there was to be a holocaust anywhere, and one regrets that there should be, it was best at Amritsar...

I motored down to Amritsar yesterday and spent some hours there, went through the city with the General Officer Commanding, Commissioner of Division and the troops. All were salaaming most profusely and are thoroughly frightened...

I think our prompt action in dominating Lahore and Amritsar by an overwhelming military force... paralysed the movement before it had time to spread.

— Lieutenant Governor O'Dwyer to
Viceroy Chelmsford, 21 April 1919

The British Army was now in charge of Amritsar and from their behaviour, it seemed they still wanted revenge. Dyer had proven, through the slaughter of innocents, that he could do as he liked, and the authorities would support him. As restrictions were imposed, more and more rights were snatched away on a daily basis. If orders were not obeyed, Dyer would kill the rebels: this, too, had been proven. And, at this peculiar time, he had the authority to do so.

Kitchin, the Commissioner of Amritsar district, came back to the city on 14 April. He made it clear who was in charge. He did not visit Jallianwala Bagh, or meet any of the bereaved. He attended a joint meeting of officials and civilians at the Kotwali at Town Hall, which was less than a six-minute stroll from Jallianwala Bagh and yet decided not to visit any of the affected areas. There was no empathy or sympathy, or even regret, for the fact that people were still hunting for their loved ones and burning or burying their dead. Instead, he literally handed over all responsibility, saying, 'The General will give orders today.'[1]

Even in the context of the bloodbath which had taken place the previous day, he still spoke as though the defenceless crowd attending the meeting had provoked the army into firing. He provided no help for the dying, the wounded or the families of the bereaved. Instead, he berated the assembled civilians:

> Do you people want peace or war? We are prepared in every way. The Government is all powerful. Sarkar has conquered Germany and is capable of doing everything. The General will give orders today. The city is in his possession. I can do nothing. You will have to obey orders.[2]

After this pronouncement in which he gave up all responsibility, Kitchin left.

The civil and military authorities had been working in tandem till then. Military assistance was being provided to civil authorities and martial law (though already proclaimed by Dyer) had not yet been formally declared. However, civilian rules and regulations were rapidly being disregarded. The British administration wanted control at any cost.

According to the Hunter Committee Report to the

---

1. INC Report, p. 59, statement 1.
2. INC Report, p. 59, statement 1.

Parliament, on 12 April, the British position 'was hardening into de facto martial law... The Commissioner had left on the night of 11th and General Dyer arrived somewhat later on that night. On the 13th formal martial law was expected, and the telegram sanctioning it was despatched at midnight. The trouble had been spreading and Amritsar was known not to be the only area involved. The proclamation of the 13th imposed permit for travel and a curfew at 8 pm; it prohibited gatherings or processions.'[3]

The odds were being stacked against the people of Amritsar. They had been grievously wounded and killed. Yet, they had not retaliated in any way. Martial law would now be formally announced, making them more vulnerable to the whims of Dyer and his men.

On the evening of 14 April, the attempt to terrorise the residents of Amritsar continued with the arrival of Dyer at the Kotwali. He made his anger evident—speaking in Urdu all through. It was a technique he had used often and successfully when stationed at the North West Frontier: browbeating the enemy. He made it clear that despite his murderous assault on 13 April, the people of Amritsar were the guilty party and if they attempted any retaliation, there would be more deaths. He too did not go to Jallianwala Bagh, nor did he offer any help. Like Kitchin, his voice and demeanour were meant to humiliate and frighten the civilians. He also wanted them to betray those who had murdered the five Europeans or participated in the destruction of the buildings on 10 April. He said he would 'shoot the badmashes'. He wasted no words on the hundreds of innocent people he had killed the previous day.

'You people know well that I am a sepoy and soldier. Do you want war or peace? If you wish for war the Government is prepared for it, and if you want peace, then obey my orders and

---

3. Parliamentary Report, pp. 32–3.

open up all your shops; else, I will shoot. For me the battlefield of France or Amritsar is the same. I am a military man and I will go straight.'[4] He wanted the shops, which had been closed because of the anti-Rowlatt Act hartal, to be opened—or they would be opened forcefully, with rifles.

'You people talk against the Government, and persons educated in Germany and Bengal talk sedition. Obey orders, I do not wish to have anything else. I have served in the Military for over 30 years. I understand the Indian Sepoy and the Sikh people very well. You will have to observe peace... you must warn me of the badmashes. I will shoot them.' The reference was to Kitchlew, who had studied in Germany. This was now being used to portray him as anti-British. The frequent references to the World War by the British speakers also made it apparent that they considered the anti-Rowlatt Act demonstrations as a declaration of war against the state. The presence of the army in large numbers and the imposition of martial law was thus being justified.

Irving spoke next and reiterated the sentiments of the General: 'You have committed a bad act in killing the English... revenge will be taken upon you and your children.'

Nothing could be clearer.

Under daily curfew, with ordinary life completely disrupted, with even electricity and water supply cut off, and constant harassment, Amritsar became a dark place. The shops were forcibly opened, and a set of punishments was imposed, some by Dyer and others by his cohorts, with the intention of debasing the population.

That this could backfire spectacularly never occurred to the soldiers who were imposing their will on a defenceless and largely innocent population: many of whom had no knowledge of exactly what had happened, and how the five Europeans had

---

4. INC Report, p. 59.

been killed. It must be remembered that by now, most of those who had attended the meeting were either dead or wounded. Those who were being savaged were in all likelihood those who had chosen a peaceful existence rather than resistance. But Dyer had tasted blood and realised that the more he humiliated the Indians, the more his stock rose with the British—he was not going to stop. And there was no one to stop him. Thirty-six miles away in Lahore, similar punishments were being meted out randomly.

The number of British Indian subjects who were stripped, jailed, whipped, made to crawl, salaam, starved, etc. grew disproportionately larger. For six weeks or more, as long as martial law was imposed, the people of Punjab became slaves who had to accept every whim of their masters.

After martial law was imposed, among the incredibly humiliating orders were the following:

1. The Crawling Order (Amritsar)
2. The Salaaming Order (Amritsar, Gujranwala)
3. The Saluting Order (Wazirabad)
4. The Descending Order (Lahore)
5. All males made to sweep and do sanitary work (Malawakal, Sheikhupura)
6. Lawyers made menials (Constable order in Amritsar)
7. Indemnities exacted for damages and taxes levied for support of troops (Akalgarh, Gujranwala, Hafizabad, Manianwala, Sheikhupura)
8. Vehicles commandeered (Lahore)
9. Crops or shop inventories confiscated (Nawan Pind, Sheikupura, Wazirabad)[5]

The list went on and on.

---

5. Helen Fein, *Imperial Crime and Punishment: The Massacre at Jallianwala Bagh and British Judgement, 1919–1920* (Honolulu: The University Press of Hawaii, 1977), p. 40.

Then there were also individual punishment orders which included flogging, forcing prisoners to rub their noses in dirt, forced marches, abuse, bombing threats. The 'rituals of abasement', as Helen Fein called them, were again long and varied—depending on the diabolical imagination of the man in charge. People were placed in cages (as in Kasur), or even evicted overnight from their homes for no reason. The martial law orders were meant to reinforce the low status of the natives.[6]

Many of the orders were petty and mean—such as those that forced men of higher status to clean drains. Others were meant to directly quell the ongoing hartal.

A notice under Martial Law Rule No. 2, issued by F.W. Berberry, the Officer Commanding in Gujranwala, stated that those shopkeepers who refused to sell articles at a reasonable price or shut their shops when someone from the army or police required something, 'would be arrested and liable to be punished by flogging'.[7]

Gujranwala had seen quite a few outbreaks of violence, and so the orders here were quite similar to those passed in Lahore and Amritsar. For instance, Martial Law No. 7, the Saluting Order, passed by L.W.Y. Campbell, also Officer Commanding, Gujranwala states:

> We have come to know that Gujranwala District inhabitants do not usually show respect to the gazetted commissioners, European Civil and Military officers of His Imperial Majesty, through which the prestige and honour of the Government is not maintained. Therefore, we order that the inhabitants of Gujranwala district should show proper respect to these respectable officers whenever they have occasion to meet them, in the same way as big and rich people in India are respected.
>
> Whenever any one is on horseback or is driving any

---

6. Fein, *Imperial Crime*, p. 41.
7. INC Report, p. 110.

kind of wheeled conveyance, he must get down. One who has opened or got an umbrella in his hand should close or lower it down and all these people should salute with their right hand respectfully.[8]

Naturally, saluting was not enough, and there were ways in which a proper salute had to be given. Instances abound of people being taken into custody in order to be 'taught' how to salute properly.

Honorary Magistrate Mian Feroze Din said: 'People used to be whipped for not standing up while salaaming the General and Mr Plomer. Those who did not salaam were at times arrested. I saw a few cases of such whipping and of such arrests myself. The people were so terrified that many had to keep standing practically the whole day to prevent any mistake on their part and to avoid any such punishment. I say "practically" because they had to stand up every time they heard the sound of a motor car. I myself did so.'[9]

There was also an order that made it a crime for more than two Indians to walk abreast. 'Whereas it is expedient to prevent violence or intimidation, if more than two natives come and do not give way to a European, that is likely to lead to a breach of peace,' is how Lieutenant Colonel Johnson, who invented this particular order, explained it.

First Amritsar and now Punjab was converted overnight into a jail in which the army was free to act in the most sadistic way possible—all they needed to do was to promulgate an order. This led to the most infamous rule of the lot—the 'crawling order'.

The 'crawling order' was created by Dyer himself and it was applied to the lane where Marcella Sherwood (also referred to as Marcia Sherwood in some accounts), a missionary, had been attacked at the beginning of the troubles in Punjab. The assault

---

8. INC Report, p. 110.

9. INC Report, p. 63.

on Sherwood took place on 10 April. Around 1 p.m., Sherwood, who was the Superintendent of the Amritsar Mission School, had been cycling through the city, when she was caught up in the violence which had been unleashed, following the shooting of the protestors on the railway bridge. She was able to wheel her bicycle around and temporarily escape from a group of protestors, when she found herself lost in the narrow streets. Unfortunately she encountered a group of around eight men who mercilessly attacked her, hitting her with lathis. She was pushed to the ground, and there were cries to kill her as she was English. She tried to get back onto her feet a few times, but she was hit on the head and left on the road, presumed dead. She tried to seek help at some houses on the street, but the doors remained closed to her. Finally, she was taken in and helped by the parents of a student in her school, who also managed to take her to safety.[10]

Sherwood was taken to Fort Gobindgarh where Dyer visited her with his wife, following the Jallianwala Bagh massacre. She lay wrapped in bandages, still recovering from the trauma. The sight of her made Dyer decide to impose a 'frightful' punishment. Unfortunately, he chose to apply the punishment to all those who passed through Gali Kaurianwala (Kucha Kuricchan, also spelt as Kutcha Kurichan). The street where the incident had taken place was around 150 yards long. Anyone who passed through it was forced to crawl; Dyer said that the site of the assault was to be seen as 'holy ground'.

He explained: 'I felt women have been beaten. We look at women as sacred. I searched my brain for a suitable punishment for these awful cases. I did not know how to meet it. There was a little bit of accident in that. Now when I visited the pickets, I went down and ordered a triangle to be erected. I felt the street ought to be looked upon as sacred; therefore, I posted pickets at

---

10. Nick Lloyd, *The Amritsar Massacre* (London: I.B. Tauris Co. Ltd., 2011), p. 76.

both ends and told them: "No Indians are to be allowed to pass along here." I then also said "If they have to pass they must go on all fours." It never entered my brain that any sensible man, any sane man, would under the circumstances voluntarily go through that street.'

Perhaps it did not occur to him that people actually lived on that street and that families needed to go out for work, for food, for other requirements. Surely, if Dyer himself were sane, he would have known that?

The pickets were placed on either side of the street from 6 a.m. to 10 p.m. Dyer apparently thought that if the people on the street needed anything, 'they could leave at all other times' that is, between 10 p.m. and 6 a.m. He said, 'It could not be helped if they had to suffer a slight amount of inconvenience.' In another part of his testimony, he said that they could have used the rooftops of their homes to exit the street.

Ultimately, more than fifty people were subjected to this barbaric and completely arbitrary crawling order; most of them were respected and respectable men who lived on the street with their families and had no choice. The women of Gali Kaurianwala became prisoners overnight as they could not step out in the presence of the jeering soldiers posted on the street, who, according to eyewitness reports, were all British.

In retrospect, it seems that the Brigadier General could have been a psychopath because he also decided that he wanted to flog a number of young men in the same lane where Sherwood had been assaulted. It did not occur to him that it made little sense to flog those who had not beaten the unfortunate woman on 10 April. Even when he was told that Gali Kaurianwala was not frequented by those who had beaten Sherwood, he replied: 'I had erected a platform there in the middle of the street and thought when I got these men who had beaten her I would lash them down, I meant to lash them.'[11]

---

11. INC Report, p. 61.

Eventually those unconnected with the incident were tied to the flogging post and whipped.

For instance, in one case, six boys were tied to the flogging post in the lane one by one and given thirty lashes regardless of the fact that they were not involved in the incident. One of them, Sundar Singh, 'became senseless, after the fourth stripe, but after some water was poured into his mouth by a soldier, he regained consciousness. Flogging was then resumed. He lost his consciousness for the second time, but the flogging never ceased till he was given 30 stripes. He was taken off the flogging post bleeding and quite unconscious.' After the whipping the boys were handcuffed and dragged to the fort as they could not walk.[12]

The crawling order also led to the humiliation of many well-known citizens of the city. Labh Chand, who lived on the street, said: 'At about 4 o'clock in the afternoon, Ishar Das, Panna Lal, Mela Ram and I wanted to go home but were refused permission by the police. We ask permission again, but it was given on condition that we would pass the street by crawling. So all of us had to pass (through) the street by crawling on our bellies. We could not go to our houses by any other road.'[13]

Lala Megha Mal, a cloth merchant who lived in an alley off the 'crawling lane', had a sick wife who needed treatment, but for seven days no doctor would attend to her as they refused to crawl through the lane. As there was no water in the house, he had to go out late at night and get water for her, even though two contradictory curfew orders were in force. One which permitted him to go out after 10 p.m. to get what he wanted and another which refused him permission, as there was a blanket ban on people going out at night.[14]

---

12. INC Report, p. 64, statements 115, 117, 118.

13. INC Report, p. 62, statement 104.

14. INC Report, p. 62, statement 114.

Dyer was allowed to issue such contradictory and illogical orders because they only impacted the Indian population of Amritsar. The more cruel the lesson, the longer they would remember it. Europeans, of course, were exempt from all punishments.

There was no interference at all from the civil administration.

Megha Mal remembered, 'On the very first day soldiers were posted in Kutcha Kurichan; I was stopped by the soldiers when I was returning home at about 5 pm and I was ordered to creep on my belly. I however ran away and kept away till the soldiers had left at 9 pm.'[15]

The discomfort and humiliation aside, denigrating remarks and physical abuse were also meted out by the British soldiers posted there. 'When I was crawling they kicked me with their boots and also gave me blows with the butt ends of their rifles. That day I did not go back home to take my food,' said Lala Rallya Ram, opium contractor, who also lived close by. 'For full eight days, not a single sweeper appeared, so the refuse of the house was never removed, nor were the latrines cleaned. The water carrier, too was throughout absent... we could neither get vegetables or other eatables.'[16]

Though the residents of Amritsar were living in their own city, many parts of it had become concentration camps, with constant supervision by armed guards who had been given the right to insult or arrest anyone who did not crawl when told to. It did not matter if the person was blind or handicapped in any way. Kahan Chand had been blind for two decades—he too was made to crawl, was insulted and kicked.[17]

Another victim who lived on the same street, described how painful it was as he had to lie on his belly and push forward

---

15. INC Report, p. 62, statement 114.
16. INC Report, p. 62, statement 102.
17. INC Report, p. 62, statement 105.

with his arms like a 'grasshopper'. He said that many people left the street altogether to avoid the humiliation and agony. 'If anybody raised his buttock in crawling he was kicked by the goras who patrolled the street. The street was patrolled by about 18 goras who came at 6 in the morning and left it at 8 in the evening for many days.'[18] Eyewitnesses recollect the soldiers photographing their humiliation.

The condition of the women inside the houses in the 'crawling lane' was deteriorating day by day. Apart from those who, like the wife of Megha Lal, were unwell and could not leave the house, others lived in constant fear that their husbands or sons or fathers would never come back. They could not leave their homes, and it was presumed that children were also not safe on the street. Many of the women were in purdah, so it would have been difficult for them to go out.

There were also reports of shocking interference in the lives of these women. One of them had to confront soldiers in her own home, when the men were away. The soldiers hit the servant who answered the door with their rifles and boots. She said, 'I am a *purdah-nashin*. I never appear in public, not even before the servants. I was, however, called down from my house. I went with a purdah. I was here peremptorily ordered to take off my purdah. I was frightened and removed the purdah. I was then asked who assaulted Miss Sahib (Sherwood). They threatened me that unless I named the assailant I would be given over to the soldiers. I said I did not know and could not name anyone falsely.'[19]

Ganga Devi, who lived close by, said, 'For four days we remained without food and water. My daughter, aged four,

---

18. K.D. Malaviya, *Open Rebellion in the Punjab: With Special Reference to Amritsar* (Allahabad: Abhyudaya Press, 1919), p. 38.

19. Vinay Lal, 'The Incident of the Crawling Lane: Women In the Punjab Disturbances of 1919', *Genders*, no. 16. Accessed at http://southasia.ucla.edu/incident-crawling-lane/.

died of fright. Her constant cry was, "Oh mother the soldiers have come to kill pigeons, they will kill me!" This constant fear brought on fever. We left the house, but the fright did not leave her. She died on the eighth day.'[20] The soldiers were known to shoot pigeons and roast them on the doorstep of the houses on the street. All the women living on the lane complained about the men exposing and relieving themselves openly. Many wept and said they were also terrorised by the cries of the young Indian boys being flogged.

The irony, of course, was that while Sherwood had been attacked on that street, it was not by anyone who lived there. Yes, some of them had refused her shelter, uncertain of the repercussions, but again, it was one of the residents of the street who ultimately took her in and smuggled her to a safe place.

Was any of the humiliation or harassment of Indian women reported? If one were to pay heed to the description by Sarojini Naidu in London on 3 June 1920 at Kingsway Hall, of the atrocities that had been inflicted on the women of Punjab, and in particular Amritsar, the situation may have looked very different to that projected by the assault on Sherwood. She spoke of the 'blood guiltiness of those who have committed murder in my country... of the thrice horrible deed... I am going to speak to you all as a woman about the wrong committed against my sisters. Englishmen, you who pride themselves upon your chivalry, you who hold more precious than all your imperial treasures the honour and chastity of your own, will you sit still and leave unavenged the dishonour and the insult and the agony inflicted upon the veiled women of Punjab. One of the speakers has said that Lord Chelmsford refused to draw the veil from the ugly face of realities, but his minion, his martial authorities rent the veil from the faces of the women in Punjab. Not only were the men mowed down as if they were grass that

---

20. INC Report, Evidence, p. 179.

is born to wither, but they tore asunder the cherished purdah, that innermost privacy of the chaste womanhood of India...' For evidence, she pointed to the INC report and said that 'women whose face had never even been touched by the curious sun, were dragged into the market place where they were stripped naked, they were flogged, they were outraged.'[21]

Was there any truth to these statements of the abuse, flogging and outraging of Indian women? Balochan, a resident of Amritsar, had testified that she and her sister were stripped naked by policemen and sticks were pushed into their vaginas. However, the testimony of these witnesses was sought to be discredited by the Viceroy, in a telegram which said these women were 'all low class prostitutes belonging to wandering tribes... settled in Amritsar for prostitution.' It was also indicated that the men accused of molesting them were Indian. Naidu's own credibility (as she belonged to the Congress) was in doubt.

But she was not the only one.

When Annie Besant, a British woman with nationalist sympathies who became the President of the Indian National Congress in 1917, alleged that British soldiers had defecated in the only well in the Kucha Kaurianwala and left women and children without water, Secretary of State Edwin Montagu was assured by Viceroy Chelmsford that the allegations were 'entirely false and unfounded'.

'It is impossible to believe,' Chelmsford wrote, employing language with which we are now familiar 'that any British soldier purposely defiled wells.'[22]

The 'crawling order' was in place from 19 to 24 April, during which it created incredible hardship for the people who lived in the 'crawling lane'. It is unlikely that O'Dwyer,

---

21. INC Report, Evidence, p. 179; Sarojini Naidu, *Words of Freedom: Ideas of a Nation*. Speech in London, 3 June 1920. Accessed online.
22. Lal, 'Incident of the Crawling Lane'.

Kitchin and Irving did not know about it. From the records it appears that daily 'pow wows', as O'Dwyer called them, were held at Government House, Lahore, where 'military officers reported on the day's events and then discussed what could be done.'[23] According to Thompson, 'there was a great deal more done orally than in normal times.'[24] Thus there are almost no records of what was approved and what was suggested afresh. Viceroy Chelmsford had begun to have some doubts about what was going on. It was as late as 30 April that he learnt about the 'crawling order' and told O'Dwyer, 'Now I have no wish to make your task harder, but I would ask, does not this particular form of punishment offend against the canons of wise punishment.' These were mild words and O'Dwyer's reply was that he had already cancelled the order as soon as he heard of it.

O'Dwyer was also to shift the blame to the military authorities, saying that while he had approved of the martial law orders in Lahore, he could not take responsibility for those about which he knew nothing.[25] For the record, between 15 April and 6 June, 64 martial law orders were passed in Lahore itself, almost one a day, creating untold difficulties for the residents.

But it was in Amritsar that the situation was becoming catastrophic. The city's streets were full of blood and garbage, and in places like the 'crawling lane', people starved for days.

Even the short distance of 36 miles between Amritsar and Lahore, which was easily covered, even twice or thrice a day, became an ever widening chasm. This would lead to serious consequences as it was claimed that much of the information about the circumstances on the ground was not communicated

---

23. Lloyd, *The Amritsar Massacre*, p. 135.

24. Lloyd, *The Amritsar Massacre*, p. 135.

25. Lloyd, *The Amritsar Massacre*, p. 137.

to the Viceroy, or to the Secretary of State, through whom it may have reached the Parliament or the Prime Minister. For a long time, the humiliation and unjustifiable barbarity being practiced in Amritsar and elsewhere would not be known outside those areas. But, in retrospect, this appears to be simply a fig leaf. In all likelihood, everyone knew, especially O'Dwyer, but chose to be wilfully ignorant.

O'Dwyer claimed that when he had checked with Dyer about this ghastly punishment of the 'crawling order', the latter had said that he had brought it in to 'restrain' his soldiers who were upset at the assault on 'English ladies'.[26]

O'Dwyer then 'told Dyer that it was an irregular and improper order, and asked him what led him to issue it. As far as I remember, he referred to his position at the time, that he had a certain number of British troops, he had the greatest difficulty in restraining them because they had seen English ladies being savagely assaulted, they had known their fellow countrymen had been killed and he thought they might break out of control; he therefore ordered this punishment to make an impression on their minds.'[27]

This was gross hyperbole, but Dyer must have known that if he spoke of how wretched the British felt over the assault on their tribe, he would have a ready audience. It was incorrect to say that 'English ladies' had been savagely assaulted—only one had been. But it was his so-called stoic defence of 'womanhood' that ultimately won him a huge audience of lady admirers in the UK.

While the order at Gali Kaurianwala continued to cause havoc, the police and the army began arresting innocent people,

---

26. V.N. Datta, *New Light On the Punjab Disturbances in 1919* (Simla: Indian Institute of Advanced Study, 1975), p. 137; Shireen Ilahi, *Imperial Violence and the Path to Independence* (I.B. Tauris & Co. Ltd., 2016), p. 66.

27. Datta, *New Light*, p. 137; Ilahi, *Imperial Violence*, p. 66.

in Amritsar and elsewhere over trivial matters; hundreds were incriminated through false testimony. Most of those arrested were unaware of what they had been arrested for.

Contrary to appearances, there was a clear agenda behind these arrests. Many of those put behind bars had been identified as having either attended or organised the anti-Rowlatt Act meetings. There were others, arrested sometimes in groups, who were accused of rioting and looting in various places. Some were arrested to provide false testimony against them. Still others were arrested without being either charged or tried. It was a free-for-all. In particular, people were intimidated to 'frame' Kitchlew and Satya Pal. The effort to nab people in connection with the riots of 10 April was relentless, although this allegation was, of course, denied by the administration.

Doctors were more often than not asked to provide lists of the wounded, so they could be questioned or placed under arrest. Dr Kidar Nath Bhandari, a Senior Assistant Surgeon who lived at Hall Gate, testified that 'On 20th April, at about 4 pm, Sewak Ram, Sub-Inspector of Police came to my house and asked for a list of the wounded I had treated on 10th April.'[28]

As Helen Fein says in *Imperial Crime and Punishment*, while it could not be proved that people were forced to invent testimony, 'they were likely to be beaten or held for long periods. During the reign of martial law, over 600 persons were detained or arrested without being charged or tried. Of the 573 for whom data is available on length of detention, we find that 91 (or 15.9 per cent) were imprisoned from four weeks to seventy-nine days, 134 (23.4 per cent) were jailed for fourteen to twenty-eight days, 108 (18.8 per cent) were jailed for seven to thirteen days and 240 (41.9 per cent) were jailed for less than one week.'[29]

---

28. INC Report, Evidence, pp. 42–5.

29. Fein, *Imperial Crime*, p. 38.

But as these arrests were arbitrary, many went unrecorded. They created enormous stress, particularly for women who may have already lost a husband or a son or a father. Neither the arrested persons nor their family members could be sure they would come back soon, or return at all. The jails remained full, often overflowing, leading many of the officers commanding various districts to prefer to flog than to incarcerate those unfortunate enough to fall into their hands.

Martial law tribunals were set up; there were also summary courts set up under the martial law order of 1919. Eight hundred fifty-two people were tried under the tribunals, out of whom 108 were sentenced to death, 265 sentenced to transportation for life, 104 to imprisonment exceeding three years and 356 to forfeiture of property. Even worse were the summary courts, where around 1,437 people were tried. These were, of course, the official figures, but within days, the law and order machinery had fallen apart as the army took complete charge. Even in September 1919, 1,229 people were still in jail.

The conditions in jail were terrible. People were often chained up without food or water, with no access to any facilities. They were forced to soil themselves where they were. They underwent other punishments as well as torture. Some of them had sticks pushed up their anus, and others were whipped or tied around trees and, in some cases, hung from them. One person even had his hand put under the leg of a charpoy, while the policemen sat on the charpoy, till he confessed. Their possessions were taken away from them, and some were evicted from their own homes. These assaults followed no rules, and guilt or evidence of alleged guilt seemed to be irrelevant. Anyone could be tortured into admitting the guilt of another.

That the allegedly fair British system could break down so swiftly, with not a single voice (within the larger administration in Amritsar or Punjab) raised against it, points to the fact that this was part of an ongoing strategy. It was acceptable behaviour because racist atrocities in Punjab had become acceptable under O'Dwyer. Those who helped him maintain law and order and suppress the nascent freedom movement were rewarded generously. Thus encouraged by the British, even the local police and others in positions of some authority became collaborators in suppressing all forms of uprising or protest in Punjab. Fraudulent evidence was a common way to trap someone, especially under martial law.

All of this may have been common practice all over the country but within a small area like the walled city of Amritsar, the impact would have been enormous. No one was safe from being hauled to the Kotwali.

One such person was Hans Raj, who had organised the satyagraha meeting at the Jallianwala Bagh on 13 April. He was taken from the Gobindgarh Fort to the Kotwali at Town Hall and kept overnight on 22 and 23 April. His statement was recorded and he turned approver. But interestingly, before he was produced before the Magistrate, Seymour, he was extensively questioned by Lala Jowahar Lal, Inspector of Police, CID, Punjab, who said that he jotted down some notes of his statement and then destroyed them because they were 'incomplete'. He conveniently forgot what Hans Raj had told him, during cross-examination by the Hunter Committee. Officials cross-examined by the Committee often 'forgot', even though testimonies such as that of Hans Raj were used extensively to implicate many in the infamous 'Amritsar Conspiracy Case'.

He said during his cross-examination: 'He (Hans Raj) was brought from the fort at about 11 o'clock and about 3 o'clock he was ready to make a statement. I ...then applied for a Magistrate. He was then put into the lock up and a Magistrate came and recorded his statement.'[30]

---

30. INC Report, Evidence, p. 153.

Lala Jowahar Lal, along with Sardar Bahadur Sardar Sukha Singh, Deputy Superintendent of Police, CID, Punjab, had been sent specially from Lahore to investigate the situation. Unfortunately, during his cross-examination, he barely appeared to remember anything.

But it was Hans Raj's evidence that led to some young boys being whipped in the 'crawling lane' for having attacked Marcella Sherwood. It is extremely doubtful that Hans Raj was an eyewitness to the event or knew much about it, for he would have been busy that morning and would have accompanied Kitchlew and Satya Pal to the District Commissioner's residence, from where they were arrested.

Ironically, even those who had tried to help the administration calm the crowds on 10 April were forced to give false evidence. One among them was Dr Maqbool Mahmood, a lawyer who was picked up and instructed to say that 'I could and would identify the murderers of Robinson and Rowland (who had been killed on the 10th). I informed the police that I had already sent a written statement to them and that I had stated that I could not recognise anybody. This statement was then brought to me and I was then asked to tear it off with my own hands and to submit a fresh statement giving the names of those whom they had found out as culprits. I refused to comply with the demand and some threats were flung at me. However, I was subsequently allowed to leave.'[31] But the threats continued—including one to cancel his lawyer's licence.[32]

Another person who had helped a European woman escape was Nelly Benjamin. She had successfully hidden Isabel Mary Easdon, the lady doctor at the IC Municipal Female Hospital at Chowk Farid, who had also been targeted by the protestors on 10 April. An agitated group had gone looking for Easdon after

---

31. INC Report, pp. 66–7, statement 5.
32. INC Report, pp. 66–7, statement 5.

she was apparently overheard saying that the Indians who were shot at had got what they deserved. But now Nelly Benjamin was also rounded up. Instead of appreciating her quick action in saving Easdon's life, Benjamin, too, was threatened with jail when she refused to falsely implicate a witness.

She said, '... when the enquiry was going on. I was taken to the Kotwali on two occasions; I was asked to say that I had seen Mohammad Amin in the crowd. As I said that was not the truth. Mr Plomer threatened to send me to jail. I told them whatever I knew but I refused to give false evidence. They also tempted me with a reward from the Government, if I supported the story of Mrs Easdon regarding the presence of Mohammad Amin. I refused again.'[33]

Mohammad Amin was a pleader. He said he was a personal friend of the Easdons and was being implicated by the police in this case. However, Mrs Easdon said she had seen him at the head of a mob on 10 April, and that his son had come looking for her. She also accused Dr Kidar Nath Bhandari, whose clinic was in front of her hospital, of refusing to help her—even though it was her chaprasi who communicated this to her. She had herself seen that Dr Nath was fairly busy treating the victims of the firing. Later, after Dr Nath's arrest, the chaprasi was to change his statement.

According to the INC report, 'On the 20th of April, he, (Amin) with his son and brother was arrested and taken to the Kotwali.' He said, 'I was taken by a constable to the door of the Havalat. A small room as it was, it contained not less than 30 unfortunate men. It was a horrible sight to see them stretching out their arms out of the iron bars and praying for a drink of water...' Amin was made to spend time inside jail and also witnessed fellow prisoners being coerced to implicate others. He found it frightening, for 'they were kept handcuffed in their

---

33. INC Report, p. 69, statement 16.

cells in pairs and thus led even to the latrines. They begged for the removal of the handcuffs, whilst they were actually in the latrines but it was no use. They were compelled to walk round and round in the hot sun—they were given no food for 36 hours and made to sleep on the bare floor...' Later, they were taken to Lahore to stand trial, 52 men chained together. Amin and his brother were finally released on 27 May, after five weeks of hell—and his son Mohammad Akram was sentenced to death, in connection with the attempt to assault Mrs Easdon. The sentence was subsequently commuted to 5 years of rigorous imprisonment.[34]

Sixty-two-year-old Dr Nath was also asked by Sardar Sukha Singh to name those who had attacked Mrs Easdon. When he refused, he was told by Plomer, Marshall and Sukha Singh that he would be arrested. The doctor replied he had not seen anyone and they could do what they liked. He was then arrested on 20 April and kept in confinement till 27 April, after which he was shifted to the subsidiary jail. He had to walk through the bazaar in the heat for about a mile, along with sixty-two other prisoners. He was kept without proper food or even a change of clothes (which he had asked for, from his home).

'On the 2nd May, the Deputy Commissioner went to the jail and the doctor asked him why he was being detained. The answer was there was nothing against him except that he had not tried to save the life of Mrs Easdon, when she was attacked by the mob. The doctor tried to reason that it was not possible for him to do so, because he did not know when the mob went to her but it was of no avail. He and his assistant were, however, released on the 12th of May, without knowing any definite charges against him.'[35]

Among the worst cases of torture was that of Gholam

---

34. INC Report, p. 68, statement 14.
35. INC Report, p. 67, statement 13.

Jilani, an Imam and deed writer, who was arrested just three days after the massacre, on 16 April. According to the INC Report, Jilani had a 'prominent part' in organising the Ram Naumi festival; this was where Hindus and Muslims had shown their unity.[36] Mohammad Shafi 'saw some of the tortures that Gholam Jilani was subjected to and heard his piteous cries.'[37] Others such as Gholam Mohammad witnessed the torture on him and on Khair Din, who died a few days later of the injuries inflicted upon him. Haji Shamsuddin, landlord and *zimindar* (sic), also witnessed the torture. 'They drove a stick into his anus. Also he was in a most pitiable condition. I saw his urine and excreta coming out. All of us, who were outside were told by the police that those, who did not give evidence, would be treated like that.' The torture and threats did in some cases have a domino effect, as more and more innocent people were brought into the net, falsely accused. Gholam Jilani, as he was being tortured, was forced to implicate at least one more person, Badrul Islam Ali Khan.

According to the INC report, the barrister Badrul Islam Ali Khan 'was arrested on 19 April. The police walked into his wife's bedroom and when she asked them to leave, they refused to do so. He was taken to the Kotwali and Mr Plomer said in a loud voice, "This is the man who wants to be the Lieutenant Governor of the Punjab."'[38] He told the Congress Sub-Committee that he was pressed to give evidence. He described the condition of the cell in which he and his fellow prisoners were locked up, how they were subjected to severe humiliation, and discussed the charges that were brought against him before he was finally discharged. He concluded that 'there was an attempt by the police to manufacture evidence against me, by torturing a man named Gholam Jilani, who admitted

---

36. INC Report, p. 71, statements 2, 6, 134, 138–40.
37. INC Report, p. 71, statements 2, 6, 134, 138–40.
38. INC Report, p. 72, statement 88.

the fact in his evidence before the Martial Law commission, in the course of my trial. Thus it was that I was arrested and kept in custody for a period of about a month and half and tried for my life.'

Arrests like his became an ongoing farce and tragedy as more and more people were forced into false admissions, leading to further illegal and motivated arrests. However, there was still no way to escape, as all the city gates were guarded. Martial law was in place and specially signed passes were required to exit or enter the walled city.

Apart from trying to nab those they considered to be the instigators of the riots on 10 April, the police (as directed by the administration and Dyer) were mainly looking for confessions that would indict Kitchlew and Satya Pal. It was their incarceration that had let to the riots of 10 April.

Seth Gul Mohammad, a glassware merchant, was arrested on 20 April while he was offering prayers and taken to the Kotwali. He was asked to give false evidence. Police Inspector Jowaharlal caught hold of his beard and slapped him so hard that it made him reel. He then asked him (Mohammad) to say that 'Doctors Satyapal and Kitchlew had instigated me to bring about the hartal on the 6th and they had encouraged me, by saying they would use bombs to drive out the English from the country.' [39] The witness refused. The officer then asked his underlings to take him aside and make him 'alright'. He was taken a few paces away from the officers' table and asked by a number of constables to please Inspector Jowaharlal by doing what he wanted. He still refused. So they caught hold of his hand, placed it under a cot, over which eight constables sat. 'When the pain became unbearable,' the witness said, 'I cried out, leave my hand, I will do whatever you ask me to do.' He was then taken to Jowaharlal again. But again he refused to implicate the doctors. He was kept confined in a room that day.

---

39. INC Report, p. 69, statement 21.

The following two days, he was beaten, slapped and caned. He was told that he would be made an accused and hanged. The beating went on for eight days. On the eighth day, he again agreed to make the desired statement. He was then taken to Aga Ibrahim, the Magistrate, before whom he repeated the same 'untrue statement' that was required of him. Hans Raj, the approver, who was also in the Kotwali, asked him to do as the police asked. After ten days' detention, he was let off, on the condition that he appear at the Kotwali from day to day, which he did, up to 9 June, when he was taken to Lahore. On 16 June, he was produced before the Martial Law Tribunal, where he made a clean breast of the whole thing and told the judges that he was tortured.'[40] He had been in police custody for approximately 56 days—without any valid reason, apart from the false statement demanded from him.

Many of those who were dragged to the Kotwali in Amritsar had survived the firing on 10 April and the massacre three days later. A number of them had already lost their friends and family members, and were being forced to betray other members of the community. The helplessness they experienced needs to be understood, as well as the rifts these forced confessions would have caused. The walled city had a close-knit life, which was now being ripped apart systematically. Those who had worked towards Hindu-Muslim unity, such as Gholam Jilani, now became special targets, and as their spirit was broken, seeds of suspicion were sown. These would come to fruition in the next few decades when even those like Kitchlew, a Muslim who strove for communal harmony, would be forced to abandon Amritsar, the city he loved, during the Partition of India in 1947.

Not only did Dyer wish to extinguish the spirit of unity through his soldiers, there was enthusiastic participation from the police as well. Even after martial law was imposed—we read in these 100-year-old testimonies—Irving would drop by

---

40. INC Report, p. 69, statement 21.

and encourage the incarcerations and torture. The army and the police came closer than ever with a dual purpose: to break the so-called rebellion, and to smash Hindu-Muslim unity forever. (This policy was also being nurtured in other parts of Punjab, often with ominous outcomes, as we will see in subsequent chapters.)

Perhaps this was all done in an attempt to prove that there was a larger conspiracy and that Kitchlew and Satya Pal were actually harbouring plans to overthrow the British (which was a far cry from the satyagraha that Gandhi had asked them to organise). The problem of course was that when the accused or witnesses appeared before the Martial Law Tribunal, they had no legal recourse, and were often produced forty or fifty at a time, making it difficult for most to argue their case. Meanwhile, arrests were taking place on a daily basis, and people had to constantly face fresh rounds of specially invented, humiliating punishments.

Irving put up notices in Amritsar during the week following the massacre on 13 April; he said the government was 'sorry' that some innocent persons had been forced by 'wicked people' to go to Jallianwala Bagh and 'get killed', but that warnings had been given beforehand. He also made it clear that obedience to the order of the 'General sahib' was obligatory, and that the 'General sahib' would not, in future, put up with any kind of unrest.[41]

For 'General sahib', that is Dyer, this was a high point in his career. For once he was completely in charge, and had been given free rein by all concerned. Considering the repressive measures he had already unleashed, word would spread that he was prepared and allowed to go to any extreme. Within a short time, other army officers had taken their cue from him and the regime of terror spread beyond Amritsar.

---

41. Notice from the Motilal Nehru papers at the Nehru Memorial Library, Delhi.

NOTICE

Ignorant and wicked people have circulated false rumours and it is the intention of the government that no such false rumours should get circulated. It is desirable that information regarding all such ridiculous news be at once communicated to the Deputy Commissioner so that he may be able to contradict false news and promulgate the correct news.

The real facts regarding the incident that took place on Sunday in the city of Amritsar are as follows—

The General Sahib had issued a proclamation that no gathering should assemble without his permission, no meeting be held and no procession take place. The General Sahib and myself went in person to the city and warned the residents of the city by beat of drum that in case any mob was held it would, if necessary, be dispersed by means of bullets. Disregarding this order of the General Sahib, some ill wishers of the Government arranged for the meeting by false pretences and gave out that a Diwan will be held there. But the people were not informed that there was danger in going there.

About 5 pm the General sahib, with about 50 Indian troops, went to the spot. There was no European soldier with him. Seeing the soldiers the people showed an attitude of defiance. On this the order to shoot was given with the result that many were wounded and many killed.

The government is sorry that some innocent persons were forced by wicked people to go there and got killed. But everyone should bear in mind that obedience to the order of the General sahib is obligatory and that the General sahib will not, in future, put up with any kind of unrest.

Dated 18th April, 1919 (Sd) Miles Irving
Deputy Commissioner
Amritsar District[42]

---

42. Motilal Nehru papers at NMML.

Despite this, all kinds of rumours persisted and the distance between the colonisers and the subjects continued to grow. There were even rumours that the bullets which had been fired on 13 April were poisoned, as the heat had caused the bullet wounds to expand.[43]

While the people feared more reprisals, government spies fed into the British insecurity that people would unite and the unrest would continue—as indeed it did, in other places like Gujranwala. But the larger expectation of the British was that the massacre would send a 'moral' message and people would not rise or rebel anymore, if they continued to be repressed.

The already terrorised, unarmed population had no intention of continuing the satyagraha so soon after the massacre. Most of the men who were active in the agitation had been either killed or wounded. Those who survived were now being demeaned or demonised. O'Dwyer never had much respect for them, in any case, as the city dwellers rarely enrolled in the army. The irony was that he had wiped out most of the young men in the villages by making them enrol in the army, and now he had managed to do the same in the city. In such a situation, it is not surprising that some chose to become collaborators.

In Amritsar, which had been a thriving city of traders, lawyers, doctors and other professionals, the massacre did not just create fear. It turned it into a city of widows and the wounded. There were fatherless children and far too many families without any source of income. We know from the sheer numbers of the dead and wounded that at least 2,000 young and old males must have been impacted, which meant that perhaps 10,000 or more family members were left devastated and in grief. Those impacted under martial law would have been at least another 2,000 in Amritsar alone, impacting approximately 10,000 more. The Congress team recording the evidence spoke

---

43. Motilal Nehru Papers at NMML.

to at least 1,700 witnesses in Punjab, out of which around 175 had been either personally impacted or were witnesses to the massacre. Not only did this change the demographics of the city, it was also to have a long lasting impact on Amritsar, changing it from an independently advancing city to a dependent economy. Many of the traders who had settled in Amritsar no longer felt secure. Of the 1,60,000 people living there 100 years ago, we can assume that at least 50,000, if not more, would have directly felt the weight of British racism.

Prior to the massacre, the riots, the death of the five Europeans and the burning of the banks would have made Europeans reconsider investing in the city. O'Dwyer's policy of repression would have itself caused further damage, reducing Amritsar to a shell of its former self. He also wrecked the possibility of Hindus and Muslims joining hands by encouraging betrayals and collaborations.

At this time, as the city continued to be isolated, with no news from the outside world, and with curfew imposed rigorously, Gandhi and the satyagraha became a distant dream. Now there was only hope of somehow surviving what O'Dwyer had called a 'holocaust'.

Dyer himself was apparently very pleased with the effect that the massacre had on the people, as was evident during his cross-examination. He was asked by Pandit Jagat Narayan:

> Q: You have told us that on the 13th the city was a model of law and order?
>
> A: It was all quiet when I went round. After the shooting it soon became a model of law and order.[44]

Even if it was a model of law and order, martial law remained in place.

Some parts of the population of Amritsar were specially

---

44. Evidence, Amritsar, p. 139.

targeted—especially the lawyers—as they had been the ones at the forefront of the satyagraha. Once again, in an attempt to humiliate them, especially as the courts were not functioning, they were appointed as 'special constables'. Even though Dyer said they did useful service and Kitchin said the lawyers liked being downgraded to 'special constables' (which meant that this order definitely was approved by O'Dwyer), the lawyers themselves, 93 in all, were aghast and humiliated. They were forced to salaam, lift tables and chairs even when 'orderlies' or servants were available to do the lifting.[45]

The INC Report contains the evidence of Lala Kanhya Lal, in whose name the meeting at Jallianwala Bagh had been called. He was the oldest lawyer in the city, but he too was given the rank of a 'special constable'. He said, '… along with all the members of the local bar, I was compelled to act as a special constable. This appointment was made on the 22nd of April, when there was absolutely no necessity for such an appointment, for the maintenance of peace and order in the city. The police force was quite sufficient for the purpose, and, as a matter of fact, the city was quiet on those days. In my old age, I was made to work like a coolie, carrying tables and chairs from one place to another, and to patrol the city in the hot sun. The abuse, which was showered upon us, and the indignities to which we were put, added a great deal to our sufferings. I cannot believe that our appointment was necessary for the maintenance of peace and order. The order was meant to punish us. The local Bar takes part in public affairs and took a prominent part in the anti-Rowlatt Act agitation, that is why the whole Bar was punished in this way.'[46]

This 'demotion' as it were, from their professions as lawyers, would not have gone unnoticed and would have harmed their

---

45. INC Report, p. 64.
46. INC Report, p. 64, statement 29.

dignity and standing in the eyes of their fellow citizens. They could be summoned at the whim of the administration, even to watch floggings, and were themselves threatened with arrest or whipping. This reduced even the respectable residents of Amritsar—even those who had gone abroad and obtained degrees from European universities and learnt their law there, and who had previously dealt with the British on equal terms—to the level of slaves. They had to obey every order on pain of death.

Lala Balmokand Bhatia, who was not just a High Court vakil, but also a Municipal Commissioner, gave evidence about the 'ceremony' of appointing special constables. After they were made to sit on the ground, 'it was then that we were called upon to witness (two) citizens being flogged after being tied to the post. We were specially ordered to see this scene. In the evening, all the members of the bar were made to stand in line.' Lieutenant Newman was placed in charge. He threatened one of them with a kicking. They were to report in thrice a day and patrol the city for the rest of the day.

'In other words,' Mr Bhatia says, 'we had to keep ourselves in attendance, the whole day, either in the (Ram Bagh) garden or in the city. We were constantly reminded that we were mere constables and the punishment for any neglect was not only flogging or imprisonment, but also death.' They were finally discharged on 12 May, after almost twenty days.[47]

All those connected in any way with the anti-Rowlatt Act movement, or with the Congress Party, were specially selected for punishment. Lala Girdhari Lal pointed out in his evidence quoted in the INC Report that 'the police began to arrest people from 12th April, as far as I remember. There was no respite after that, and people from every sphere of life were arrested from day to day while employed peacefully in their occupations. No

---

47. INC Report, pp. 64–5, statement 91.

charge was stated.' They were then 'handcuffed at once and put into the lock up, for days and months, without being informed what they were accused of...'

While the residents of Amritsar were trapped, flogged, demeaned, arrested and tortured at whim, other cities and small towns of Punjab were also suffering.

For several years during Lieutenant Governor O'Dwyer's regime, it had been felt that Punjab was in a state of unrest, some of it led by the advocates of the Ghadr Movement, which was based in the US. O'Dwyer had been tracking the return of these apparently foreign-trained revolutionaries and according to his memoirs, *India As I Knew It*, he had managed to persuade 'leading Sikhs' while in a conference with the commissioners and deputy commissioners that this movement would bring them 'discredit'.[48] He also added helpfully, 'I put the situation very frankly before them—it is only our latter-day politicians who think that candour is not appreciated by Orientals—and told them the Government was strong enough to crush the Ghadr rebellion by its own resources, but that this could be done more promptly and with less bloodshed if I had the hearty co-operation of the Sikhs themselves.'

According to him, they gave many suggestions, including wanting to 'intern in jail the whole three thousand two hundred emigrants who had upto then returned and of whom we had only interned some two hundred in jail and seven hundred in their villages.' He then set up a system whereby the prominent Sikhs would inform the Deputy Commissioner of the 'conduct and reputation of the returned emigrants and their supporters'. While this led to a smooth system of functioning, according to him, it also led to the murder of some of the 'loyal Sikh Sirdars'.

He was also extremely proud of another conspiracy that he had managed to scuttle: 'Early in 1915, the Bengali Rash Behari,

---

48. Sir Michael O'Dwyer, *India As I Knew It* (London: Constable and Company, 1925), p. 204.

with the Mahratta Brahmin, Pingle, were the brains directing the revolutionary activities of the Ghadr Party, who were mainly Sikhs. Rash Bihari had established his headquarters at Amritsar, where he lived with other Bengalis, whom he and Pingle had brought up from Bengal to assist in bomb-making. These leaders were also active in endeavouring to enlist the support of Indian troops, specially Sikhs and Rajputs, in Northern India.' Using informants, the British managed to quell the rebellion and on 19 February 1915, there was a raid on four homes in Lahore, during which they captured thirteen of the 'most dangerous revolutionaries, with arms, bombs, bomb making material'. Though Rash Bihari escaped, Pingle was captured and later hanged. According to O'Dwyer, this conspiracy had 'tainted' a Sikh Squadron, which was eventually court-martialled. Eighteen of the regiment were sentenced to death and twelve were actually executed.

By 1919, O'Dwyer had managed to build an even larger network of informants—though he continued to fear a mutiny in the forces—and other conspiracies. As in Amritsar, and elsewhere in Lahore too, the policy of divide and rule (in this case, within the Sikh community itself) had worked and he was now looking forward to leaving his post in Punjab with an enviable reputation. Unfortunately for his plans, this was when the anti-Rowlatt Act movement began to have some repercussions in Lahore, where O'Dwyer was based, at Government House. Fond as he was of his shikar and his anecdotes of how he had cleansed Punjab of rebellion, he was determined not to leave behind a disorderly mess for his successor, MacLagan; he was sanguine about using strong measures.

In Lahore, a city of about 250,000 at the time, people had begun to show an increased interest in political activity, especially against the Rowlatt Acts. When Gandhi announced his Satyagraha Movement, very few in Lahore (unlike in Amritsar) actually took the satyagraha oath. It was the leaders in the city who spread the word about the proposed hartal, and the accompanying call to fast. According to the Hunter Committee Report, a notice was issued on 2 April by the Superintendent of Police that anyone convening or collecting an assembly or directing or promoting a procession in the public streets would have to apply for a licence.

When some leaders met with Fyson, the Deputy Commissioner of Lahore, on 5 April (they were even prepared to abandon the proposed meeting on 6 April), Fyson handed out the following regulations, according to the INC report:

1. All may endeavour, upto the evening of the 5th, to convince the citizens either for or against the hartal on the 6th April.
2. On the 6th there should be no canvassing one way or the other.
3. The meeting may take place, but there should be no inflammatory speech making.[49]

However, the hartal, probably to the surprise of all, was successful and attended by thousands, including women and children, who also bathed in the river. In this case, women formed part of the satyagrahis. The entire group then formed a procession which went down to the Mall. This was in contravention to the earlier order issued on 2 April, but the police did not interfere, despite some provocation. For instance, the crowd (referred to constantly in the official reports as a mob, even though they were peaceful) chanted '*Hai Hai George Mar Gaya*' (King George is dead)—which could be considered sedition.

Based on the evidence of witnesses, the INC Report states that on 6 April afternoon there was a meeting at Bradlaugh Hall which was attended by 'thousands' and also, on the order of O'Dwyer, by the Superintendent of the CID.[50] Once again,

---

49. INC Report, p. 75.
50. INC Report, p. 76.

it was peaceful, although speeches against the Rowlatt Acts were made.

Interestingly, there are some clear diversions in the memories of those reporting the events in Lahore, depending on whether they were giving their evidence in front of the Hunter Committee or the Congress Sub-Committee.

Thus, the Hunter Committee reported some tensions at an event that was otherwise reported as 'peaceful'. European police officers who attended the meeting were loudly hooted and hissed at. Resolutions were passed condemning the authorities in Delhi for 'having fired upon innocent people without justification', on 30 March. The congregation viewed with alarm and disapproval the orders passed on Kitchlew, Satya Pal and others (banning them from attending and speaking at public meetings, etc.), in the first week of April.

As in Amritsar, on 9 April, which was Ram Naumi, Lahore witnessed fraternisation amongst Hindus and Muslims, and the officials who were with the procession were cheered. Thus far everything was calm, even though Hindus and Muslims were coming together, and this would have alarmed the British.

According to the INC Report, on 10 April, things were about to change, as the news of Gandhi's arrest spread (the news was published in the *Civil and Military Gazette*). A spontaneous hartal took place and all businesses were closed at 4 p.m. The Hunter Committee Report also says that word of the resistance and rioting at Amritsar reached Lahore around 3.30 p.m.

Concerned about the death of five Europeans in Amritsar, the administration placed protective pickets in Lahore wherever Europeans were likely to be, such as at the Gymkhana Club, the telegraph office, Government House and European hotels. At 6 p.m., a meeting was held by O'Dwyer at Government

A view of Jallianwala Bagh from the eastern side, 1919.

People pointing at bullet marks at Jallianwala Bagh, 1919.

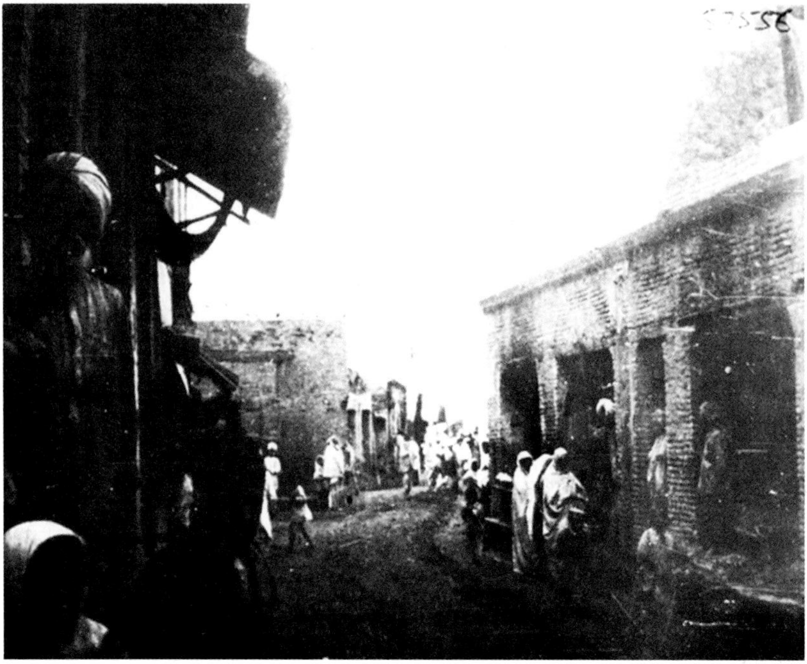

Nehru Memorial Library and Museum; courtesy Partition Museum, Amritsar

The street through which General Dyer approached Jallianwala Bagh.

INC Report; courtesy Partition Museum, Amritsar

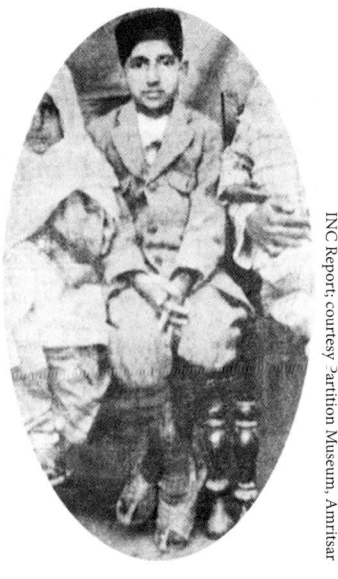

Thirteen-year-old Madan Mohan, shot and killed at Jallianwala Bagh.

INC Report; courtesy Partition Museum, Amritsar

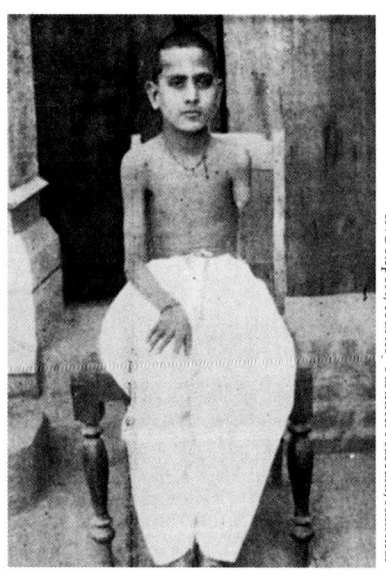

Sardari Lal, whose left arm had to be amputated on account of injuries from the bombing at Gujranwala.

Uttam Chand, wounded at Jallianwala Bagh.

An eleven-year-old boy in Kasur, charged with waging war against the King.

Sunder Singh, wounded in the left eye at Jallianwala Bagh.

Arrests in Amritsar under martial law, 1919.

The crawling order being executed, Amritsar, 1919. This photograph was probably taken by a British soldier posted there.

Dr Satya Pal, B.A., M.B., Amritsar.

Dr Saifuddin Kitchlew, B.A., Ph.D., Barrister-at-Law, Amritsar.

Brigadier General R.E.H. Dyer.

Sir Michael O' Dwyer.

S. Udham Singh, who killed Sir Michael O'Dwyer more than twenty years after the incident.

House with all concerned officials, and they were apprised of the situation.[51]

This is where the two accounts of the incidents at Lahore—of the INC Sub-Committee and the Hunter Committee Report—begin to diverge, even more.

Since the Hunter Committee was confined mainly to the official narrative and its witnesses were also from among those who worked for the administration, the evidence that was recorded carried a definite bias. What the victims experienced was vastly different from what the Government of India had recorded and indeed presented before the British Parliament. The evidence was recorded often in camera (as was the O'Dwyer statement), in a very formal environment. Witnesses stuck to the official lines.

But the Congress Sub-Committee recorded its evidences in very different circumstances. None of the witnesses who appeared before it appeared before the Hunter Committee. But the Congress at least used the Hunter Committee Report to verify their facts. It is unlikely that the opposite was true. The principal places where martial law was declared were all visited by the Congress Sub-Committee. The members led by Gandhi stated: 'In most places, large public meetings were held and (the) public were invited to make their statements to us. The nature of the evidence already recorded was placed before the meetings, and those who wished to challenge the accuracy of the statements made, were invited to send their statements even under the pledge of confidence if they so desired. No contradiction was received by us.'[52]

About Lahore, the INC report maintains that people formed a peaceful procession but were stopped at Foreman's Christian College as they were going up the Mall. 300 or 400

---

51. Hunter Committee Report, p. 55.

52. INC Report, p. 2.

of the protestors broke away and wanted to go to Government House and request Gandhi's release. They were halted again at O'Dwyer Soldier's Club. It was a repeat of the incidents that took place in Amritsar on 10 April afternoon. In the firing, 'two or three' were killed, and many more wounded.[53] While the crowd was pushed back till it reached Anarkali Bazaar, near Lohari Gate, it was the police who carried away the dead and wounded. Some effort was made by Pandit Rambhaj Dutt Chowdhari, who lived just outside the city, to calm the crowd, but to no avail, as there was too much noise and he could not be heard. The Deputy Commissioner Fyson gave him just two more minutes and started to fire. Three men were killed in the firing. Many more were wounded.[54]

The Hunter Committee Report, however, does not give such a peaceful image of the crowd, and mentions a lower casualty rate. According to it, the crowd was shouting 'Mahatma Gandhi ki jai' and some people were carrying black flags. The police were driven back, despite the joint presence of Fyson, Cocks, Deputy Inspector General (CID), and Clarke, Deputy Superintendent of Police. According to the report, 'the mob was getting completely out of hand, and, as he had no means of stopping their progress, Mr Fyson ordered the police to fire'. Somewhere between a dozen and twenty shots were fired with the result that one man was killed and around seven wounded.

Cocks, the DIG, also felt that 'serious consequences might result', and it was essential to shoot. He said there was imminent danger of the police being overpowered. The HC report goes on to say that though a party of cavalry arrived, the mayhem continued. The crowd refused to disperse and, finally, around Anarkali Bazaar, the gathering swelled to approximately 20,000. Broadway, the Superintendent of Police, and his men

---

53. INC Report, p. 76.
54. INC Report, pp. 76–7.

had bricks and mud thrown at them for 45 minutes and he was hit five or six times. In retaliation, 'two or three rounds' of buckshot were once again fired into the crowd. When it still did not disperse—despite the entreaties of Pandit Rambhaj Dutt Chowdhari—another half a dozen rounds of buckshot were fired. This time, around eighteen men were wounded, of whom three died.

By now, even according to the Hunter Committee witnesses, four Indians had been shot dead, and around 25 injured.

The HC Report is noticeably more precise as it received inputs from the officers but the INC Report continuously gives the overall impression that the crowd was peaceful and unarmed. This reflects the vastly different mood on the two sides. The crowd, as requested by Gandhi, was only prepared for a non-violent protest. However, the administration, as in Amritsar, was alarmed by the sheer numbers. Secondly, the administration would have been unsettled because this was the first time they were seeing an organised crowd comprised of people from all communities. To them this looked even more dangerous. O'Dwyer himself had constantly raised the specter of a brewing 'revolution'—akin to that of 1857—and so his men would have been on alert, and lastly, the report of the murder of Europeans in Amritsar (regardless of who instigated the disorders) would have put them on edge.

From all accounts, the misreading of the crowd, the reluctance of the British to enter into a dialogue with the satyagrahis and the alacrity with which force was used led to another tragic encounter.

The official account contains no information about those who were wounded—their names or their professions. Even if Indians (who were also British subjects at the time) died brutally due to gunshot wounds, that fact is not described in the official version with the same level of detail and gore as accounts in which Europeans were burnt or beaten to death by sticks. Anyway, if the crowd wanted to be avenged for the murders, they had no guns or ammunition.

In Amritsar, they had to resort to throwing sticks and stones, and burning buildings and sadly, people as well. In Lahore, they threw some bricks and mud. No European was killed in Lahore. Though many Indians were shot, the precise numbers are not found anywhere in the official records.

People in Lahore were upset because the dead and wounded were retained by the authorities and not handed over to their relatives, according to the INC Report. All that the HC Report points out is that the city was 'dangerously disturbed' for days.

In many ways, the situation was similar to that in Amritsar. It was felt by the administration that no European could enter the city. Even police posts inside the city were abandoned as it was felt that the presence of European officers could lead to more loss of life. This is despite the fact that the British continued to be safe in Lahore. They were not attacked —but as in Amritsar there was fear that Hindus and Muslims combined could present a formidable force.

Officially it was said that: 'For about two days the city was controlled by the mob. The Superintendent of Police and Deputy Commissioner took up their quarters in the Telegraph Office.'[55] Plainly, this fear was exaggerated. While people may have been gathering in the city, and were obviously troubled and restless, they had not resorted to violence as yet.

The variance between the official and Indian version of events continues into the accounts of the following day. The INC Report for the next day, 11 April, says that the impasse continued; while the HC Report reads many more meanings in the occurrences. The INC Report is quite matter of fact in stating that Badshahi Mosque had seen another large meeting where feelings 'ran high', and yet the closeness between Hindus

---

55. Hunter Committee Report, p. 58.

and Muslims persisted. This was an important and unusual turn of events: Hindus were present inside the mosque along with Sikhs and Muslims and yet there was no acrimony.

Perhaps it was to break this visible bond that the police fired upon the crowds coming out of the mosque and returning home, leading to more casualties. Undeterred, the communities drew even closer together in order to help each other. As the hartal was still ongoing, there was a need to provide food kitchens and so langarkhanas were opened for the needy. But they lasted only till 15 April, at which point they were ordered to be shut down.

The HC Report provides more detail, giving a different texture to the events:

> On the morning of the 11th April, all the shops were closed, and a huge crowd of Hindus and Mohammedans (said to be around 25,000) collected in the Badshahi Mosque. This crowd was addressed by Rambhaj and others. Inside the gate of the mosque a banner was hung bearing the inscription 'The king who practices tyranny cuts his own roots underneath.' Inflammatory speeches were delivered in the course of which allegations were made that the police had fired on the crowd the preceding day after they had retreated and that this action was a tyrannical action. People who wanted to know whether the hartal should be continued or not were told that a committee would decide and that later on this committee was nominated. Towards the end of the meeting, an ex sepoy shouted to the people a false story that the Indian regiments had mutinied in Lahore Cantonment and were marching on Amritsar and Lahore. He added that about 200 or 250 British soldiers had been killed and that he himself had killed six. His announcement was received with great enthusiasm by the people who garlanded him and carried him in triumph to the pulpit of the mosque. A subscription was opened and at least one large sum promised to establish *langar khana* during the *hartal*, i.e., free food shops. At the

conclusion of the meeting, the mob headed by hooligans carrying sticks marched through the city shouting. On the way they destroyed pictures of the King-Emperor and the Queen-Empress shouting that King George is dead. The band of hooligans referred to was known as the *Danda Fauj*.[56]

Far more worrying for the authorities was the continuing closeness between Hindus and Mohammedans: '...the meeting itself was a very extraordinary one to be held in a mosque. From a Mohammedan point of view, it was a violation of every religious instinct. It represents the highest pitch of the Hindu Mohammedan unity which at this time was spreading rapidly by dint of hatred of the Government.'[57] It was an extraordinary admission: the recognition that government antipathy was uniting Hindus and Muslims. There was growing resentment over the fact that Gandhi and other leaders had been peremptorily arrested. Yet the meetings, apart from using abusive language and anti-British propaganda, had been peaceful.

As in Amritsar, this unity became a cause for great concern to the British. There was no empathy or attempt to understand the cause for the unrest and no sympathy was shown for those murdered or wounded by the police, nor for their families. These were all nameless 'hooligans' and possibly deserved no better. This instance of blatant racism would have irked Indians immensely, especially those who already had a grouse against O'Dwyer's regime.

On 12 April, another meeting was held at Badshahi Mosque. This time, the CID Inspector was beaten with 'sticks'. Obviously, the protestors were irked by the constant monitoring of their movements. On the morning of 12 April itself, the army began to move in for the first time, under Lieutenant Colonel Frank Johnson (who, as the unfortunate residents

---

56. Hunter Committee Report, pp. 58–9.
57. Hunter Committee Report, p. 59.

of Lahore were to find out shortly, was a 'trained expert' in the administering of martial law, having spent many years in Bechuanaland—now known as the Republic of Botswana). He arrived with a mixed column of 800 police and army personnel. Two aeroplanes flew overhead to ensure there was no attack on the troops with 'bombs' and that they were not 'fired' upon.

As in Amritsar, there was fear that the 'mob' would attack. Nobody stopped to ask where the unarmed crowd was likely to get guns or bombs or even aircraft from. However, these were the grim conditions under which Johnson came to rescue the city.

The city remained peaceful, though the crowds were said to be 'bad tempered'. This was not surprising as, by now, news of the attack by the police and army on the defenceless crowds in Amritsar must have spread. Soldiers travelling between Amritsar and Lahore would have brought the news. These cities did not have large populations. Had just one official phone call been overheard, word would have spread. The hartal meant that all establishments owned by Indians were closed, and so people were free and wandering about.

There were particularly large crowds 'moving to and fro' between the Badshahi Mosque and Hira Mandi—which were practically next to each other. The sight of people moving back and forth restlessly made the administration even more nervous. The cavalry was brought in as the DC, Fyson, tried to disperse the crowds. Once again, the crowd retaliated by throwing stones, and was fired upon. One man died and 28 people were wounded in the encounter. It appears that only eight rounds were fired. It must have been a very dense crowd for such a high casualty rate of 29. The police who fired into the crowd had used buckshot (which had a wider impact) and also some rounds of ball cartridge.[58] The HC Report later approved of the firing.

---

58. Hunter Committee Report, p. 60.

Posters and other reports in the papers apparently further incited the 'mobs'. One poster said: 'We are the Indian nation whose bravery and honour have been acknowledged by all the kings of the world. The English are the worst of the lot and are like monkeys whose deceit and cunning are obvious to all, high and low. Have these monkeys forgotten their original conditions? Now these faithless people have forgotten the loyalty of Indians, are bent upon exercising limitless tyranny. O brethren, gird up your loins and fight. Kill and be killed. Do not lose courage and try your utmost to turn those mean monkeys from your holy city.'[59]

This was obviously meant for the soldiers who had fought alongside the allies in the World War, and who came back home only to face bullets from those on whose behalf they had fought. 'Monkey' was a term often used for the British in Punjab, and even though it was a fairly mild term of abuse, it was one that the British could not tolerate.

The posters also called for unity, defying all attempts to divide the communities.

'Oh Hindu, Muhammadan and Sikh brethren raise the cry of Allah Akbar and kill the Kaffirs. Get ready for the war and God will grant victory to India very soon. Fight with enthusiasm and enlist yourselves in the Danda army.' The last was again a reference to the danda fauj—the people's army which used sticks as weapons to fight a 'duplicitous' colonial power.

However, all such attempts by the people to demonstrate their rights would soon come to naught. Following pre-censorship on 10 April, the district of Lahore was brought under the Seditious Meetings Act on 13 April. All assemblies of more than ten persons were banned, as were liquor shops.[60]

---

59. Hunter Committee Report, pp. 60–1.
60. Hunter Committee Report, pp. 60–1.

It was thought that the idle crowds would be fuelled by liquor to confront the British.

On 14 April, some of the leaders in Lahore, who had participated in the anti-Rowlatt Act movement peacefully, were now arrested and deported. 'Lala Harkishan Lal, one of the magnates of the Punjab, Lala Duni Chand, one of the most popular Municipal Commissioners of Lahore, with a record of unbroken public service, and Pundit Rambhaj Dutt Chowdhari, who had tried to help on the 10th of April, by calming the crowds were arrested and deported.'[61]

Despite all the provocations and trials before them, and despite the fact that nothing was known of their struggles outside Lahore, the residents carried on with the hartal—from 11 to 18 April. This meant enormous hardship, as everything in the city was shut.

Even though, according to the official tally, at least 5 residents had been killed and more than 50 wounded, the people of Lahore remained calm. In fact, some of them even tried to reason with the authorities and sent a proposal to Chief Secretary, Thompson, asking that:

1. The military be removed from the city
2. Arrested people should be released on bail and
3. The bodies of the men killed in the firing by the police should be released.

The government did not entertain the bargain offered and the bodies of two men killed on 10 April were 'not returned but the burial was carried out by the authorities in the jail though relatives were allowed to attend. One man (who had died) was not identified. The reason was that any other course was thought likely to lead to a demonstration and probably would have given a new occasion for hartal.'[62] One can only wonder

---

61. INC Report, p. 79.
62. Hunter Committee Report, p. 62.

who these men were, whose funerals had to be carried out in such secrecy.

This essentially was the problem now agitating the crowds: the refusal to recognise the martyrs and the obvious lack of respect for those who had lost a family member, as the corpses were not handed over.

The hartal was finally lifted, with 'direct action of the military under the operation of Martial Law',[63] which was proclaimed on 15 April.

But more importantly, was there any necessity to impose martial law in Lahore, at all?

Not if one looks at the social diary of O'Dwyer, because it was a pretty busy social week for him. On 10 April (as Amritsar was burning, and Lahore was 'disturbed'), O'Dwyer had a garden party in the Lawrence Gardens, attended by 'people from the town'. On 12 April he was called for dinner by Sir Zulfikar Ali Khan, and on 14 April a big Durbar was held by him, attended by people from the district. There were meetings being held by the officials throughout and the law courts functioned normally. Yet, the town was militarised, and on 15 April, the military strength 'was 406 British troops, 250 Indian Defence Force, (European Section), 381 Indian Troops, 460 armed police, 800 unarmed police and 3 armoured cars. By the 20th, more British troops came, making an aggregate of 1000.'[64]

Even the most enthusiastic advocates of martial law had to eventually concede that there was no compelling reason for it to be imposed in Lahore.[65]

When Kitchin, Commissioner of Lahore, who as such was in charge of the Districts of Amritsar, Lahore and Gujranwala

---

63. Hunter Committee Report, p. 62.
64. Hunter Committee Report, p. 168.
65. Parliamentary Report, p. 102.

was cross-examined by the Hunter Committee he felt that there were only a few reasons to impose Martial Law:

> Q: If there were no other considerations the civil authority could soon after the 11th that is, on the 12th, 13th and 14th as the case may be, have taken back control and carried on with such aid as might have been necessary from the military?
>
> A: Yes, in individual places.
>
> Q: According to your statement in almost all places?
>
> A: Yes.
>
> Q: But your view is that martial law was wanted not for the purpose of getting control but for the purpose of what you describe as preventing the spread of infection?
>
> A: Yes.
>
> Q: And that is your only justification for martial law being declared.
>
> A: That was the immediate reason.
>
> Q: And I also take it the second important reason from your point of view was to provide for the speedy disposal of the cases of persons who had already been arrested between the 10th and 13th?
>
> A: That is the reason which weighed with me. I have no reason to suppose it weighed with anyone else.
>
> Q: In your view those were the two main reasons for the declaration of martial law, preventing the spread of infection, and finding some speedy method of disposing of the cases of persons already arrested?
>
> A: Yes.

Yet, as the HC pointed out, most of these emergency measures already existed with the civil authorities under the Defence of India Act, and the Seditious Meetings Act.

But for those who were so inclined, martial law provided

an immense opportunity to humiliate and harrass. No one was better qualified to do this (with the exception perhaps of Dyer) than Johnson. Many regulations were imposed in Lahore, some that he had thought up himself, and some that were suggested by Civil Service officers.

Johnson administered martial law 'intensively' and conditions were equally depressing in Lahore and Amritsar. Anyone breaking a rule, such as the curfew order of being out after 8 p.m., was likely to be 'shot, flogged, fined or imprisoned to otherwise punished'.[66]

To begin with, Johnson wanted four Lahore representatives (Europeans were exempt) to be present every day at the water works of every ward from 8 a.m. to 5 p.m. to disseminate his orders to the people. As it was their responsibility to ensure that orders were widely known, this was the only work they could do. He also imposed a special curfew order, by which Indians (once again, Europeans or those in possession of special military permits were exempt) could not leave their homes or be on the streets between 8 p.m. and 5 a.m. (The timings were amended to between 12 a.m. and 2 a.m., six weeks later.)

Among the first things he did was to break the hartal and force the shops to open, but he also went ahead and fixed the prices. The price of non-compliance was to be shot or have the shops forcibly opened and *their contents distributed free to the public*.[67]

Even worse was his restriction on mobility and transport. He took away all motor cars and other vehicles from Indians, and gave them to Europeans to teach the so-called rebels a lesson they would not forget.

In his written statement submitted to the Hunter Committee, he said: 'Under Order III all motor cars had to

---

66. Benjamin Guy Horniman, *Amritsar and Our Duty To India* (London: T. Fisher Unwin Ltd., 1920), p. 133.

67. Horniman, *Amritsar and Our Duty*, p. 133.

be surrendered for military service, but in cases where I was satisfied that cars were essential to the business or profession of a European, their cars were at once released and an exemption certificate issued. I refrained from granting exemptions in the case of Indian residents in Lahore as I thought it desirable to bring home to them all—loyal or disloyal alike—some of the inconveniences of martial law in the hope and belief that in future the weight of their influence will be wholeheartedly thrown against seditious movements likely to lead to the introduction of martial law.'[68]

> Q: What were the reasons for commandeering tongas and vehicles which were plying for hire? Was it not that they also took place in (the) hartal?
>
> A: That was the main reason. They were taking part in (the) hartal. No one could move in Lahore if he wanted to; they refused to carry him.[69]

Not only did he take away motor cars and tongas, he even ordered that the ordinary bicycles belonging to Indians be delivered up to military authorities; they were then handed over to officials for their own use. Electric fans and other electric fittings belonging to Indians were commandeered and stripped from the houses for the use of British soldiers.[70] Even public conveyances were not allowed into the city and were parked outside. This was April, and it was very hot: to deprive people of all means of transport, and even fans, indicated that he wanted to inconvenience and punish all income groups among Indians, from the poor to the rich. As in Amritsar, it was this latter section, and the upper-middle-class professionals—lawyers, doctors, businessmen, traders—who had been organising the

---

68. Hunter Committee Report, p. 198.
69. Hunter Committee Report, p. 198.
70. Horniman, *Amritsar and Our Duty*, p. 134.

hartals. Students had also been helping in the satyagraha and they were to be specially humiliated by his orders.

The reason for choosing petty discriminations was that if anyone broke a rule (which was fairly easy to do), they could be arrested and punished. It made people fearful and worried even when stepping out of the house, in case they made a mistake. None of the rules applied to Europeans. In Hitler's Germany, Jews had to wear a star to distinguish them from the rest—here the colour of the skin was enough.

Johnson made it 'unlawful' for two Indians to walk abreast and all meetings and gathering of more than ten persons were banned. He also specifically chose the homes on which he wanted his martial law orders pasted.

While appearing before the Hunter Committee, he was asked:

> Q: You left the selection of these houses to the Criminal Investigative Department?
>
> A: They submitted a list. I requested them to submit a list of people who were not notoriously loyal. I selected the houses from the geographical position from the map.[71]

Through Order VIII issued on 16 April, Johnson notified: 'All orders to be issued under martial law will be handed to such owners of property as I may select and it will be the duty of such owners of property to exhibit and keep exhibiting all such orders. The duty of protecting such orders will, therefore, devolve on the owners of property and failure to ensure the proper protection and continued exhibition of my orders will result in severe punishment.'

The owners of the property ran the risk that if someone else tore down the order or defaced it, they—the owners of the property—were likely to be arrested and severely punished.

---

71. Hunter Committee Report, p. 199.

Johnson, when asked about the order, said he thought it was reasonable and that he would do it again: 'It was one of the few brainwaves I had.'[72]

This 'brainwave' created a nightmare for Sanatan Dharam College where a poster was torn off, leading to the arrest of all 'male persons' in the compound.

The Hunter Committee Report documented that more than 65 students and all the professors were taken to the Fort three miles away and interned for 30 hours. Of course, they were threatened with dire consequences were the posters torn again.

In his cross-examination, Johnson was asked again if he thought this had been a reasonable order to make.

Quite unfazed, he replied he had to make an example of someone in order to stop the posters from being torn down.

> Q: And your frame of mind then was, as you indicate in your report on page 11, that you were waiting for an opportunity to bring home to all concerned the power of martial law?
>
> A: That was so, Sir.
>
> Q: You were longing for an opportunity?
>
> A: Only in the interest of the people themselves.

And then, in another case, he was asked:

> Q: And you marched these 500 students and their professors in the sun three miles?
>
> A: That is so.
>
> Q: And you still maintain that was a proper exercise of your authority as martial law administrator?
>
> A: Absolutely. I would do it again tomorrow in similar circumstances.[73]

---

72. Hunter Committee Report, p. 199.
73. Hunter Committee Report, p. 200.

He had a definite madness to his method.

For instance, he ordered that students from three colleges—the DAV College, the Dyal Singh College and the Medical College—should attend roll call four times a day, which meant they had to walk 16 miles in the hot sun. He said that this was meant to keep them out of mischief. Over 1,000 students were punished thus and many were expelled and rusticated, while others had their scholarships and stipends stopped.

All such punishments were indiscriminate and not related to any particular misdeed. For instance, he decided that a certain percentage of students should be punished from each college. The principals of each college were obliged to send him the numbers he demanded. 'When the Principals of the various colleges sent up the list of punishments, in cases in which he thought the punishments were either not adequate or did not come up to proper percentages, he remitted the list to the Principals to bring up the lists to the proper percentages.'[74]

Given below is an extract from letter No 111-4, dated 10 May 1919, from the Staff Officer, Lahore (Civil) Command, Punjab Club, Lahore to the address of the Principal, DAV College, Lahore:

> In order to assist you in framing a scale of punishments, I am directed to inform you that in the case of the Government College, 6 students are being expelled and debarred from ever entering any other college in the University, 6 are not to be allowed to proceed to any further examination, 6 are to be rusticated for a year, 15 forfeit their scholarships, besides minor punishments in 112 other cases.
>
> In the Dayal Singh College, 7 students are to be expelled, 5 are to be rusticated for a year, 14 will be put back one year, 14 are suspended for three months, 2 are temporarily deprived of their scholarships, and 224 are to suffer minor punishments, while 245 are required to furnish substantial securities for their future behaviours.

---

74. Hunter Committee Report, p. 201.

The Officer Commanding thinks that it may help you to submit proposals which will save him the necessity of closing your college... I add that he expects disciplinary action to be in no degree less than those to which I have drawn your attention.

Signed W. Barns Major
Staff Officer
Lahore Civil Command[75]

While some of the students might have been out on the streets of Lahore on 10 or 14 April, the desire to punish a 'percentage' of them, many of whom may have been entirely uninvolved, is inexplicable. Undoubtedly, these bizarre punishments would have ruined hundreds of young lives. These students, because of the composition of the population of Lahore, would have included Hindus, Muslims and Sikhs.

Q: Because you got reports of the character you mention with regard to 20, 30, or even 50 (students), you thought that was enough to justify in making orders of this character affecting thousands?

A: I thought I was justified in making the orders at the time; I still think, and I shall always think so.

When two students who were to be punished with rustication asked that they withdraw their names from the current year, Johnson replied adamantly that they should be reinstated in the list or two other names included.[76]

Other orders also made no effort to distinguish between those who were guilty or innocent.

In Order No. 1 issued by him, it was suggested that: 'If any firearm is discharged or bomb thrown at the military or the police, the most drastic reprisals will instantly be made

---

75. INC Report, p. 90.
76. Hunter Committee Report, p. 202.

against the properties surrounding the outrage.' He proceeded to call a hundred leading persons from the city to tell them that if any 'bomb fell or that if any British soldier or anybody was wounded or injured as a result of that bomb, that spot would be deemed the centre of a circle having a diameter of a hundred yards and that he would give them one hour in which to remove everything living from that circle and at the end of that time the demolition of every building other than mosques or temples would take place inside that circle'.

He also declared that the 'continuation of electric lights and water will depend on the good behaviour of the inhabitants and their obedience to our orders'. This was an open threat and was meant to make life as insecure as possible for the residents of Lahore.

It was almost as though Dyer and Johnson were competing with each other. If one was to be eventually known as the Butcher of Amritsar, the other was already known as the Physician from Bechuanaland, which was the appellation given to him by *The Independent* in an ironical allusion 'to the panegyrics of *The Pioneer*, which hailed him as the "physician" with expert experience of Martial Law in Bechuanaland'. Johnson, on his part, said 'he had been longing to show the people of the Punjab the might of Martial Law.'[77] Overseeing all of this was the triumvirate of O'Dwyer, Kitchin and Thompson. They were quite content to let the army do as it pleased, while giving suggestions.

Among the many racially motivated and distasteful punishments were the public floggings. Johnson 'declared that these were not public but quasi-public floggings, whatever that may mean. They were only inflicted on people of low social status. He was not a doctor, and could not say whether whipping might affect the health of the victim. But he thought it was an

---

77. Horniman, *Amritsar and Our Duty*, p. 155.

essential punishment. People liked going to gaol, and flogging was a better deterrent.' A particularly horrible instance of this was the whipping of an entire wedding party, including the priest, for breaking curfew hours. Johnson called it a 'regrettable incident'.[78]

It appears that Johnson's reign of terror spread to the villages surrounding Lahore as well. One example demonstrates how perfunctory the entire business was. While no European was ever touched, all Indians—whether in the city or the village—were fair game.

On 20 April, 'another flying column went to Muridke and Kamske, between which the telegraph wire had been cut; this column was accompanied by a civil officer, and the latter, acting as a Summary Court, sentenced the headman of Kamske to a fine of Rs 200 and a whipping for obstructive behavior.' The headman was tied to a tree and publicly flogged. As Jacob, the Civil Officer who performed the whipping described it, there was no judicial procedure followed.[79]

Johnson, who was permitted to inflict his sadistic fantasies on the residents of Lahore for six weeks, considered himself a 'benevolent autocrat' and was convinced that his methods had a reformatory effect on his victims. He also maintained that people could not 'wage war' without suffering hardships. The truth was that nobody was interested in waging war; they had only been trying to organise protest meetings.[80]

The gatherings at the Badshahi Mosque were halted by Fyson, the Deputy Commissioner; the order was confirmed by Johnson. The Badshahi Mosque was closed and permitted to be opened only on an undertaking by the trustees that 'No Hindus would be allowed to enter the Mosque.' This was a huge blow

---

78. Horniman, *Amritsar and Our Duty*, p. 138.

79. An official report, quoted in Horniman, *Amritsar and Our Duty*, p. 188–9.

80. INC Report, p. 81.

to the unity that was being forged among Hindus, Muslims and Sikhs, with the mosque becoming a meeting place. The effort now was to take everyone back to the 'divide and rule' system, which had worked so well for the British.

The ever-energetic Johnson was also trying cases in the summary courts. He tried 227 cases in less than 45 days; most of those tried (201), unsurprisingly, received convictions. Punishments included imprisonment, fines and floggings. Around 66 people were whipped in Lahore: the maximum number of stripes they were given were thirty and the least were five. Johnson felt 'this was the kindest method of punishment'. His answer to the Hunter Committee when Justice Rankin asked him if this was the most efficacious method of dealing with minor breaches, was: 'I hardly agree with you. You have a very great population. You are creating new offences by the issue of these orders. If the jail is the only punishment, it would not effect this population here very much. The jails are an extraordinarily comfortable place from the general standard of household in the city. They are well fed in the Central Jail and one would soon have got used to the conditions. We were going to have the whole lot of them. I feared the jail would be too filled.' He also said that the value of a whipping was equal to the use of 1,000 soldiers.[81]

The press and the legal profession were specially chosen for punitive measures. One among them was Manohar Lal, who was a trustee of *The Tribune* newspaper as well as a well-known lawyer. It did not help that he had been a foundation scholar of St John's College, Cambridge, from where he had completed his BA. He had received his MA from Punjab and was now a well-established lawyer as well as the President of the High Court Bar Association. On 18 April, he was arrested at around 7.30 a.m., without a warrant, and till he was released on 16

---

81. INC Report, p. 82.

May, he had no idea what he had been charged with. In his absence, his home was searched on 19 April. His wife, who was an invalid, and his children had to take shelter in the servants' quarters. He was kept in unsanitary conditions, with very few facilities—just 'stinking earthen vessels cleaned twice daily', for almost five days. Then he was shifted into the European ward, which was much more comfortable. But the reason for his arrest remained a mystery, for he was neither involved in the organisation of the hartal, nor was he politically inclined. Yet he was kept in jail for almost 20 days.[82]

Other members of the press, such as Kalinath Roy, the editor of *The Tribune*, along with the editor of *The Pratap* were arrested and tried. During the period when martial law was in place, *The Tribune*, *The Punjabee* and *The Pratap* were not published. Pre-censorship of the newspapers had already been in place since 10 April.

Apart from Amritsar and Lahore, bizarre martial law orders were passed in Gujranwala and Kasur as well, following an uprising of the people. The reasons for the unrest were similar, except that contrary to Dyer's claim that the Jallianwala Bagh massacre would subdue Punjab, these two areas experienced disturbances even after 13 April.

Gujranwala lies just 36 miles from Lahore, and at the time had a population of 30,000. There was a local meeting on 5 April at which the action of the authorities in Delhi, of firing at the anti-Rowlatt Act protestors, was condemned. It was proposed that 6 April should be a national protest day. It passed off without any problems. This was despite the fact that there was a complete hartal. Colonel O'Brien, the Deputy Commissioner, had already issued a warning that if there was violence, he would take action against the protestors.

Everything remained peaceful, but as news of the

---

82. INC Report, p. 83.

disturbances of 10 April trickled in from Amritsar and Lahore, the organisers felt that perhaps another protest meet should be held to communicate their dismay. The chosen date was 14 April. In the meantime, O'Brien left Gujranwala on 12 April, and Khan Bahadur Mirza Sultan Ahmed became the acting Deputy Commissioner. Anticipating some backlash after the troubles in Amritsar and Lahore, all European and American missionaries left Gujranwala on the advice of O'Brien and the Superintendent of Police, Heron.

As already noted, there was a close-knit understanding between the Indian communities in their common cause against the British. This was visible at Gujranwala as well, but it became clear that someone was trying to deliberately foment trouble between them. In Amritsar and Lahore, steps were already being taken to ensure that Hindus and Muslims did not put up a united front. The same methods that would be used during the Partition of India to incite communal violence were used here, possibly for the first time.

Oddly enough, at 7 a.m., the body of a dead calf was found hanging on the Katchi Bridge near the railway station. It was removed by the Deputy Superintendent of Police but no trouble ensued as it was suspected that the calf had been hung there by the police themselves to engender suspicion among the Hindus and Muslims.[83] According to the INC Report, pork was found to have been thrown 'by someone in a mosque'.[84] Wisely, the crowd that had gathered to protest against the British did not react or harm each other.

Also, according to the INC Report, the complete hartal continued. Unfortunately, with nothing to do, the crowd was fuelled with drink and resentment and became increasingly unruly. A train to Wazirabad had arrived with holidaymakers.

---

83. Hunter Committee Report, p. 69.
84. INC Report, p. 105.

The Fancy Punishments 163

Following an attempt to stop the train, the crowd set fire to the Arya Samaj Gurukul Bridge.[85] After that, local leaders such as the Governor of the Gurukul, Lala Rallya Ram, barrister Labh Singh, and pleader Din Mohammed arrived and together with some policemen and a few others, they helped put out the fire. The crowd then moved to the other side of the station, to Katchi Bridge. Meanwhile, the leaders called a meeting to get the crowd to calm down. However, before their words could have any effect, Heron, the SP, fired on the crowd at the bridge, leading to casualties. As before, since these were Indians, the HC Report barely mentioned them and there are no precise numbers.

Immediately upon seeing the wounded, the crowd became uncontrollable and destroyed the church, the post office, the tahsil office and the Court House, and attacked the railway station. Here, too, the Hunter Committee account and the INC account vary. The former has little local colour and, as before, the latter is unclear about the names of the British officials who were there, and the exact timeline.

Meanwhile, the Gurukul Bridge fire had been doused by Nevill, the Assistant Superintendent of Police, with a guard of seven men. The telegraph wires had also been cut and the SP could only send a message to Lahore by telephone. By midday, most of the telephone and telegraph wires were cut for around three miles. The damage to Katchi Bridge was also quite serious and the area was rendered unsafe for trains.

The Deputy Superintendent of Police was able to rescue a guard who had been surrounded by a crowd of protestors. Events moved fast after that, as another crowd had gathered behind the railway fencing on the Grand Trunk Road, on the Lahore side. Now 'armed' with whatever they could lay their hands on—crowbars, hammers, lathis, and railway implements—they

---

85. INC Report, p. 105.

wanted to break up the railway line, as one of the objectives of the hartal was that nothing should be in operation, not even trains. (Interestingly, till today, the destruction of public property remains a popular form of protest in India.)

The confrontation steadily grew more serious. When Heron tried to prevent them from breaking up the railway lines, someone in the crowd made a move to attack him, and stone throwing followed. Heron fired and ordered his men to do so as well. As a result, 'upto three men were wounded, one seriously.'[86]

According to the INC Report, local leaders tried to pacify the crowds and lead them back to the city. However, 'the temper of the crowd seems to have got worse than before'.[87] Heron was now the chief target; one person accused him of having shot his brother, and threatened to kill him.

At this crucial moment, the burning post office, which was close to the station, distracted everyone. The fire engine was not allowed in by the protestors who kept waving black flags and throwing bricks 'mostly at Mr Heron (and) upon the police'.[88] Heron and the DSP were keen to shoot at them, but the acting Deputy Commissioner, Khan Bahadur Mirza Sultan Ahmed, restrained them. He was concerned about the young boys in the crowd, and hoped that the leaders would be able to achieve some calm. This pacific approach was later said to be a mistake by the Hunter Committee. It is debatable whether firing would have dispersed the crowd or made it angrier as they set the tahsil (the revenue office), the church, the dak bungalow and the district courts ablaze. The police then mostly fired from a distance, as they were not equipped for riots at this scale. This carried on as the crowds kept regrouping and coming back. The firing on them also continued. The railway station buildings and

---

86. Hunter Committee Report, p. 70.

87. Hunter Committee Report, p. 71.

88. Hunter Committee Report, p. 71.

goods shed were set on fire and looted. The Casson Industrial School was set on fire.

Though there is no mention of the massacre in Amritsar on 13 April (the previous day) as a reason for the anger of the crowd, it is likely that they were aware of what had happened. Given that trains had come in and stopped at the station, the news would have spread by the afternoon. The crowd entered Civil Lines, and the District Engineer and his family took shelter in the Treasury, where they were protected by a small guard under a Havildar.

Things changed rapidly at around 3.10 p.m. Three aeroplanes flew in from Lahore and over Gujranwala. This was probably done on the instructions of O'Dwyer, for whom an opportunity had appeared at last for actual bombing, which had eluded him in both Amritsar and Lahore.

The first to enter air space was then Captain (he was later promoted to Major) D.H.M. Carberry, MC, DFC, Flight Commander, No. 31 Squadron. 'He had received his orders from Lieutenant Colonel FF Minchen, DSO, MC, Wing Commander, who had himself received them verbally from the General Staff of the 16th Division. They were to the following effect:

- that the native city was not to be bombed unless necessary;
- that crowds were to be bombed if in the open;
- that gatherings near the local villages were to be dispersed if coming or going from Gujranwala.'[89]

As O'Dwyer was to state later in his testimony:

We knew a very dangerous situation had arisen in Gujranwala; there were no troops there and very few police. The Deputy Commissioner had just been transferred and an Indian officer of very little executive experience was in charge of the district...

---

89. Hunter Committee Report, pp. 72–3.

O'Dwyer had asked O'Brien to motor back and had also sent the Deputy Inspector General of Police, but he doubted that either of them could reach in time or even reach at all. So he suggested to General Beynon, General Commanding Officer, 16th Division, that aeroplanes be sent out. O'Dwyer said in his evidence: 'We know that these aeroplanes could fly at a very low level and it was agreed that they should use their Lewis guns in the same conditions as troops would use their rifles.' He said that he could not obviously give any instructions to the pilots and all instructions were given by the General.

There had been a discussion at Government House a few days earlier whether aircraft could be sent and it was decided that crowded areas should be avoided, but the request to send aeroplanes to Gujranwala was made by O'Dwyer. The following entry appears in the Government House War Diary:

> General Staff Officer, 16th Division, asked to send aeroplanes and drop bombs if necessary and a good target presents itself. The opportunity for an aeroplane seems good.

The General Staff Diary has similar notations:

> His Honour considers this to be a good opportunity for aeroplanes to use bombs as there is little opportunity for hurting friends.[90]

The Hunter Committee notes that the orders given to the Wing Commander by the General Staff were 'to send machines out with bombs and machine guns to disperse the rioters at Gujranwala with the object of saving the lives of any of the white population who were in danger'. This was despite the fact that not a single European had been harmed in Gujranwala.

There is no discussion anywhere of the thousands of peaceful Indian men, women and children who had probably stayed indoors during the disturbances on 14 April or were

---

90. Hunter Committee Report, p. 225.

continuing with their daily lives. As indiscriminate bombing and shooting began, it would soon become obvious that many innocent people would be wounded or killed. Yet, O'Brien, who reached Gujranwala around the same time as the aircraft, gave the number of victims, including those killed by bombs and machine guns and those shot by the police, as 11 killed and 27 wounded.

It is very likely that these figures were incorrect, as there were instances in which firing took place from the aircraft, and bombs were dropped as well, but there is no account of the resulting casualties. It is also important to remember that some of the wounds were grievous—people lost limbs and young children and students were also affected. Not just the physical trauma but the mental trauma has also gone unrecorded. Most people in Gujranwala would have never seen an aircraft before, let alone have these machines shoot at them and drop bombs upon them. The fact that the Indians, injured and killed, mostly remain nameless is another travesty of the evidence that was given before the Hunter Committee. These were smaller numbers than the thousands affected in Jallianwala Bagh. Yet here, too, there was no attempt to gather information about them—apart from the arrests which would follow, if ever any unfortunate men, women and children were identified. There is no account of any medical help given to them either. Later, the Congress Sub-Committee gathered evidence, and recorded a few names. However, given the persistent firing and bombing that took place, it is obvious that more casualties would have occurred than we know of.

Major Carberry was flying at 100 to 700 feet within an area of three miles. He saw the railway station burning, as well as the goods shed. He said there was a train on fire as well (there is no account of that in the evidence presented before the Hunter Committee or in the INC Report). He saw large crowds around the station, on the roads, as well as in Civil Lines. He also saw that the church and four homes in Civil Lines were on fire.

According to the evidence provided by Carberry, he first took action outside the town of Gujranwala. As stated in the Hunter Committee Report, he dropped 'three bombs on a party of Indians 150 strong which was making for Gujranwala. This was outside a village around two miles north-west of Gujranwala. (We are informed that the name of this village was Dhulla.) One of the bombs failed to explode; the others fell near the party and scattered it. Three people were seen to drop as a result of this bombing. We are informed by the Punjab government that a woman and boy were killed and two men slightly wounded. The rest ran back to the village, and fifty rounds were fired at them with the machine-gun to ensure that they were effectively dispersed. A few minutes later, Major Carberry took action on a group of about 50 Indians outside a village about a mile south of the first... Major Cranberry tells us that the party was apparently returning from Gujranwala, and that he dropped two bombs, only one of which burst, but this, though it dropped near the party, did not cause any casualties. The party disappeared into the village, 25 rounds from the machine gun being fired after them without any visible effect...'[91]

Interestingly, while he was flying and dropping bombs as well as shooting, Cranberry also had the time to count the number of people in the crowd. And he also knew the direction they were coming from, and because they were coming from Gujranwala, he presumed it was fine to bomb them. Yet, he could not see that there were children and women among them, who were obviously not indulging in any violent activity. Still he bombed them. We are back to the 'moral effect' doctrine: No matter who you kill, you are killing the enemy, and the people of Gujranwala had to be taught a lesson.

---

91. Hunter Committee Report, p. 73.

> The aeroplane was now returning to Gujranwala. Major Carberry observed a party of about 200 Indians in a field near a large red building on the north-west outskirts of the town. This was the Khalsa High School and Boarding House. He dropped a bomb in the courtyard and several people appeared to be wounded. Thirty rounds were fired at the party with the machine-gun and took cover in the house... one man (was) hit by a bullet, one student by a splinter and one small boy stunned.[92]

According to the INC Report, a student of Khalsa College described the scene: 'We heard the noise of aeroplanes about 3 pm... They remained hovering over the boarding house for about 10 minutes... suddenly a noise was heard and a shell came down which struck our confectioner Ganda Singh... A small piece of it injured the finger of my right hand. A boy fell down because of the shock.'[93] As no incendiary activity was going on at the school, was it deliberately targeted because so many young boys were participating in the anti-Rowlatt Act protests? This was possible, because as in Amritsar and Lahore, more and more imaginative punishments would be meted out to the male youth of Gujranwala over the following weeks.

Carberry dropped eight bombs in all. One came down on a large crowd inside the town, and another near the station. Apparently the first bomb killed four and wounded five. And the second killed two and wounded six. 'He also fired 100 to 150 rounds upon parties of Indians coming from the railway station and going to the civil lines. He returned to Lahore around ten minutes to four.'[94] He had spent 45 minutes over Gujranwala.

In the War Diary of the 2nd (Rawalpindi) Division, an entry dated 14 April, 6 p.m., is by another pilot who also flew

---

92. Hunter Committee Report, p. 73.
93. INC Report, p. 107.
94. Parliamentary Report, p. 46.

over Gujranwala: 'Lieutenant Kirby, RAF, confirmed report of bombing of Gujranwala and stated he had fired successfully into rioters. Subsequently had forced landing near Wazirabad. Rioters proposed to burn his aeroplane, but he was able to start his engine and get away.'[95]

The sorry saga of the bombing did not end there. The next day, Lieutenant Bodkins was once again sent to check on the situation, reconnoitre the damage to the railway lines, and also 'take offensive action on any large gathering of people.'[96] While Gujranwala itself was quiet (the terrified residents would have remained indoors following the assaults), Bodkins saw approximately 20 people one mile to the west, whom he scattered by firing his machine gun. More worryingly, he bombed a gathering of about 50 men, in a semi-circle outside a house, being addressed by a man standing at the door. They could have collected there for any purpose at all. But Bodkins dropped a bomb, which hit the adjoining house, and blew up the side of it. Nothing was, or is, known of the damage. For all we know, 50 people could have been either killed or wounded just that day alone.

In the evidence he gave to the Hunter Committee, Carberry said he had been ordered to disperse the crowds 'going or coming'.[97] This was clearly not the case at the Khalsa Boarding House, and yet bombs were dropped there.

However, when questioned further, he said he was bombing and shooting the people in 'their own interest'.

Q: You first bombed and they began to run away into the village?

A: Yes.

Q: That is over the houses in the village?

---

95. Parliamentary Report, p. 46.
96. Hunter Committee Report, p. 79.
97. INC Report, p. 107.

A: Yes. I suppose some of the shots hit the houses.

...

Q: You fired the machine gun into the village; you may be thereby hitting not those people whom you dispersed, but other innocent people into their homes?

A: I could not discriminate between the innocent people and other people. I tried to shoot the people, who ran away and who I thought were coming to do damage.

...

Q: Your object seems to be to hit or kill more people of that crowd, although they had begun to disperse, and were running away after the bombs were thrown?

A: I was trying to do it in their own interest. I also realised that if I tried to kill people, they would not gather again and do damage.

He told the Hunter Committee he had fired 150 rounds, adding for clarity, 'You must understand it was no good firing at the houses. I was firing at the natives into the native city.'

As we know from Amritsar and Lahore, this was only the beginning of the miseries that the people of Gujranwala would have to endure. To begin with, when O'Brien came back to Gujranwala, he said he was given a 'blank cheque'.

During the cross-examination by Setalvad, he said, 'I had a conversation with the Chief Secretary on the telephone on the 15th and said to him, I might probably have to take certain actions and I hope they will be legalised afterwards if done in good faith.'

'But that was before the declaration of Martial Law?' asked Setalvad.

The answer was 'yes'.[98]

This was probably the beginning of the Indemnity Act,

---

98. INC Report, p. 106.

which was subsequently introduced to protect all those who had been officially asked to terrorise the people of Punjab.

Having got his clean chit in advance, O'Brien could now begin to teach the natives a 'moral lesson' they would not forget. On 16 April, the day after the second bombing of Gujranwala, while things remained quiet, martial law was declared, and the arrests began. As in other towns and districts, most people had no idea what their crime was. They were picked up—sometimes not even allowed to get dressed, if roused from sleep.

In Gujranwala, as in Amritsar and Lahore, even those who had tried to help the administration in the riots of 14 April, like the Governor of the Arya Samaj Gurukul, Ram Rallya, found themselves handcuffed on 16 April. Twenty of them were chained and made to march through the streets. They were taken to Lahore in an open truck. No facilities were provided of any kind.[99]

Next, O'Brien wanted to force the shops open and keep them open. So a notice was issued called 'Notice under Martial Law Rule No. 2':

> As we have come to know that some shop-keepers, who live within the Municipal limits of Gujranwala, shut up their shops when the army and the police people go to them to purchase articles, or that they refuse to sell the articles to the army or the police soldiers for a reasonable price. Therefore, the undermentioned orders are issued that after the publication of this Notice, those shopkeepers, who would be found acting as mentioned above, would be arrested, and they would be liable to be punished by flogging.

(Sd) F.W. Berberry
Lieutenant Colonel
Officer Commanding, Dist Gujranwala
18/4/1919[100]

---

99. INC Report, p. 388, statement 282.
100. INC Report, p. 110; Motilal Nehru papers at NMML.

Martial Law Notice No 7 was another harsh and racist measure, in which Indians were forced to salute all Europeans (as mentioned earlier in the chapter). Even British soldiers had to be saluted, and offenders were likely to be flogged.

In other orders, students had daily compulsory attendance to salute the Union Jack. Curfew had been imposed and railway travel was forbidden. According to the INC Report, 'Men of status were made to clean drains in the bazar, although in some cases the municipal sweeper had already cleaned them.'[101]

Almost all the important leaders of Gujranwala were eventually arrested and though summary courts had been set up, many among them were never even tried. Not everyone who was punished was arrested; however, sometimes the treatment outside the jails was far worse. In many areas of Gujranwala people were flogged, arrested, and their properties taken away.

Given that such difficult conditions prevailed in other places in Punjab as well, it was only natural that the disorders would spread.

Kasur, a small town of 25,000 in Lahore district, also felt the full weight of martial law. There had been a reluctance in Kasur to participate in the hartal or satyagraha until early April. It was only on 11 April that Nadir Ali Shah, a local shopkeeper, went about requesting that the shops be closed—possibly following the news of Gandhi's arrest and the events in Amritsar and Lahore on 10 April.

Everyone, including school children, joined in enthusiastically. A meeting was held where lawyers showed their solidarity with the anti-Rowlatt Act Movement and Gandhi's call for a hartal.

On 12 April, as the hartal continued, Shah, definitely an unsung hero of the agitation (he was among those who were later hanged for their role in the agitation) took out a funeral march for 'liberty' using an upturned charpoy with a black flag

---

101. INC Report, p. 111, statement 304.

on it. There were cries of lamentation, and the beating of breasts just as in a Muharram procession.[102] This form of grieving had been propagated by Durga Das, editor of *Waqt*.

In the evidence recorded by the Hunter Committee, it was suggested that some of the people who behaved defiantly during the 'disorders' at Kasur had come from Amritsar. In that case, their anger would have been palpable as they would have escaped the increasingly miserable conditions in the city, following the violence on 10 April.

Once again, understandably, there is a divergence in the details given about the disorders in Kasur, in the INC Report and the Hunter Committee Report. The INC Report focusses more on the travails of the people, while the Hunter Committee Report is more conscious of the official stance.

The crowd at Kasur threw stones at windows and broke down doors of government buildings. The telegraph office was ransacked and furniture set on fire, telegraph wires were cut, and all the goods inside the railway building were looted or wrecked. No one, including the constable posted there, tried to stop the protestors. The railway stations were key points for agitators to target for a variety of reasons: they were a symbol of British governance, and as part of the hartal, the protestors wanted to halt the trains, and stop all movement and activity at the station.

However, the situation in Kasur quickly got out of hand. When the crowd reached the station, there were three trains, which had arrived from Lahore, Patti and Ferozepur (also spelt as Ferozepore in the HC Report) respectively. The Ferozepur train had eleven Europeans on board, including a British family with three children. Their presence immediately escalated the violence, leading to the death of two Europeans and around five or six of the Indian protesters. As always, we know precisely,

---

102. Hunter Committee Report, p. 63.

by name, what happened to the Europeans, but we know very little about the Indians, except for those like Khair Din, an Inspector in the Railway Accounts, who helped the British family to safety.

Two of the British officers were badly beaten but managed to escape and found shelter in a nearby village. The family with the three children found refuge in a gatekeeper's hut with Khair Din. It was he who finally, with the help of another lawyer, Mohi-ud-din, took the family to the nearby village of Kot Halim, and from there to the bungalow of the DSP, Sardar Ahmad Khan. Two other British officers escaped, though one of them was badly beaten.

However, two warrant officers on the train who were armed with revolvers, were killed. They had been standing at the door of the compartment when the train halted at the station and fired at the crowd, hurting one man on the foot. They were chased down the platform and beaten to death with sticks. By the time the DSP arrived, it was too late.

The events at Kasur seem extremely violent when seen in isolation but if we see them in the context of the killings and oppression underway in Amritsar and Lahore, and even Gujranwala, as well as other small towns and villages of Punjab (of which we will see a few more examples), the anger in the crowd, though reprehensible, is not difficult to understand.

As the violence spread, there were attempts to loot the tahsil (or the Revenue Office) and the Munsif's Court (or the Civil Court). Sub Inspector Bawa Kharak Singh defended the tahsil along with some armed men. It is important to note that so far, at Kasur, many of the officers coming into contact with the crowd were Indians. They were trying to protect government property, as well as save European lives, all the while trying to persuade the crowd to disperse.

Around this time, it seems slogans in praise and support of Mahatma Gandhi, Kitchlew and Satya Pal were raised.

Slogans against the British Raj were also raised. To the credit of the outnumbered police officials—as the crowd was said to be around 1,500 to 2,000—no aggressive moves were made by them. The crowd asked the police to join the agitation, which they resisted. Thus far, the Sub Inspector had only flung bricks at the crowd and received them back as well. Now, as things began to spiral out of hand, he fired a few shots in the air.

Up to this point, there had been no casualties in this particular encounter.

Things changed with the arrival of Sub Divisional Officer Mitter, when orders were given to fire. Fifty-seven rounds were fired with 'some ten or a dozen muskets taking part'.[103] Four men died and many more were wounded. Some were arrested. It is important to note that the crowd is described in the HC Report as 'low class people, sweepers, skin-dyers etc., and not of the more respectable classes. The Deputy Superintendent of Police noticed in it some strangers to Kasur.' The report goes on to state that 'We uphold the decision to fire upon this mob and think it should have been fired upon before the Deputy Superintendent of Police arrived.'

The comment on the status of the crowd is important as it shows how deeply the anti-Rowlatt Act agitation had affected everyone; even the poor, mostly daily wagers, were driven to protest the arrest of their leaders. The common assumption by the British would have been that these were 'hooligans'. In actuality, these were probably just very ordinary people protesting not just the recent oppression, but also the economic hardships they had been experiencing in Punjab under the regime of O'Dwyer.

It was only in the afternoon of 12 April that troops arrived from Ferozepur. On 15 April, more reinforcements were brought in and on 16 April, martial law was imposed, though by then, all

---

103. Hunter Committee Report, p. 66.

was quiet. According to the HC Report, an 'Indian gentleman' on the Ferozepur train had gone on a tonga to summon the troops from Ferozepur. We also know from the HC Report that Sherbourne (whose family had been rescued from the train) had been disguised as an Indian—wearing a turban and armed with a revolver—and had gone to Ferozepur to get help.

At Kasur, the fury of the people had subsided in a few hours. But as it was thought that the Indian Sub Divisional Officer had not been tough enough, he was replaced by a British officer, Marsden, and the administration of martial law was given over to Colonel Macrae and later to Captain Doveton.[104] Both these officers excelled at brutality.

People were punished as cruelly as they were elsewhere. More arrests started from 16 April. As in the other five districts under martial law, whipping was a popular way of inflicting punishment and initially it was conducted in public places. Between five to thirty stripes were administered. Below are the official records of these sentences; Kasur is high on the list, but there were many more which have possibly gone unrecorded:

Lahore—80
Kasur—79
Chuharkhana S.D.—40
Gujranwala—24
Amritsar—32
Gujrat—3
Lyallpur—nil[105]

Totalling 257, this does not include the flogging of six school boys at Kasur, and the other six flogged in Amritsar who were under trial, supposedly for the attack on Sherwood. It also does not include the flogging resorted to when mobile columns visited the villages. 'The normal procedure adopted was to strip

---

104. INC Report, p. 98.
105. Hunter Committee Report, p. 231.

the person to be whipped and tie him to a frame-work and then lash him.'[106]

Initially, the flogging was public. Viceroy Chelmsford had written to O'Dwyer, and the latter had replied to him on 21 April, saying that he had told the military authorities that it was 'very undesirable to have public flogging'. O'Dwyer also told the Hunter Committee that he did not think 'that there was really any harm in having on the first day a few public floggings which would make the people realise that law was re-established and people who had infringed the law must accept some chastisement.' But the orders to cease public flogging did not mean that it was discontinued. On 25 April, a railway employee was flogged at the Kasur railway station and the sentences of whipping inflicted by Bosworth Smith of the Sheikhupura sub-division used to be carried out in the court compound after the rising of the court. As the court was at the canal bungalow, this place was, according to Bosworth Smith, 'not altogether private, and it was not public.'[107]

However, in Kasur, flogging posts were (according to the INC Report) erected on the railway station platform, and even school boys were flogged. As in other places, they had been part of the agitation, and now they had to be 'chastised'. In one bizarre case, when the headmaster of a school said that the boys were becoming insubordinate and asked for military help, it was suggested by the Officer Commanding in Kasur that they should be whipped. Therefore, boys from this school and others were assembled in one place. However, the boys who were selected by the headmaster were found to be physically weak. The Officer Commanding rejected these boys and asked Marsden to select more schoolboys from the same school as well as others—the only criteria was that they should be fit to receive

---

106. Hunter Committee Report, p. 231.
107. Hunter Committee Minority Report, p. 231.

the punishment. Marsden (according to the INC Report) said that there was no particular objective to this punishment. There was no investigation and no trial.[108]

In his cross-examination, Colonel MacRae, who was in charge at Kasur, gave laconic answers to the Hunter Committee, as quoted in the INC Report:

> Q: As regards the whipping of school boys, you gave directions that the biggest six boys were to be selected for whipping?
>
> A: Yes, generally speaking.
>
> Q: Their misfortune was that they happened to be big?
>
> A: Of course.
>
> Q: Because they were big, therefore they had to suffer these lashes?
>
> A: Yes.
>
> Q: Do you think it was a reasonable thing to do?
>
> A: I thought so under the circumstances, and I still think so.[109]

Just as Johnson in Lahore had a whole wedding party flogged, Doveton in Kasur had men flogged in the presence of prostitutes. He said he had asked the Sub Inspector to round up some bad characters in front of whom to conduct the flogging and was 'horrified' when prostitutes showed up. He added that he could not send them away as he could not find an escort for them. The number of 'minor punishments' that Doveton came up with was quite astonishing, including having people whitewashed. There was no one to stop him from humiliating the population in any way that he wished.[110]

---

108. INC Report, pp. 99–100.

109. INC Report, p. 103.

110. INC Report, p. 103.

In Kasur, another common punishment for anyone who did not salaam a white person was to have them rub their nose on the ground. Doveton suggested that people 'liked' martial law, and they were amused at these punishments, rather than humiliated or terrified. He would have people mark time, skip, climb ladders and even work as 'coolies' at the railway station. Like Johnson or Dyer, he too thought of himself as a benevolent dictator. Just as Dyer got himself declared an honorary Sikh at the Golden Temple, Doveton had verses composed in his favour by a Muslim poet.[111]

'What happened was,' said Marsden, 'Captain Doveton did not want to go through the formalities of trial and sentence. He wanted to do things summarily.'[112]

Undoubtedly, Punjab was enslaved. Doveton described the terrified population as 'willing slaves' while deposing to the Hunter Committee. When asked to explain during the cross-examination by Setalvad, he said, 'It (willing slaves) means, willing to work in the way you require.'[113]

After the initial arrests following the events on 12 April at Kasur, the next round of arrests was made on 16 April. One hundred seventy-two people were arrested in Kasur, of whom 97 were discharged without trial. Of the rest, 51 were convicted. Sadly, here too, people who had tried to help the police by calming the protestors were arrested, including Maulvi Ghulam Mohiyuddin and Maulvi Abdul Kadir, who had, in fact, protected the Sherbournes. On 1 May, there was an identification parade in which women and children were included; they had to sit at the railway station, bareheaded, without food or drink, till 2 p.m. Everyone was forced to attend these identity parades. What if someone did not turn up when

---

111. INC Report, p. 100.
112. INC Report, p. 100.
113. INC Report, p. 100.

summoned? Well, then their homes would be destroyed, and their belongings burnt.[114]

Apart from other punishments that were meted out in Punjab, gallows were set up in public spaces, as close to the scenes of 'mob outrage' as possible. At Kasur, they were erected but apparently never used. A large public cage was also set up near the railway station, which could accommodate around 150 persons. The entire male population of the town was paraded for identification.[115]

Capital punishment was also meted out in Punjab. Eighteen people were hanged due to the unrest in the province. Pandit Motilal Nehru had to intervene and write to the Secretary of State to get hundreds of sentences commuted. The INC Report states: 'We much suspect that many of those who were hanged and over whose heads the death sentences are still hanging, were or are totally innocent.'

This sentiment was not shared by the British civilian officers, who were busy supporting martial law. Officers like Bosworth Smith at the sub-division of Sheikhupura felt that martial law was not only essential but desirable. In total, he would have tried 477 persons between 6 May and 20 May and the accused usually pleaded guilty, with very few exceptions. 'This was peculiar to Mr Bosworth Smith's Court. He seemed to exercise a subtle influence over the persons brought before him, which produced wholesale admissions of guilt. Convictions, it is alleged were based on the evidence of three or four railway officials.'[116] Like Johnson, he managed to get the maximum number of convictions in a few short weeks.

Most of the army and civilian officers who imposed martial law in Punjab confessed to being sceptical about the

---

114. INC Report, p. 101.

115. Horniman, *Amritsar and Our Duty*, p. 155.

116. Horniman, *Amritsar and Our Duty*, p. 158.

loyalty of Indians. Bosworth Smith even said, 'There is no place where disloyalty is so deep as in Delhi, Lahore and Amritsar.' He suggested this, in particular, about the legal profession. As we know, lawyers were at the forefront of the anti-Rowlatt Act agitation everywhere and Gandhi himself, of course, was a lawyer.

In reality, many Indians in the official machinery, in the army and the Civil Service, remained loyal to the British, and even among the lawyers, many tried very hard to keep the agitation peaceful.

Having made this 'sweeping statement', Bosworth Smith could provide no proof of it. In the cross-examination by Setalvad, he was questioned about his statement of 'disloyalty':

Q: Have you any personal experience of Delhi?

A: I spent some months there.

Q: Had you ever been officially connected with that place?

A: No.

Q: On what material did you base your statement?

A: It was a confidential report to the Government.

Q: But when you make a confidential report surely any opinion you may express therein must be based on some material?

A: I had my own opinion.

Q: You don't arrive at opinions without material. What is the material on which you based your opinion?

A: I prefer not to say.

Q: Why don't you care to enlighten the Committee in the matter? Is it against public interest or were you ordered by the government not to say? Why are you so unwilling?

A: I don't care to say.

Q: I want to have your position clear. You don't want to answer the question?

A: I have already said I don't think it is desirable.

Q: Is it against public interest?

A: I don't wish to answer this.

Q: May I know your reason?

A: I don't wish to give it to you.

Q: You don't wish to answer the question and you don't wish to give your reasons?

A: Yes.

Q: You think this is the way in which to come here to assist the committee?

Silence.

Q: Does the same thing apply to your assertion regarding Lahore and Amritsar?

A: The same.[117]

Given that there was a pre-existing bias and prejudice against the residents of Punjab, it is hardly surprising that sadistic methods were used to deal with the anti-Rowlatt Act Movement. While the satyagraha had spread to other places such as Delhi, Mumbai and Ahmedabad, 'fancy punishments' which converted Indians into 'slaves' were not used there. This was O'Dwyer's special parting gift to Punjab, along with the Jallianwala Bagh massacre.

---

117. Hunter Committee Report, quoted in Horniman, *Amritsar and Our Duty*, p. 159–60.

5

Fascist, Racist or Both?

Punjab 1919

How shall our love console thee, or assuage
Thy hapless woe; how shall our grief requite
The hearts that scourge thee and the hands that smite
Thy beauty with their rods of bitter rage!
Lo! let our sorrow be thy battle-gauge
To wreck the terror of the tyrant's might
Who mocks with ribald wrath thy tragic plight.
And stains with shame thy radiant heritage!
O beautiful! O broken hearted and betrayed!
O mournful queen! O martyred Draupadi!
Endure thou still, unconquered, undismayed!
The sacred rivers of thy stricken blood
Shall prove the five-fold stream of Freedom's flood,
To guard the watch-towers of our Liberty.

—Sarojini Naidu[1]

The policy of the British towards India, at the start of the twentieth century, appeared confused. They owed a huge debt

---

1. Quoted in Pandit Pearay Mohan, *An Imaginary Rebellion and How It Was Suppressed* (Lahore: Kholsa Bros., 1920).

to the Indian soldiers who had fought on their side in World War I, but the colony was still regarded through the prism of the 'mutiny' of 1857. Resistance was brewing all over India, and Punjab, Bengal and Maharashtra were among the most rebellious. 'By 1918, the government held 806 political prisoners in Bengal... a preliminary investigation committee reported that 70 to 80 per cent of them are inexperienced and young students' as well as teachers, clerks and 'persons of no occupation'.[2]

Yet, as Helen Fein points out, the Rowlatt Committee claimed that 'all these plots have been directed towards one and the same objective, the overthrow by force of British rule in India... All have been successfully encountered with the support of Indian loyalty.' Why, given such an optimistic conclusion, asks Fein, were the British in need of new legislation? 'Although they had been able to foil all attempts at armed revolt and had subverted plans to obtain German arms, they were unable to squash the underground movement. Most crimes were never solved, fewer were persecuted, and even fewer defendants were convicted. The police, as the Rowlatt Committee described them, were generally illiterate, untrained in detection, and lacked modern communication devices.'[3] (Here the reference is specifically to so-called acts of sedition against the British, which were poorly investigated) Fein further points out that while witnesses were reluctant to appear, as some who did had been murdered in the past, government lawyers were hopeless at presenting cases that could 'stand up'.

The one person who understood the need for greater freedoms in India was Sir Edwin Montagu, the British Secretary of State. He had proposed the Montagu-Chelmsford Reforms, which were bitterly resented by many who were ruling India at the time. The Governors and Lieutenant Governors did

---

2. Helen Fein, *Imperial Crime and Punishment* (Honolulu: The University Press of Hawaii, 1977), p. 77.

3. Op. cit., p. 77.

not appreciate the idea of diarchy, according to which Indians would gradually be absorbed into positions of power. These local satraps had got used to ruling independently. They reported directly to the Viceroy, who was either in Delhi or Simla, and who in turn passed all information on to the Secretary of State in London. There were many loopholes in this system, which could easily be exploited in a vast country like India. The agitation over the Rowlatt Acts grew quickly, precisely because of these lacunae.

Gandhi, having spent his formative years in London and then South Africa, understood the importance of collective agitation. There was a strength in numbers that he wanted to tap into, and this was exactly what the British feared.

Why did the anti-Rowlatt Act protests expand so swiftly into a movement, which was then squashed with such great cruelty? Perhaps because many of the top leaders of the time—Gandhi, Malaviya, Mohammed Ali Jinnah—were lawyers and understood the dark side of the Acts only too well.

The Anarchical and Revolutionary Crimes Act, or the Rowlatt Acts, were actually two bills. They had been gazetted in early 1919 and were then quickly introduced in the Imperial Legislature. They were drafted following the concern that the Defence of India Act, the Indian DORA, had been a 'war emergency' measure and something equivalent was needed in peace time. An English judge, Sir Sydney Rowlatt, presided over a committee which included two Indian judges as well, but they conducted their deliberations in-camera, and the material they dealt with were mostly secret police records. None of the men whom they considered 'revolutionary' appeared or spoke in their own defence. Except for four sittings in Lahore, the rest were conducted in Calcutta.

There was stiff opposition to the passing of the bills. Bill No 1 was actually the weaker of the two bills and strangely, it was enacted before it was published. The usual procedure was for a bill to first be published in all the provincial gazettes, and then become law after a period of time.[4] But this was not how it happened in this case.

'It has been stated that the Secretary of State cabled his sanction only for the publication of the bills, but the Government of India misunderstood or misread the cable, and took as conveying sanction to proceed with its enactment, with the result that the first intimation of this fact that Mr Montagu had came to him in the newspapers. The error was rectified too late and the first Bill was then allowed…'[5]

The first bill, though not as drastic as the second, provided for an amendment of the Indian Penal Code and the Code of Criminal Procedure. It made the Sedition Law even more severe. Section 124 B was added, which made the possession of seditious literature punishable with imprisonment and/or with a fine as well. This meant that one could be punished even for accidental possession of any literature that was considered seditious. A seditious document, as per the code, could be one 'which instigates or is likely to instigate the use of criminal force against the King, the Government, or a public servant or servants.'[6] Even historical documents or books could be misconstrued as seditious. The onus would be on the possessor of the document to prove his or her innocence.

The bill also contained some added provisions under Chapter VI of the Indian Penal Code, which stated that in case the accused had a previous conviction, or had been associated, habitually or voluntarily, with a person who had been convicted under that chapter, it would affect his or her own case. This meant that even friends and relations of the previously convicted person would have to shun him or her, so as to not be accused.

---

4. Benjamin Guy Horniman, *Amritsar and Our Duty To India* (London: T. Fisher Unwin Ltd., 1920), pp. 53–4.

5. Horniman, *Amritsar and Our Duty*, pp. 53–4.

6. Op. cit., p. 55.

Further, the bill stated that even those convicted only once would be under the scrutiny of the state and could even be prohibited from public speech and writing. Eventually, this bill was dropped.

Bill No 2, Part 1, was far more dangerous in its limitation of safeguards and checks. People could be tried by courts, which could sit in-camera, and there would be no juries, no preliminary proceedings for committal, and no appeal allowed either. Extraordinarily, evidence could be accepted from dead or missing persons and any previous conviction could also be admitted as evidence. The tribunals comprised of three persons, who could be either high court judges or person of similar stature, and their judgement could send the convicted to Kala Paani in the Andamans or to the gallows.

Part II of the bill empowered the Executive to restrict and restrain anyone thought to be complicit in 'anarchical and revolutionary movements'. This could also mean restrictions through bonds and keeping the police notified of one's movements. Disobedience of any order would attract a fine of ₹500 (a huge sum in those days), imprisonment for six months, or both.

However, it was Part III which was found to be the most 'alarming'. It empowered the Executive to arrest and search without warrant and to confine persons thus arrested 'without trial in any part of a prison or place not actually used for confinement'. These so-called criminals could be kept in solitary confinement as well. In Part IV, there was provision for an automatic continuance of persons to be confined or restricted, were they already confined or restricted under the Defence of India Act. Part V added a few more provisions to make these punishments watertight.

Clearly, the odds were heavily stacked against anyone who was being investigated or arrested as he would not be represented by a lawyer. B.G. Horniman, the editor of *Bombay*

Chronicle, who was closely associated with the Satyagraha Movement and had been externed to England because of his writings, lucidly articulated the concerns of the time. (It was Horniman who smuggled out photographs of the massacre and was one of the first to publish reports on Jallianwala Bagh in the *Daily Herald* in England.[7]) He wrote, 'The position of a person attempting to defend himself against vague allegations supported by an untested police dossier before a secret inquiry of this character would be obviously hopeless.' The act was to be put into operation with the 'formal declaration of the prevalence of anarchical or revolutionary movements'. The worry, of course, was that any political movement could be considered 'anarchical and revolutionary'.[8]

Despite the fact that not a single Indian on the Imperial Legislative Council voted for the bill on 6 February (barring Sankaran Nair, who was on the Viceroy's Executive Council), it was passed on 18 March. There were three major resignations from the Council: Pandit Malaviya, Mazurul Haque and Mohammad Ali Jinnah. These were important names, and the movement against the 'Black Act' picked up in tempo and awareness.

Even though some British historians have tried to downplay the resentment towards the Rowlatt Acts as unreasonable, just as the British administration did at the time, Gandhi stepped up the argument in a letter to the press. This was at the start of his Satyagraha Movement. He said, presciently, that the decision to launch the satyagraha was 'probably the most momentous in the history of India. I give my assurance that it has not been hastily taken. Personally I have passed many a sleepless night over it. I have endeavoured duly to appreciate the government's position.' He went on to add that while there might be a slight danger

---

7. Op. cit.
8. Op. cit., pp. 59–64.

from 'secret violence' in a few parts of the country as stated in the bill, he was more concerned about 'arming the Government with powers, out of all proportion to the situation...'

In his powerful letter, which was to ignite the rebellion against the Act, Gandhi added, '... I consider the Bills to be an unmistakable symptom of a deep rooted disease in the Governing Body. It needs therefore to be drastically treated... If the Covenanters know the use of this remedy, I fear no ill from it. I have no business to doubt their ability. They must ascertain whether the disease is sufficiently great to justify the strong remedy, and whether all milder ones have been tried. They have convinced themselves that the disease is serious enough and that milder measures have utterly failed. The rest lies in the lap of the gods.'[9]

The agitation against the Rowlatt Acts united people across India and they began to look to Gandhi for leadership. While nowhere in the country did the Satyagraha Movement, even when it turned violent, provoke the large-scale repercussions it did in Punjab, one must remember that racism was widespread.

As Helen Fein notes in her book, *Imperial Crime and Punishment*, Indians could be killed by Europeans with impunity—so long as the murderer was white:

> Lord Curzon was vexed during his viceroyalty (1899-1905) by the failure of juries to punish Europeans who maliciously wounded or killed natives either out of personal pique (sometimes randomly vented) or desire to retaliate for some previous crime of an Indian:
>
> I grieve to say that, since I came to India, I have not found a single man among 'the better class' to whose feelings you think that we might safely appeal, who either shares my views, or could be relied upon to back them, at the cost of clamour or unpopularity. They all admit privately that the occurrence of these incidents is regrettable... (but) contend

---

9. INC Report, p. 26.

that the blame rests with the Natives (which certainly in my experience, have not found to be the case) and as for the judicial scandals—well they shrug their shoulders and smile.[10]

Fein quotes Philp Woodruff who, writing from the 'perspective of a civil servant', noted the changes that had begun to take place, and the awkward relationships that resulted. Woodruff attributed the growing racial hostility 'to the emergence of an educated class of Indians from whom deference would not be automatically expected.' A young artillery officer put the popular feeling in a nutshell. He said, 'I know nothing of politics, but I do know that if a nigger cheeks us, we must lick him...'[11]

Such sentiments were becoming increasingly problematic in India, with educated Indians looking for more powerful positions and even speaking of equality. Lord Minto, for instance, recommended Sir Satyendra Prasanna Sinha (later Lord Sinha) to be elevated to the Viceroy's Executive Council, somewhat biased by the 'comparatively' white colour of his skin:

> Sinha stands high in public estimation as well as in his profession—and he and his family are socially in touch with European society... In making a great change like this I think we should consider the line of least resistance as well as the ability of an individual. Moreover—please do not think me terribly narrow! but Sinha is comparatively white, while Mookerjee is as black as my hat! and opposition in the official world would not be regardless of mere shades of colour![12]

Skin colour was essentially what differentiated the ruling class from the masses. While this racism was a difficult reality for Indians to accept in civilian life, it was easier to live with within

---

10. Fein, *Imperial Crime*, p. 56.
11. Fein, *Imperial Crime*, pp. 56–7.
12. Fein, *Imperial Crime*, p. 57.

the armed forces and the police. The uniforms, the regimental banners and badges, and the advantages that came with these were attractive. The narrative was clearly in favour of the British and many Indians were thus seduced. When native soldiers were used to kill fellow Indians, they accepted their orders from the white sahibs unquestioningly, as their first loyalty lay with the sahib, and then the king, from whom flowed all kinds of benefits and titles.

However, if ever a native civilian appeared to 'cheek' an army or police officer, there would be grave consequences for the offender, no matter how minor the 'insult'. The various officers commanding the disturbed areas in Punjab usually reacted with extreme measures because they were not used to any form of retaliation or disrespect.

When Montagu tried to point out his concerns, particularly regarding the 'crawling order' in Amritsar to Viceroy Chelmsford, he did not get the response he was looking for. Montagu wrote to Chelmsford:

> Dyer's judgment and temper have in my opinion proved so unreliable that I am of the opinion that he cannot be fit to retain command. I consider in fact it very undesirable that he should continue in the Army of India. Unless the military authority has something to urge on his behalf beyond his previous excellent record of which I am not aware, I think you should relieve him of command and send him to England.[13]

Despite being the author of the Montagu-Chelmsford Reforms, and driven perhaps by the fact that these actions had taken place on his watch, Chelmsford took a very different stand. He responded:

> I was extremely sorry to get your telegram with regard to Dyer, not that I think it was unnatural in the circumstances...
> I have heard that Dyer administered Martial Law in Amritsar very reasonably and in no sense tyrannously. In

---

13. Montagu Papers, British Library, MSS, Eur D 523, 523/8.

these circumstances you will understand why it is that both the Commander-in-Chief and I feel very strongly that an error of judgment, transitory in its consequences, should not bring down upon him a penalty which would be out of all proportion to the offence and which must be balanced against the very notable services which he rendered at an extremely critical time. I should add further that Dyer took part in the recent operations at Thal and again distinguished himself as a military leader of great push and determination.[14]

Meanwhile, in Punjab, with this kind of protection, false evidence continued to be concocted against those who were arrested under martial law. Naturally, when anyone could be arrested on trumped-up charges, corruption also became widespread. Authorities dismissed allegations of army brutality, police corruption and false accusations.[15]

Ironically, Major S.R. Shirley, the Area Officer and Provost Marshal for Amritsar District, blamed the inhabitants of Amritsar for all the miseries heaped upon them. His disposition was very similar to that of Dyer, Johnson and Beynon. According to Shirley, if the authorities had behaved badly, the Indians deserved it. 'After all,' he explained, many Punjabis proved reluctant to provide information that could help arrest 'conspirators and rioters'. Therefore, 'if doubtful methods were used to obtain evidence or if prosecution by the police took place, the inhabitants of Amritsar themselves are more to blame than anyone else.' With this sort of attitude, it was no surprise that Indians 'became sullen and resentful as arrests and investigations proceeded'.[16]

The British Missionary C.F. Andrews, who had visited Amritsar in early May 1919, noted:

---

14. Chelmsford Papers, 264/1, 264/5, British Library, 523/8.

15. Shireen Ilahi, *Imperial Violence and the Path to Independence: India, Ireland and the Crisis of Empire*, (London: I.B. Tauris Co. Ltd., 2016), p. 68.

16. Ilahi, *Imperial Violence*, p. 68.

I have seen with my own eyes just such a sudden rush of panic. I have also seen the police, at every corner, dominating the city. I have seen the long lines of cavalry patrolling the streets. I have understood from the lips of many witnesses, the terror which these forces have inspired.[17]

When Kapil Deva Malaviya visited Amritsar on 18 July 1919, he found that there was still ongoing surveillance on anyone arriving in the city; he was trailed by two constables wherever he went. There were armed guards at the station and though martial law had been abolished, 'for all practical purposes the so called precautionary or punitive measures that are in vogue, serve as an unmistakable reminder of the "reign of terror" that was introduced on the 15th of April last'.[18]

Amritsar, Kasur, Gujranwala and Lyallpur were under martial law until 9 June 1919, and Lahore till 11 June. In Gujarat, military rule was abolished after one month and railway lands were released on 25 August 1919. However, the area had become peaceful much before that, or rather had been terrorised into an uneasy calm. This was partly due to the fact that thousands of people had been arrested, many of whom were innocent, while quite a few were trapped through false testimony.

In the words of Kapil Deva Malaviya:

> The Government professes ignorance of the actual number of persons arrested and detained in custody in connection with the Punjab disturbances. It is generally believed that the total figures must be appalling and 5,000 is not an overestimate.
>
> The number of persons actually tried by Martial Law Commissions was 852. The number of those tried by the Summary Courts established under Martial Law was 1437.

---

17. Ilahi, *Imperial Violence*, p. 68.

18. K.D. Malaviya, *Open Rebellion In The Punjab: With Special Reference To Amritsar* (Allahabad: Abhyudya Press, 1919), pp. 1–3.

Out of those tried by the Martial Law Commissions 581 were convicted.

Altogether 18 persons were executed, 26 transported for life and 1,229 confined in jails.[19]

The number of Europeans who died was seven in all: five in Amritsar and two in Kasur. The number of Indians who died was over 1,000 and many more simply vanished.

The war on Punjab had been 'won' according to O'Dwyer, but there was no war to begin with. There was only a brutally suppressed satyagraha and a forced attempt to disrupt the political unity between Hindus and Muslims, which ultimately succeeded. People found it impossible to continue the agitation; Gandhi himself conceded he could not continue with it.

In the week preceding the events in Punjab, the first city to witness anti-Rowlatt Act protests was the capital, Delhi. Gandhi had proposed that Satyagraha Societies or Sabhas be set up in various places so that people could take oaths against the Rowlatt Acts. After that they would go onto the streets, observe a fast, and ensure a peaceful shutdown of all work, as the instrument of hartal was key to the Satyagraha Movement. Once he arrived in Delhi on 7 March, a local branch of the society was organized and several people took the oath.

Gandhi then decided that a countrywide hartal would be organised in order to impress upon the British the seriousness of their intent. Delhi was already politically sensitised and the previous winter meetings of the All India Congress and the Muslim League had been held there. In February 1919, the meetings of the Legislative Council had led to discussion and unrest as rumours had begun to spread about the Rowlatt Acts. Some information was certainly incorrect, for instance, that police could arrest any 'three or four men conversing together, that nobody would be allowed to own more than a

---

19. Op. cit., p. 56.

certain amount of land, and that nobody would be allowed to marry without leave from the Government'.[20] It all added to the growing resentment against the Acts.

Other factors could have also contributed to the rise of discontent in specific places. For instance, in Delhi, it was felt that the Deputy Commissioner was 'unsympathetic' towards political activities, that there was a general dislike of the police, and that the prices of commodities continued to be high despite the armistice, following the World War.

Unlike in the Punjab, however, there are no detailed eyewitness accounts from this difficult period. In any case the disorders were over within a few days. It could be argued that because the authorities did not react with the same severity as in Punjab, the disorders lasted for a shorter period in Delhi and everywhere else in the country.

The first clash in Delhi between the satyagrahis and the British authorities occurred on 30 March while a hartal was being observed. It was a day of abstinence and 'general mourning to protest against the Government's plan in passing Rowlatt Act No 2'.[21] It was apparently very successful as both Hindus and Muslims shut their businesses for the day. In the morning, as part of the satyagraha, and in order to bring the city to a halt, people riding in tongas and cars were also asked to alight and walk.

At the railway station, where the crowd went next, they tried to persuade the vendor at the third-class refreshment room to abstain from work. A scuffle ensued, as the vendor, who was old and deaf, resisted, saying he was under contract with the Railways. Matthews, the Deputy Station Superintendent, had his coat torn off, and the vendor was hurt as well.

Two men were arrested but later let off, as the crowd

---

20. Hunter Committee Report, p. 6.
21. Hunter Committee Report, p. 1.

continued to protest outside. While they stopped traffic and carried on with the demonstration, Currie, the acting Additional District Magistrate, and Jeffreys, Additional Superintendent of Police, arrived at the station at around 1 p.m. A military force was also summoned. The civil authorities contacted General Drake Brockman, and a picket of thirty men and a Sergeant under Lieutenant Shelford were deployed at the railway station. It is important to note that they were armed with rifles, bayonets and twenty rounds of ammunition each. A train on which some fifteen to twenty British soldiers were travelling was stopped at the station. Around 250 Manipuri soldiers had arrived from Mesopotamia; even though they did not understand either Urdu or English and could not be of much help, they were detained in Delhi to provide reinforcements. Shelford divided his force into two parties after requesting the British soldiers on the train to join them. They were given arms from the ammunition store at the railway station.

Obviously, the British were preparing for a confrontation.

The senior officials tried to break up the crowd of satyagrahis, but the numbers were growing. According to the Hunter Committee Report, they kept asking for the release of the arrested men. The British countered by saying that the men had already been released. By about 1.45 p.m., the Senior Superintendent of Police also arrived, with a small force of mounted police.

Possibly enraged at the increasing number of police and military personnel, and the fact that the arrested men were, allegedly, not released, the crowd—whose leaders and members remained nameless throughout—started throwing stones and bricks at the police and the soldiers. Marshall told Currie to give instructions to open fire and finally the ADM agreed. In the firing, 'two or three men' were killed. The crowd continued to retaliate and Barron, the Chief Commissioner, 'found the place littered with bricks and stones'. Some of the policemen were wounded by 'missiles' flung by the protestors. The bodies of the protestors who had been killed were taken to the station. The exact number of the dead remained unknown.

The crowd then moved on from Queens Gardens to Town Hall and Chandni Chowk. At Town Hall, there was another confrontation, as they pelted the police force of about seventeen constables, headed by Jeffreys, with stones. Jeffreys himself was hit, whereupon he instructed his troops to fire and one more protestor was killed. Had it been a British soldier, we would have known the name and the circumstances of his death, but there was minimal detail or interest in an Indian.[22]

The crowd continued to advance. Fifteen soldiers under Sergeant Kemslety arrived and the troops fired into the air. This did not settle the crowd, but it 'charged' the British party, and in the volley of firing from the soldiers, the death toll apparently rose to eight, though the number of wounded would have been much higher. The next day, only around a dozen protestors showed up for treatment at the hospital. As at Jallianwala Bagh and other places in Punjab, hospitals were to be avoided because doctors were being questioned and there was a real fear that the patients—and doctors—could be arrested.

On 30 March, Munshi Ram, also known as Swami Shraddhanand, President of the Reception Committee of the Indian National Congress (1919), addressed a large crowd at People's Park in Delhi, but the meeting was dispersed peacefully after Superintendent Orde of the CID persuaded Shraddhanand to call it off. Things began to quieten down after that. Even though large funeral processions were taken out on 31 March, no further clashes took place.

All was peaceful until Sunday, 6 April, when there was another hartal, part of an all-India shutdown. There was a total

---

22. Op. cit., pp. 3–4.

strike in Delhi and, importantly, open evidence of Hindu-Muslim unity. 'A meeting was held at the Fatehpuri mosque where, contrary to Mohammedan custom, Hindus were allowed to speak.'[23]

This would have raised concerns among the authorities, who would have been keen to end the hartal and the emerging unity in the communities. Possibly under government pressure, on 7, 8 and 9 April a few shops were reopened. However, with the news spreading that Gandhi would be travelling through Delhi on 9 April, there was growing excitement. The authorities, on their part, feared another gathering. Ultimately, as we know, orders were issued at the behest of O'Dwyer, preventing Gandhi from entering Punjab. The Chief Commissioner of Delhi also received an order to stop Gandhi from entering the capital; he was to be confined to the Bombay Presidency. As news of this and of the trouble in Amritsar and Lahore spread through Delhi, shops remained closed on 10 April.

It is notable that there was no attack on any European, though a CID inspector was assaulted at a meeting that took place in King Edward's Park. He, too, must have been an Indian as there are no details to be found about him.

Since the authorities and the leaders of the Satyagraha Movement (unnamed in the HC Report and also in the INC Report) were in conversation, it was felt that the hartal could be lifted. On 17 April (by which time it is likely that news would have trickled in from Punjab despite censorship and the ban on travel), there was one more attempt to enforce the hartal. Clashes ensued when the crowd managed to go around the police pickets to close the shops which were being opened. An arrest led to another assault on a head constable. There was an attack on a police picket at Ballimaran Street in Chandni Chowk. In the police firing that followed (in 'self protection'),

---

23. Hunter Committee Report, p. 5.

eighteen people were reported wounded, while two others were killed.

In total, even though there had not been any organised violence on the part of the crowd, up to ten people were killed, and perhaps two or three dozen more wounded. Of these individuals we know nothing beyond the tentative numbers.

By 19 April, the hartal was over and shops reopened. Nevertheless, around 17 April, the Chief Commissioner asked for martial law to be imposed in Delhi. The request was inexplicable as the city was entirely peaceful.

Perhaps the authorities thought the trouble in Punjab might infect Delhi. Or was there fear that in case a 'hartal' was called again and the 'lower orders found themselves with nothing to do', there might be violence again?[24]

Even though martial law was not imposed, some of the punishments that were doled out in Punjab were introduced in Delhi too; for instance, the practice of enrolling leading citizens as 'special constables'. There was an attempt to issue uniforms and have them report at the police station. The move was 'strongly resented' by those to whom this stricture was applied.

However, the handling of the situation in Delhi was vastly different from that in Amritsar or Lahore. The fact that there was a dialogue between the officers and the protestors, at least in some instances, meant that a few potentially dangerous situations were defused. The Chief Commissioner of Delhi, Barron, came in for praise from the Hunter Committee (both the Majority and Minority Reports) for this.

In Ahmedabad, a city with a population of nearly 400,000, things were not to be so quickly managed. The 49-year-old Gandhi had already achieved a near-spiritual status there. As a member of the Gujarat Sabha said, 'Mr Gandhi has honoured Ahmedabad by making it his headquarters, and while he is loved

---

24. Hunter Committee Report, p. 7.

and respected as a spiritual and political leader in the whole of India, the feelings of love and reverence cherished for him in this city are extraordinary.'[25]

The Gujarat Sabha worked as a District Congress Committee for the District of Ahmedabad. It was in Ahmedabad that the satyagraha oath was formulated, an outcome of a meeting of the Home Rule League at Gandhi's ashram, on 24 February 1919. It was attended by representative 'Home Rulers' from Ahmedabad and Bombay, and a decision was taken to 'start a passive resistance campaign against the proposed Rowlatt resolution'. Gandhi signed the oath, as did Anasuya Sarabhai and other Home Rulers, including a number of barristers and pleaders. Many meetings were held all over Gujarat and posters were deployed as well. These posters, as quoted in the Disorders Report, stated that civil disobedience had to be used side by side with passive resistance.

While passive resistance would have meant literally 'resisting' laws, civil disobedience was rather more active. This was the dichotomy that many found difficult to understand. Perhaps this was why the first round of satyagraha ended in some form of violence in most places, especially when crowds began to enforce the hartal and the authorities tried to stop them. But there was an agreement on all sides, that these clashes could have been controlled had the leaders, especially Gandhi, not been arrested.

The posters also advocated disobedience, such as not paying taxes. (Gandhi would later refine this further, but at this point, there were general pointers towards the kind of action ordinary people could take to show their opposition to the Rowlatt Acts.)

One of the posters said:

> How can the atrocities of the Rowlatt Bill be stopped? There is no atrocity if a thousand men refuse to pay taxes;

---

25. Op. cit., p. 10.

but to pay taxes to a Government which commits atrocities is to support such a rule and thus encourage atrocities.

Posters like this would have stirred up the people and worried the government. They popped up in Gujarat, Bombay, Delhi and Punjab. The anti-Rowlatt Act movement was basically a franchise and its main contribution would be to create leaders in different parts of the country. Anyone could show their anger towards their foreign ruler and participate in the political movement by shutting shop or fasting or making a poster. This was the first truly unifying movement of the people, led by Gandhi, who was by then a revered, if eccentric, leader.

Gandhi's popularity in Ahmedabad also stemmed from the fact that both he and Anasuya Sarabhai were held in special esteem after their intervention in favour of mill workers in 1918. At that point, Ahmedabad had 78 mills, employing around 40,000 workers, so they formed a sizeable part of the population. Thus when the mill workers heard of Gandhi's exclusion from Punjab on 9 April, they went on a rampage. The situation was to become worse the following day when Anasuya Sarabhai failed to arrive as expected and it was thought that she, too, had been arrested. In the two terrible days that followed, there were two casualties on the British side—an armed constable was thrown from a balcony (he must have been an Indian, as he remained nameless) and a Sergeant Fraser was killed. On the Indian side, the numbers were much higher. According to official reports, at least 28 were killed and 123 wounded. The Hunter Committee Report admitted that there could have been many more casualties, which were not traced. It also referred to 'one woman and four children wounded by the firing'.[26] The woman had been inside her house when she was struck by a stray bullet. We do not know her name.

Subsequently, the rioting and violence took off on a very large scale.

---

26. Hunter Committee Report, p. 19.

When the news of Gandhi's detention first reached Ahmedabad, it was followed by a circular issued by the Secretary of the Satyagraha Sabha:

> The day before yesterday, Mahatma Gandhi started from Bombay for Delhi, Lahore, Amritsar, etc. On reaching Delhi yesterday night an order under the Defence of India act was served on him requiring him not to go to Delhi, Punjab and other places and restricting him to Bombay. He disregarded the order; he is therefore arrested. He has expressed his desire that that all residing in the Ashram will celebrate this day and will do their work with double zeal and faith. It is requested that the whole public will respect his desire.[27]

Instead of calming them down, the circular caused many to become emotional and angry. They stoned the police, damaged a cinema hall and tried to observe hartal once again. Yet, there was no overreaction from the authorities at any stage, nor was martial law imposed in Ahmedabad. The similarity between the manner in which events unfolded in Ahmedabad and Amritsar is evident; the difference lay in the handling of the volatile situation.

However, some worrying incidents did take place.

Two European employees of a mill, Sagar and Steeples, were driving through the city when they were forced to alight. (The crowd was forcing everyone to walk as a sign of mourning.) They tried to get a ride on another vehicle but were stoned and chased into a police chowki. They tried to go further and, following another attack, took shelter in Beehive Mill near Prem Gate. Here, too, they were forced to leave, as people inside the mill did not want them to stay. They were accompanied by a small group of policemen, who had previously tried firing over the heads of the protestors.

Once they left the mill, the policemen fired into the

---

27. Hunter Committee Report, p. 12.

crowd, wounding twelve men. The defending party were then forced into the balcony of a house from which one policeman fell and was beaten up. He was to die later in the day from the injuries he received. Meanwhile, around 24 policemen arrived on the scene, followed by the District Magistrate and the Superintendent of Police. When they saw the policemen surrounded by a large crowd, the officials sent a driver with a message to Colonel Frazer, the Officer Commanding, requesting a dispatch of troops.

The 24 policemen managed to keep guard over the dying constable as well as some people they had arrested. The tense situation was managed by the DM and SP until the troops under Colonel Frazer arrived at 6.45 p.m.

Despite a quiet night, the unrest continued the following morning, when Anasuya Sarabhai did not arrive by the early train as expected. The police and the large, suspicious crowd clashed once again at Prem Gate.

The DM, Chatfield, described the events thus: 'The first incident on the 11th was when the District Superintendent of Police and I went down to the Prem Gate where the riot had occurred on the previous day. We discovered that the platoon which was stationed there was confronted by a crowd and the officer in charge complained to us that his men were annoyed. They were jeered at and it appeared to us that there was some danger and that trouble might arise on this account.'[28]

As the DM and the DSP drove around the city, they saw that the situation was spiraling out of control. Large crowds continued to gather, and their car was stoned. The hartal was still on, the mills and the shops were shut. Meanwhile, 300 soldiers under Major Kirkwood had been sent into the city, followed by 200 more. It was clearly a difficult situation as the crowd began to burn down government buildings including the

---

28. Hunter Committee Report, p. 14.

Collector's office, the record rooms, the Sub Registrar's office, the City Magistrate's office, and the City Survey Office over the gate of the Sub-Jail. They were fired upon by the armed police guard and so the Sub-Jail was saved, but they did burn down Mamlatdar's Court House, the telegraph office, the post office at Delhi Gate and two police chowkies.

As the attacks continued, a few Europeans were caught up in them, but fortunately, some like Mrs Tuke, the wife of the Civil Surgeon, managed to use a gun (actually, just brandished it about) very judiciously. She was finally rescued by some medical students. The electric power station was attacked next and Brown, who was in charge, was chased, till a worker put the crowd on a false scent. The situation grew worse as people got after Lieutenant MacDonald of the Army Clothing Department; he was saved only after a Parsee student, Laher, went across to the camp and brought back motor lorries. Meanwhile, an entrapped MacDonald managed to keep the crowd at bay on a narrow staircase of the Delhi Chala Chowki for more than an hour, while being pelted with missiles, even a broken bottle. He was saved by the arrival of the troops, thanks to the intrepid Laher.

From eyewitness accounts found in the Hunter Committee Report, it is clear that while the mill workers were determined to inflict maximum damage to ensure the release of Gandhi (who had not yet arrived in Ahmedabad), many other Indians kept trying to help the Europeans who were trapped.

By 11 a.m., several government buildings were on fire. The protestors were now playing hide-and-seek with the troops that had arrived under the command of Lieutenant Larkin. They continued to abuse and throw stones at the troops but by noon, troops had been deployed to protect the waterworks, the police headquarter lines and the railway bridge across the Sabarmati river. The defiant crowd continued to attack and even raided two temples from where they apparently procured guns and swords. They also murdered a European police officer. Sergeant Fraser was dragged out of hiding from a shop on Richey Road and killed.

Two Indian magistrates were attacked and so were some Indian policemen, but the crowd was primarily interested in targeting Europeans and government property. Orders were given to the troops that controlled fire was to be opened, but only if, after a warning, the crowd still came within 25 yards, and if they indulged in incendiarism.

Kirkwood stated that Lieutenant Larkin was wounded and one of the rioters killed, but he advanced as far as Panch Kor Naka. In the ensuing confrontation, he estimated the total number of casualties to have been six or seven.[29] Later, when Lieutenant Fitzpatrick was posted at the Panch Kor Naka, from 11.30 a.m. till the evening, he too had to fire on the crowd that kept advancing closer, despite warnings.

Interestingly, in Ahmedabad, where the crowd was far more organised than in Amritsar and had even managed to access guns and swords (though this might have been exaggerated by the British officers), the violence was more or less under control and at no point was there any indiscriminate firing. However, it is also apparent that the number of casualties on the Indian side must have been higher than the numbers stated in the HC Report.

Other officers, such as Lieutenant Morris, who were in charge of the troops, also had to resort to firing. The trouble went on through the night, with some more government buildings being burnt. It was a very difficult situation and the police joined in the firing alongside, as per the testimonies of Sub Inspector Kothawala and Deputy Superintendent Shirgaonkar. However, there was no large-scale attack on Europeans in the mill area (barring the few incidents already

---

29. Hunter Committee Report, p. 17.

mentioned) or the suburbs, and they were given shelter at Shahibagh and the railway station, where they remained under military protection.

Meanwhile, it was felt that the troops, which had been on their feet all day needed to be relieved, but the train bringing British troops from Bombay had been derailed and the telegraph wires connecting Bombay and Ahmedabad had been cut. Sanitation was an issue. The electric power station had been shut down and the drainage pumping system no longer worked. The municipal staff had gone on leave.

On 12 April, Colonel Frazer, the Officer Commanding, with the concurrence of Chatfield, the District Magistrate, issued a proclamation which stated:

1. Any gathering of over 10 individuals collected in one spot will be fired at;
2. Any single individual seen outside any house who does not stop and come up when challenged between the hours of 7 p.m. and 6 a.m. will be shot.

Unlike Amritsar, however, good care was taken to ensure that the orders were properly distributed and understood. The British troops arrived from Bombay and the situation rapidly returned to normal. There were still a few occasions when firing was resorted to as crowds refused to disperse, but by the afternoon of 13 April, everything was peaceful. Following Gandhi's arrival and a calming speech by him on 14 April, all bans and restrictions were also removed.[30]

Meanwhile, some other areas in Ahmedabad district had experienced violence, such as Viramgam, where a Junior Magistrate was murdered by a violent group of protestors on 13 April. MacIlvride, a Traffic Inspector, was brutally attacked at the railway station and escaped only in disguise. Six Indians were said to have been killed and eighteen wounded. The

---

30. Hunter Committee Report, p. 18.

treasury was looted (₹58,499 was the estimate) and 25 undertrial prisoners were released from jail by the rioters.[31]

In all these areas, the situation was quickly brought under control. Of course, there were arrests. The number of people placed on trial was 167 in Ahmedabad, 50 in Viramgam, and 82 in Kaira. A total of 123 were convicted and 25 were given transportation for life (this included one death sentence, which was later commuted). Rigorous imprisonment was pronounced for the rest, with sentences varying between 6 weeks and 14 years. A further 140 in Ahmedabad and 41 in Kaira district were released after their arrest as there was no evidence to convict them.[32] This again was in sharp contrast to the situation in Punjab where the war against the people carried on for months and evidence continued to be concocted against those who were arrested.

The unrest continued till Gandhi and Sarabhai arrived back in Ahmedabad, and Gandhi met the Commissioner. Prohibitory orders were later withdrawn and on 14 April, Gandhi addressed a large gathering, which he chastised for violent behavior, urging them all to return to work. With this the Satyagraha Movement was called off and the violence came to an immediate halt, barring an incident at Sarkhej, around six miles from Ahmedabad, where a police post was burnt and the police were stripped and beaten.

Despite the spread of violence outside Ahmedabad, there was no attempt to make it appear as though a large-scale revolution was taking place. There was no call to impose martial law, and there were no fancy punishments.

In Bombay too, the disturbances following the news of Gandhi's arrest (published in *Bombay Chronicle* on 10 April) were brought under control fairly quickly, even though the

---

31. Op. cit., pp. 20, 22.

32. Op. cit., p. 28.

police remained on high alert. Close to midnight on 10 April, a wire was received by the Bombay Commissioner of Police that told of disturbances in Lahore and Amritsar. Even as crowds began to gather, shouting 'Hindu Mussalman ki jai' and 'Mahatma Gandhi ki jai', and a request was sent for more troops at around 3 p.m., Gandhi arrived in Bombay. The crowds thronged to Chowpatty Beach where he addressed them, and things calmed down again.

Was this the simple solution that, if implemented by O'Dwyer, could have saved Punjab from cruel repression and the loss of thousands of lives? What if he had allowed Gandhi to address the people, or even allowed freedom for Kitchlew and Satya Pal? On hindsight, was a great mistake made by removing the leaders and leaving the large crowds, who were already restless, rudderless as well?

The Government of Bombay (unlike the Government of Punjab, which had claimed all kinds of conspiracy theories to justify the large-scale loss of life) told the Hunter Committee that the disturbances 'were attended by no fatal casualties, or extensive destruction of public or private property. There was no suspension of the normal course of administration or of civil control over law and order. Offences committed in the course of the disturbances were dealt with by the permanent magisterial courts. There was no serious dislocation for any considerable time of the normal life of the city.'[33]

The question asks itself then: If the situation in other places could be quickly brought under control, what was so different about what transpired in Amritsar and other parts of Punjab?

---

33. Hunter Committee Report, p. 26.

6

'You Cannot Kill a Tiger Gently'

> They say that it was brutal and horrible to kill so many people. There are three ideas which occur to me. You cannot put out a fire in a warehouse, which has caught well alight, with a teacup. Equally, as has been said, if your house catches fire, it is no use telling the fireman, after he has put your fire out, that he has used too much water to do it. You cannot kill a tiger gently, I defy you to do it. Lastly, supposing a burglar came into your house, and you had a life preserver, and hit him on the head with the intention of stunning him, it is impossible to say what force you would use.
>
> —Lieutenant Colonel James, MP[1]

Looking at the evidence a hundred years on, it is difficult to escape the reality that Punjab had been enslaved by a group of men led by O'Dwyer who believed that the natives were incapable of self-rule or having a voice. Anyone who challenged the system had to be wiped out. There was no space for dialogue since the British always knew best and the Indians, like naughty children, had to be punished, coerced or rewarded into good behaviour.

---

1. UK Parliamentary Hansard, 1920.

One year before the Amritsar massacre, on a trip to India, the embattled Secretary of State for India, Edwin Montagu, was not complimentary in his description of O'Dwyer, whom he met several times. Though the proposed Montagu-Chelmsford Reforms were being hammered out to build up a power-sharing module, it was staunchly resisted by administrators like O'Dwyer. Montagu said after meeting him, 'O'Dwyer frankly wants… that the Government of India may protect him against the inhabitants of Punjab.' Calling him 'long, pugnacious, narrow,' Montagu said O'Dwyer 'would not have anything, particularly no elected majority.'[2]

He added that 'O'Dwyer… is still opposed to everything. As his memoranda show, he is determined to maintain his position as the idol of the reactionary forces and to try and govern by the iron hand.'[3]

But O'Dwyer had his supporters.

While in India, Montagu wrote in January 1918, after a meeting with Viceroy Chelmsford and others, 'I heard them say, to my amazement, that it was a most disquieting sign that agitation was spreading to the villages. What was the unfortunate politician in India to do? He was told he could not have self government because there were no electorate, because only the educated wanted it, because the villagers had no political instincts; and then when he went out into the villages to try and make an electorate, to try and create a political desire, he was told he was agitating, and that the agitation must be put a stop to.' He did not think that interning the politician was an answer.[4]

Meanwhile, British historians have spent years digging

---

2. Edwin Montagu, *An Indian Diary* (London: William Heinemann Ltd., London, 1930), pp. 207–9.

3. Montagu, *An Indian Diary*, pp. 207–9.

4. Montagu, *An Indian Diary*, p. 216.

into Dyer's life to find some evidence that could foreshadow his murder of hundreds of innocents. He was actually a classic, patriarchal representative of the deep schisms that existed at the time and he did what so many others in his place would have easily done. There was underlying mistrust and suspicion of the natives, who had risen once before in 1857 and could do so again. The British may have been fewer in number, and yet they ruled and encouraged men like Dyer to believe that they, the British, were superior. But no one, not even an officer bent upon saving the Empire, should have been congratulated for murdering subjects of his own country, in cold blood. Even if they had a different skin colour.

But discrimination did exist—and Montagu felt that Indians were despised by the British. While in 1919, the Suffragettes in England succeeded in getting the vote for women, in India self-government remained a distant dream. Montagu had said in 1917, on his Indian trip. 'I am confirmed in my belief that the reasons which make self government impossible in this country now are not really distrust or unfitness or lack of ability or want of character. Unfortunately, there are some people, many people, who agree on this fact that self government is impossible now, but agree because they despise the Indian...'[5]

Gandhi, along with the commissioners of the Congress Sub-Committee Report, condemned the system rather than any one individual and requested that the officers who had suppressed the disorders be relieved from duty—O'Dwyer, General Dyer, Colonel O'Brien, Bosworth Smith, as well as two Indians: Rai Sahib Sri Ram Sud and Malik Saieb Khan. (The brutalities were often supported and perpetuated by Indian collaborators, who were generously rewarded.) They said that Colonel MacRae and Captain Doveton had failed too, but they were young and inexperienced, and 'their brutality was not so studied and calculated as that of the experienced Officers'.

---

5. Montagu, *An Indian Diary*, p. 136.

The INC Report, as well as the Minority Report of the Hunter Committee, were far more critical than the Hunter Committee Majority Report. The INC Report also requested that Viceroy Chelmsford be recalled as he had ignored 'telegrams and letters from individual and public bodies. He endorsed the action of the Punjab government without enquiry. He clothed the officials with indemnity in indecent haste. He never went to Punjab to make a personal inquiry even after the occurrences. He ought to have known, at least in May, everything that the various officials have admitted, and yet he failed to inform the public or the imperial Government of the full nature of the Jallianwala Bagh massacre or the subsequent acts done under law.' It was a long list of omissions, made worse by the fact that there were plenty of warnings. Even when responsible people like Pandit Malaviya had raised questions in the Imperial Legislative Council, he chose to ignore them.

As has already been pointed out, there was enough physical distance between the Lieutenant Governor and the Viceroy for anyone to go rogue. Information took a long time to reach, so it wasn't hard to keep something quiet. This was nowhere more evident than in Punjab, where bans were placed on the most vocal newspapers and martial law curtailed the free movement of people.

In many ways, O'Dwyer created the conditions in which someone like Dyer could kill with impunity—just as he gave an opportunity to Johnson to whip people in public and Bosworth Smith to humiliate. He was in agreement with Sir Aukland Colvin, once Governor of the United Provinces (UP) who said:

> Whatever may be hazarded with the educated minority, the real India is only to be found in the masses of the ignorant millions. To govern this real India, authority and justice should be in full view, but in reserve must be ample force. These are the only methods which under their own rule the masses of that country have ever respected, not even at the

desire of the British Government will they readily adopt any other.[6]

O'Dwyer found Colvin's words so moving that he wrote: 'The views (Colvin's) so admirably expresses are those which many of us, more crudely, in vain endeavoured to impress on those responsible for the Reforms (of 1919).'[7] O'Dwyer lamented the fact that 'a change has come over the spirit of (India's) rulers' as men like Montagu worked to reform the imperial system and to share power with their subjects. He was certain this would only lead to anarchy in India.

That O'Dwyer believed in 'ample force' was quite apparent in the manner in which he ruled Punjab, even before the disorders. For instance, he was very proud of how many soldiers Punjab was able to provide to fight in the World War. In fact, it could be argued that it was precisely this forced recruitment—largely done through a programme of coercion, inducement and rewards—which caused unrest, especially as recruitment carried on after the war as well.

Most families in Punjab—given the scale of recruitment—would have had someone in the army, posted in some distant land, with whom their only connection was through the 'goras'. This gave O'Dwyer and his kind enormous power, more than in other 'non-martial' states.

There are, of course, romantic stories of Indians fighting for the British and the close links this created; of friendship and shared concerns. In actuality, these were terrible postings. Soldiers were away from home for months on end and expected to perform heroic tasks for European countries they barely recognised. They were separated from their families at a young age, and had to deal with post-traumatic stress disorders when

---

6. Shireen Ilahi, *Imperial Violence and the Path to Independence: India, Ireland and the Crisis of Empire* (London: I.B. Tauris, 2016), p. 168.

7. Ilahi, *Imperial Violence*, p. 168.

they returned, with little or no help available. Their families, in turn, had to deal with a lack of young, able-bodied men in the state, leaving many young women either unmarried or widowed at a very young age. The impact of this ruthless militarisation may have propagated the myth of the 'macho' martial races, but the consequences, including gender imbalance and a marked preference for a male child, are still being felt today.

In the early 1900s, especially following World War I, it would have come as a rude shock to the British that the urban youth of Punjab and their families were choosing to go into professions other than the army, such as law, in which they were not subservient to their colonisers. Education was not widespread, nor was it a priority with the British, as admitted by Montagu.

The British were desperate to keep the 'martial races' of Punjab on their side. It was the one state where the soldiers had stood by them even in 1857. The thought that they may have begun to lose faith in the Empire was difficult to bear.

This was also a state where rebellions were becoming more and more frequent. To counter this, public gestures of loyalty were encouraged—indeed, enforced. In Punjab, school children and college-going youth were expected to salute the Union Jack multiple times, every day.

O'Dwyer, who was posted in Punjab between 1913 and 1919 as Lieutenant Governor, notes in his memoir that while in 1914, 28,000 men were raised, of whom 14,000 came from Punjab, by the end of 1916, 'the Punjab which had started the War with 100,000 men in the Army, had supplied 110,000 out of the 192,000 fighting men raised in India'.[8] This was obviously a proud moment for him.

He pushed the numbers ever higher, and believed that there was enthusiasm for the war among the 'martial races'. As he

---

8. Michael O'Dwyer, *India As I Knew It* (London: Constable & Company Ltd., 1925), p. 217.

puts it: 'The association of the martial races with the Army had become steadily closer, the material benefits of military service had been realised, interest and enthusiasm for the War were stimulated by the civil authorities; the announcement that Indian troops were to fight against a European foe on the Western front caused widespread enthusiasm...'

He adds that civil officials and rural 'men of influence' were asked to help in recruitment. New depots were opened and 'Finally, and this was the most effective of all, inducements to the Punjab peasant.' He said that as soon as the war broke out, 'I put at the disposal of the Commander-in-Chief one hundred and eighty thousand acres of valuable canal irrigated land for allotment to Indian officers and men who served with special distinction in the field. I also set aside some fifteen thousand acres for reward grants to those who gave most effective help in raising recruits.' These thousands of acres of land in inducements turned Punjab into a hunting ground for agents who began to scout for suitable men and boys to place in the army. These agents grew rich and owned large landholdings. Many of these collaborators would sustain their material and social dominance in independent India as well.

Even more effort was put into the recruitment process from February 1917 onwards, and 'all assistance in raising men for the Army was made a duty of all executive and village officials and of all who were enjoying grants of land or other marks of consideration from Government, and one of the main qualifications in establishing claims on Government.'[9]

Recruitment became a primary function of all government officials and anyone who wanted anything at all from the government. O'Dwyer, without much concern for the freedom of the people he was governing—who were, after all, British subjects enjoying some amount of liberty—commented:

---

9. O'Dwyer, *India As I Knew It*, p. 219.

'... the recruiting organisation was rapidly expanded by the appointment of experienced civilians, official and non-official, with a knowledge of the people, as assistants to the military recruiting officers; Indian officials or non-officials of influence were employed on recruiting work in nearly every district; the territorial force of recruitment by which suitable men of every class could be enrolled in nearly every district was substituted for the old class system under which there were only four recruiting centres, Rawal Pindi for Mohammedans, Amritsar for Sikhs, Jullundur for Dogras and Delhi for Jats; while in the more backward districts, unaccustomed to military service local depots were established for the training of the young recruits near their homes.' The system of rewards continued to be applied and 'were such as would appeal to the Oriental mind, such as Indian titles of honour from "Raja" and "nawab" down to "Rai Sahib" and "Khan Sahib", robes of honour, swords of honour, guns... cash rewards.' Depending on how much help the individual had given in recruitment, the grants could go up to 15,000 acres of land.[10]

While O'Dwyer insisted in his memoir that these and other recruitment processes were not meant to 'denude the martial tribes of the flower of their manhood,' the fact was that the target for the year beginning 1 July 1917, for the province, was set at over 200,000 men.[11] He explains that the quotas for each district were based on knowledgeable assessments by local experts. A War League or a Recruitment Board was set up, headed by the Deputy Commissioner as President. Each village 'was told what further numbers it was expected to provide'. As they ventured into newer territory for recruitment, some resistance did arise, and O'Dwyer admitted to at least a few cases of people refusing to join the army in Punjab.

---

10. O'Dwyer, *India As I Knew It*, pp. 219, 224.

11. O'Dwyer, *India As I Knew It*, p. 221.

He hit out at Montagu and his visit in 1917–18 to India as diverting attention from the war effort towards political reform. 'The visit of the then Secretary of State (Mr Montagu) to work out the scheme of reforms at the end of 1917, gave the "politically minded" classes an excuse for forgetting that India, with the rest of the Empire, was still in the throes of a death struggle.' But he claimed that the 'fighting races' were unlikely to forget that those clamouring for 'Swaraj' showed little inclination to defend their country.[12]

Punjab grew more and more uneasy following the King Emperor's appeal in April 1918. At a public meeting in Lahore in May 1918, it was 'unanimously decided' to furnish the quota of 200,000 men. It was also decided that if voluntary measures failed, 'other means' were to be adopted.

The pressure remained even after the armistice was announced. In August and September, 21,000 were recruited each month. This was not a happy time, as more than half a million people succumbed to an influenza epidemic. The price of food was shooting up. In the cities, there was growing restlessness: the idea of political reform, introduced by Montagu, was gaining currency.

According to the INC Report, there were instances of recruitment in the rural areas in particular, which amounted to coercion.[13] In Shahpur district, a tahsildar, Nadir Hussain Shah, was murdered because of his methods of pressure and persuasion. According to a witness, Shah would get hold of a list of possible recruits prepared by the patwari. He would then visit the village to find out more and gauge whether there were any objections to his recruiting men. He would usually ask a family for their consent, but the witness admitted that the zamindars of the area used to run away when they heard

---

12. O'Dwyer, *India As I Knew It*, p. 229.
13. INC Report, p. 19.

the tahsildar was coming as they did not want to be employed. Some form of force was undoubtedly used—some of the men were stripped naked in front of the women of the household, and women were allegedly abducted in order to force men to join the army.

In another case, in the village of Yara in Karnal district, a number of boys were induced to offer themselves as recruits.[14] However, the father of one of them 'entreated the Magistrate not to take from him his only son'. In the scuffle that followed, five people were convicted under the Defence of India Act. 'It appears from the judgement that the lower court had acted under the express orders of Mr Hamilton, the District Magistrate,' the Appellate Court stated and added, 'The various orders passed by the District Magistrate from time to time clearly show that if these appellants had also supplied recruits from among their near relations or if they were fit for enlistment themselves, they would have been let off, provided twenty recruits were made up from the villages as was originally demanded from it.' Indeed, twenty recruits were supplied, but the District Magistrate wanted twenty from the same family. This was a bizarre demand and was only meant, no doubt, to create more trouble for the already distressed family.

It is particularly interesting to note what happened in Gujranwala, which had been picked as a bombing site just after the massacre at Jallianwala Bagh. Was it to firmly quell any open defiance over the recruitment drive?

Recruitment in Gujranwala had shot up once Colonel O'Brien took charge. From a contribution of 3,888 (or one in every 150 of the male population) it increased, in August 1918, to 11,795. This was hailed as a triumph by O'Dwyer at a durbar at Gujranwala. He said it 'gives a ratio of one in every 44 of the total male population and one in every 14 of military

---

14. INC Report, p. 21.

age. Thus within a year you have raised 8,500 men. This is a triumphant instance of successful organisation, mainly due to the untiring activities of your admirable District War League, under the inspiring and energetic guidance of your Deputy Commissioner, Colonel O'Brien, and his assistants, backed up by the Divisional Recruiting Officer, Major Barnes, and his recruiting staff.'

The INC Report records another instance of forced recruitment. Sardar Khan, from Gujranwala district, described how everyone was summoned to the village daira one morning. A man had gone around the previous night, beating a drum and making the announcement. He also described how, as it was Baisakhi and harvest time, only a small number showed up, worried that they would be recruited. The tahsildar then levied a fine on around 60 people, which amounted to ₹1,600.

However, the matter did not end there. They were asked to come to Gujranwala, which was 18 miles away. 'When the people went there on the fixed date, they were made to stand in a row and seven young men were picked out... The other people were abused and beaten and told to bring more recruits.'[15]

These coercive methods led to desperate families purchasing recruits, or forcing those from a lower strata to go in place of their own children, as happened in Multan. In Ambala, the Commissioner reported: 'In order to make up the quota, the people resorted to the not unnatural expedient of subscribing large sums to be given to young men to enlist, 500 or 1000 rupees being the price of a recruit.'[16]

Not just forcible recruitment, but war loans were levied too, and money was collected for the Imperial War Fund. The war loan was particularly attractive to the title hunter, as Sardar Sant Singh Vakil of Lyallpur put it. 'Title hunters exacted the war

---

15. INC Report, p. 22.
16. INC Report, pp. 20–1.

loan from the masses in order to win honour for themselves... No exception was made. Even an adjudged bankrupt had to pay it.'

Due to this combination of forcible recruitment—war loans and the Imperial War Fund—large parts of rural Punjab were at the mercy of touts and agents. People were also forced to pay into an Aeroplane Fund. Ironically, the aircraft they helped purchase were used to bomb Gujranwala.

Not much of this was known in England and till the incident at Jallianwala Bagh became public knowledge, it is possible that even the Secretary of State was oblivious to the true state of affairs in Punjab. It was only after 9 June 1919, when martial law ended and censorship was lifted, that information began to pour out of Punjab. Prior to that, there was even a ban on lawyers entering Punjab and offering help to the undertrials. Many of these cases therefore received scant attention, and even prominent people like Dr Kitchlew were treated poorly while in jail and during the so-called trial stage.

He was to state in his evidence that he had been kept in solitary confinement, in dreadful conditions, for a month and a half, before he was shifted to a larger jail room in the Central Jail at Lahore. But he had little opportunity to instruct his counsel as the English Superintendent insisted on being present. He said: 'The trial was a huge farce. The attitude of the presiding Judge was obviously hostile to the accused persons. Prosecution witnesses who deposed in our favour were bullied by the court. Our counsel were often told that they were allowed to appear for the defence only as a matter of courtesy, otherwise they had no right to be there. They were treated not only with scant courtesy but were not even allowed to cross examine prosecution witnesses at length. Even answers given by the prosecution witnesses were not recorded fully. The defence witnesses were maltreated by the Police as well as by the presiding Judge. In short, Mr Broadway behaved not as a judge but as a prosecutor. On the day when the judgement was delivered we were brought from the Jail to the court house, handcuffed two together. After conviction we were taken back to the Jail in the same condition.'[17]

Gandhi asked for a Royal Commission of Inquiry and the All India Congress Committee meeting at Allahabad had passed a resolution demanding an inquiry on 8 June. Letters and telegrams began to flow to the Government of India and to the Secretary of State, who had already begun the process of setting up an inquiry. On 11 June, Montagu asked the Government of India to 'submit proposals for its term and composition'. Meanwhile, the poet Rabindranath Tagore shocked the Western world by surrendering his knighthood because of the 'insults and sufferings endured by our brothers in the Punjab'.[18]

O'Dwyer had met Montagu in London on 30 June and 24 July, but did not share the details of the massacre at Jallianwala Bagh. He gave the impression that Dyer had fired at the crowd because he was worried about being assaulted. Chelmsford stated that it was an error in judgement on Dyer's part and that he had the opportunity 'of discussing the situation in the Punjab with the Bishop of Lahore, who reported... Indian villagers saying... that it was Dyer's prompt action which saved the situation from being infinitely worse.' It is unlikely that anyone would have said this—unless they were fearful of the consequences of disagreeing. There is little doubt that after the events in Punjab—taking into account the ruthless behaviour of O'Dwyer's men—fear was widespread, especially amongst the more vulnerable sections of society.

This was in sharp contrast to the attitude of the British in India, who regarded Dyer as a hero. European women spoke of facing a fate worse than death had Dyer not taken 'prompt

---

17. INC Report, Volume II, pp. 713–14.
18. Mohan, *An Imaginary Rebellion*, p. 1009.

action'. The story of the narrow escape by Sherwood, and Easdon in Amritsar, received wide circulation. Slowly, some parts of the British and English press in India began to follow that line. The word spread that Dyer had saved the Empire.

However, the Congress had, through Pandit Malaviya, a former member of the Imperial Legislative Council, and others, begun relief work in Punjab; they were also gathering information about all that had happened in the past three months. Sankaran Nair, who had just resigned from the Viceroy's Executive Council, was sent to England in July, to try to promote the idea of an official inquiry.

The official Committee of Inquiry that was eventually set up was presided over by Lord Hunter, and it recorded evidence at Delhi, Lahore and Bombay. However, in Punjab, there was an impasse because the jailed Punjab leaders were not given permission to appear before the Committee. Also, some of the evidence was recorded in camera, such as much of that of O'Dwyer, due to security reasons. It would be many decades before this was released into the public domain.

The All India Congress Committee, meanwhile, set up their own Sub-Committee under Pandit Malaviya, with Pandit Motilal Nehru and Mohandas Karamchand Gandhi as members.

Acting quickly, the Government of India sought to protect those whose actions would be questioned by the Hunter Committee and an Indemnity Bill came up for discussion on 19 September 1919. Reacting to the discussions, O'Dwyer said, 'Pandit Malaviya and others, who for months had been carrying on a virulent campaign against the Punjab Government and the officials who had crushed the rebellion, came forward with the wildest allegations against my misdeeds and Dyer's action at Amritsar.'[19] Needless to say, the Indemnity Bill was passed.

---

19. Rupert Furneaux, *Massacre at Amritsar* (George Allen and Unwin Ltd., 1963), p. 113.

Meanwhile, Dyer continued to serve in the army. There was no question of reprisals. Some red flags, however, began to be raised. While speaking about the Jallianwala Bagh massacre, Dyer had begun to change his narrative, saying he had wanted to issue a 'moral lesson'. His initial report, received on 14 April by General Beynon, revealed no such introspection, only a matter-of-fact documentation of events.

> I entered Jallianwala Bagh by a very narrow lane which necessitated my leaving my armoured cars behind.
> On entering I saw a dense crowd estimated at about 5000, a man on a raised platform addressing the audience and making gesticulations with his hands.
> I realised my force was small and to hesitate might induce attack. I immediately opened fire and dispersed the crowd.
> I estimate that between 200 and 300 of the crowd were killed. My party fired 1,650 rounds.

This information was passed on to London and, on 18 April 1919, the India Office had issued the following, almost terse, statement: 'At Amritsar April 13th the mob defied the proclamation forbidding public meetings. Firing ensued and 200 casualties occurred.' That was all that was known of the Jallianwala Bagh incident for a long time.

Nearly five months after the event, on 25 August 1919, Dyer wrote a detailed report of what happened on 13 April. Martial law had been lifted in Punjab and stories about the massacre were circulating in India and abroad.

Dyer exaggerated every step (those who have read his rather unbelievable autobiographical record in *The Raiders of the Sarhad* would be familiar with the strategy) to show that he had no choice but to fire.[20] He established the 'fact' that in Amritsar the

---

20. Reginald Dyer, *The Raiders Of The Sarhad: Being The Account of a Campaign of Arms and Bluff Against the Brigands of the Persian-Baluchi Border during the Great War* (London: H.F.&G Witherby, 1921).

crowd defied him and forced his hand. He gave the example of insolence shown by the mobs who, when his columns marched through the city, raised slogans of Hindu–Muslim unity. He pointed out that instead of firing at the crowd he had issued a proclamation banning meetings and warning that they would be fired upon. Yet the crowd had gathered at Jallianwala Bagh.

He added:

> The responsibility was very great. If I fired I must fire with good effect, a small amount of firing would be a criminal act of folly. I had the choice of carrying out very distasteful or horrible duty or of neglecting to do my duty, of suppressing disorder or of becoming responsible for all future bloodshed.
>
> We cannot be very brave unless we be possessed of a greater fear. I had considered the matter from every point of view, my duty and my military instincts told me to fire. My conscience was also clear on that point. What faced me was, what on the morrow would be the Danda Fauj.
>
> I fired and continued to fire until the crowd dispersed and I consider this the least amount of firing which would produce the necessary moral and widespread effect it was my duty to produce, if I was to justify my action. If more troops had been at hand the casualties would have been greater in proportion. It was no longer a question of merely dispersing the crowd; but one producing a sufficient moral effect, from a military point of view, not only those who were present but more specifically throughout the Punjab. There could be no question of undue severity.

He claimed, 'Many inhabitants have thanked me and recognised that I had committed a just and merciful act.' He said that he had been thanked by thousands and that Honorary Magistrates, leading citizens and Municipal Councillors had expressed their admiration for 'his firm action and told him he had saved Amritsar and indeed, all of Punjab, from plunder and bloodshed'.

Never one to shy away from self-praise, he added that 'acts of violence, plunder and bloodshed would immediately have been perpetrated on a much larger scale through India' had he not fired. In this bombast was true self-belief that by killing and wounding hundreds of people, he had prevented further bloodshed. There was also the confidence that he had sent out a 'moral' message.

However, his report (in August 1919) was the first confirmation that he had fired without warning and continued to fire for ten minutes, and it was the first time that the Government of India learnt about the actual circumstances.[21]

Despite all precautions, when he gave his evidence to the Hunter Committee, the reaction was one of shock. When he was questioned in Lahore on 19 November, 1919, even O'Dwyer found him 'indefensible'. Overall, the Committee listened to evidence for twenty-nine days in Lahore, three days in Bombay and eight days in Delhi.

Later, some would question why Dyer had not been provided with counsel. He was even warned by Beynon to be careful of the 'clever' Indian lawyers on the committee—Pandit Jagat Narayan, Sir Chimanlal Harilal Setalvad, and Sardar Sahibzada Sultan Ahmed Khan.

Sir George Barrow wrote in *The Life of General Sir Charles Carmichael Monro, Bart*: 'It would be interesting to know who it was denied Dyer the assistance of counsel. It was certainly not the Government of India, nor the Commander in Chief, not the Hunter Committee. On the contrary, counsel was pressed on Dyer by the government; and his friends, knowing his tendency to excitability, begged him to accept the assistance offered to him. Dyer obstinately refused saying he would and conduct his own case. Neither was he cross examined without warning. He had many days in which to prepare his evidence...'[22]

---

21. Furneaux, *Massacre at Amritsar*, p. 112.
22. Furneaux, *Massacre at Amritsar*, p. 119.

But his answers pleased no one.

The Pioneer reported that 'he was jeered by a gallery of students at the back of the improvised court and Lord Hunter signally failed to keep order or protect the witness against overzealous cross examination... that was fatal with a man of Dyer's temperament. He lost his temper.'

The interrogation by one of the 'clever' Indian lawyers, Setalvad, didn't go very well for Dyer.

Q: You took two armoured cars with you?

A: Yes.

Q: Those cars had machine guns?

A: Yes.

...

Q: Supposing the passage was sufficient to allow the armoured cars to go in, would you have opened fire with the machine guns?

A: I think probably yes.

Q: In that case the casualties would have been very much higher?

A: Yes.

Q: And you did not open fire with the machine guns simply by the accident of the armoured cars not being able to get in?

A: I have answered you. I have said that if they had been there the probability is that I would have opened fire with them.

Q: With the machine guns straight?

A: With the machine guns.

...

Q: Did it occur to you that by adopting this method of 'frightfulness'—excuse the term—you were really doing a great disservice to the British Raj by driving discontent deep?

A: No, it only struck me that at the time it was my duty to do this and that it was a horrible duty. I did not like the idea of doing it but I also realised that it was the only means of saving life and that any reasonable man with justice in his mind would realise that I had done the right thing: and it was a merciful through horrible act and they ought to be thankful to me for doing it.[23]

He added that it would be 'doing a jolly lot of good' and they (the people of Amritsar) would realise that they were not to be 'wicked'.

The 'brave' Brigadier General went on to admit that he had shot even those who were lying down. 'I wanted to punish the naughty boy.' Worse, he even admitted that he would have fired even if he had not made the proclamation in the morning, in which public meetings were banned.[24]

His arrogance was apparent to a 33-year-old Jawaharlal Nehru, as he was to write in his autobiography:

Towards the end of that year (1919) I travelled from Amritsar to Delhi by the night train. The compartment I entered was almost full and the berths, except the upper one, were occupied by sleeping passengers. I took the vacant upper berth. In the morning I discovered that all my fellow passengers were military officers. They conversed with each other in loud voices which I could not help overhearing. One of them was holding forth in an aggressive and triumphant tone and soon I discovered that he was Dyer, the hero of Jallianwala Bagh and he was describing his Amritsar experiences. He pointed out how he had the whole town at his mercy and he felt like reducing the rebellious city to a heap of ashes, but he took pity on it and refrained. He was evidently coming back from Lahore after giving his evidence before the Hunter Committee of Enquiry. I was greatly shocked to hear his conversation and to observe his

---

23. Parliamentary Report, pp. 112–14.

24. Parliamentary Report, pp. 112–14.

callous manner. He descended at Delhi station in pyjamas with bright pink stripes and a dressing gown.[25]

Following the revelations of the Hunter Committee, Edwin Montagu had to admit in the House of Commons that he had no idea of the 'details' of the massacre till he read about it in the press.

The 200-page Hunter Committee Report that was issued on 26 May 1920 shocked many. The Committee criticised Dyer for giving the crowd insufficient time to disperse; they felt that he should not have continued to fire after the crowd at Jallianwala Bagh began to disperse and that his intent to produce a moral effect on both the crowd and the Punjab was in error and should be condemned. They also upheld that the administration of 'fancy punishments' was in error.

The Hunter Committee concluded that while Dyer had wanted to create a 'wide impression', he had, by indiscriminately killing innocent people, 'produced such a deep impression throughout the length and breadth of the country, so prejudicial to the British Government that it would take a good deal and a long time to rub it out.' His action could only be compared to the acts of frightfulness committed by some of the German military commanders during the war in Belgium and France.

Dyer was shown to be clearly in the wrong. The Committee said he thought 'he had crushed the rebellion, and Sir Micahel O' Dwyer was of the same view. There was no rebellion which required to be crushed. We feel that General Dyer by adopting an inhuman and un-British method of dealing with subjects of His Majesty the King Emperor has done great disservice to the interest of British rule in India. This aspect it was not possible for the people of the mentality of General Dyer to realise...'[26]

The battleground to determine what had happened in

---

25. Jawaharlal Nehru, *An Autobiography* (1936), pp. 43–4. Accessed at https://archive.org/details/in.ernet.dli.2015.98834.

26. Parliamentary Report, p. 115.

Punjab now shifted to the British Parliament. In India, finally, some steps were taken to ensure that punitive measures were taken against Dyer. It is important to note that he was the only one singled out, as perhaps his was the greatest folly. None of the others—O'Dwyer, Kitchin, Irving, Johnson, O'Brien, Bosworth Smith and so on—were punished.

Ironically, despite the Hunter Committee Report and widespread recriminations in the press, Dyer was promoted as head of a Division on 30 January 1920. However, the order was withdrawn on 14 February 1920. Ian Colvin, Dyer's biographer, suspected it was due to a question asked in the Legislative Council by Babu Kamini Kumar Chanda. The question was: 'Is it a fact that General Dyer received promotion after the firing in Jallianwala Bagh?' The Commander-in-Chief, General Sir Charles Munro, denied it. It would have quickly become obvious to all from that point onwards that Dyer had become a liability.

Dyer, who had fallen ill with gout and jaundice and also suffered from arteriosclerosis, was summoned to Delhi on 23 March 1920, to meet Munro. Sir Havelock Hudson, the Adjutant General, who had thus far been a supporter, now told him bluntly that following censure from the Hunter Committee, he was to be deprived of his command. This was confirmed by Munro.

On 27 March 1920, about a year after the killings at Jallianwala Bagh, Dyer wrote to his immediate superior, the General commanding the 2nd Division: 'Sir, I have the honour to state that during my recent visit to Delhi, the Adjutant General in India informed me that, owing to the opinion expressed by the Hunter Committee regarding my action in Amritsar during April 1919, it was necessary for me to resign my appointment as Brigadier-General commanding the Infantry Brigade. Accordingly, I hereby ask that I be relieved of that appointment.'

Still convinced of his own righteous behaviour, Dyer reached

London and constructed, with the help of a law firm—Messrs Sharp and Pritchard—a lengthy statement to place in front of the Army Council, which was to take the final decision on his case. He gave ever more reasons for the influences prevailing on him on 13 April 1919, as he entered Jallianwala Bagh, including the situation on the Afghan frontier, the possible threat to the lives of British men, women and children in Amritsar and throughout the Punjab, the danger of an uprising in rural areas for the purpose of committing other atrocities, the need to send out a strong message, and so on.

The Army Council's decision on the Dyer Case was announced on 7 July in the House of Commons. The Secretary of State for War, Sir Winston Churchill, who had forcefully argued against Dyer, said the Council felt Dyer had committed an error of judgment; he was to be retired on half pay with no prospects of future employment.

Almost immediately after the pronouncement, there was a popular outpouring of support for Dyer. A fund started by the rightwing newspaper, *Morning Post*, climbed to £26,317 within a few weeks. The contributors included a 'mutiny widow', 'a patriot', 'a beggar who loves justice', 'a widow and her daughter who know more about Amritsar than did Mr Montagu', and so on. This sum was much larger than the amount that would eventually be distributed among the families of those who had died in Jallianwala Bagh. Nothing could demonstrate the growing chasm between England and her colony than their starkly differing stand on the motivations and actions of Dyer.

In the House of Commons, though, there was a concentrated effort by both the Secretaries of State, Montagu and Winston Churchill, to condemn the actions of Dyer. Montagu, aware of the importance of the debate and battling stress, did not manage to make the case forcefully enough, although he made some very salient points.

Montagu was himself attacked for his liberal views, and his Jewish background was used to colour his actions at the India

Office. He became a victim of widespread anger during the debate in the House of Commons. Both Dyer and O'Dwyer were in the visitors' gallery, along with some Indian princes. The benches were notably crowded as the press was also closely covering the proceedings. Austin Chamberlain, the Chancellor of the Exchequer, described the scene when Montagu began to condemn Dyer, in the face of palpable animosity:

> I hope that I shall not have such a house as confronted Montagu on Thursday, and that, if I do, I shall not handle it so maladroitly. With the House in that temper nothing could have been so infuriating to it as his opening remarks—no word of sympathy with Dyer, no sign that Montagu appreciated his difficulties, but as it were a passionate peroration to a speech that had not been delivered, a grand finale to a debate which had not begun. Our party has always disliked and distrusted him. On this occasion all their English and racial feeling was stirred to a passionate display—I think I have never seen the House so fiercely angry—and he threw fuel on the flames. A Jew, rounding on an Englishman and throwing him to the wolves—that was the feeling.[27]

Opening the debate, which lasted for over nine hours, Montagu asked: 'Are you going to keep your hold upon India by terrorism, racial humiliation and subordination and frightfulness, or are you going to rest it upon the goodwill, and the growing goodwill, of the people of your Indian empire? I believe that to be the whole question at issue.'[28]

He went on to say, 'Once you are entitled to have regard neither to the intentions nor to the conduct of a particular gathering, and to shoot and go on shooting with all the horrors that were here involved, in order to teach somebody else a lesson, you are embarking on terrorism, to which there is no end.'

---

27. Sir Charles Petrie, *The Life and Letters of Sir Austen Chamberlain* (London: Cassell, 1940), pp. 152–3.

28. UK Parliamentary Hansard.

As Meghnad Desai writes in *Rediscovery of India*, it was Churchill who rescued Montagu that evening. He made a powerful speech against Dyer, whom he criticised for 'resorting to a doctrine of "frightfulness".'

> What I meant by frightfulness is the inflicting of great slaughter or massacre upon a particular crowd of people with the intention of terrorising not merely the rest of the crowd, but the whole district or country...Frightfulness is not a remedy known to British pharmacopoeia. This is not a British way of doing business.

Pointing squarely at the pro-Dyer Tories, he added:

> However we may dwell upon the difficulties of General Dyer, during the Amritsar riots, upon the anxious and critical situation in the Punjab, upon the danger to Europeans throughout that province, upon the long delays which have taken place in reaching a decision about his office, upon the procedure that was at this point or that point adopted, however we may dwell upon all this, one tremendous fact stands out—I mean the slaughter of nearly 400 persons and the wounding of probably three or four times as many at the Jallian Wallah Bagh on 13 April.
>
> This is an episode which appears to me to be without precedent or parallel in the modern history of the British Empire. It is an event of an entirely different order from any of those tragical occurrences which take place when troops are brought into collision with the civil population. It is an extraordinary event, a monstrous event, an event which stands in singular and sinister isolation.[29]

Leading Liberal politicians forced a vote but the government was only successful by 101 votes. One hundred and nineteen of the 129 votes against the motion came from the government's

---

29. Meghnad Desai, *The Rediscovery of India* (Penguin Books India, 2009), pp. 138–9.

own Conservative coalition. This caused a split in the governing coalition that would eventually lead to the demise of Lloyd George's government.

The matter was not yet over; there was another round of debates in Parliament, this time in the House of Lords, on 19 and 20 July 1920. Here, 129 voted in favour of Dyer. He may have felt vindicated by such a large majority, especially as the session was well-attended. He was certainly 'pleased with the division... many peers greeted him afterwards in the lobby', reported the *Pall Mall Gazette*, on 21 July 1920.[30]

'There was a really brilliant scene in the House of Lords last night... Not since before the war', wrote the 'Clubman', 'had there been such a gathering of peeresses and the Stranger's Gallery was crowded with distinguished Ango-Indians and Indians. The Indians, many of them, wore gorgeous turbans, and the ladies wonderful robes of silk.'[31] Also present was the recently invested Duke of York (the future George VI), attending his first House of Lords debate.[32]

Among the sixteen speakers were five former Governors of Indian provinces, one former Viceroy, and three former Secretaries of State for India. Only six of them supported Viscount Finlay's motion that 'This House deplores the conduct of the case of General Dyer as unjust to that officer and as establishing a precedent dangerous to the preservation of order in the face of rebellion.'[33]

But the upholding of the motion, as the *Guardian* reported was 'A vote in favour—even indirectly—of Prussianism' in India by a House representing especially old British governing classes

---

30. As quoted by Derek Sayer in his paper on Jallianwala Bagh. Accessed online.
31. As quoted by Derek Sayer, *Pall Mall Gazette*, 20 July 1920.
32. As quoted by Derek Sayer, 21 July 1920.
33. UK Parliamentary Hansard.

'must not merely do harm in India... It must also do harm at home...'[34]

Prominent Indians were aghast. Rabindranath Tagore wrote from London on 22d July:

> The result of the Dyer debates in both Houses of Parliament makes painfully evident the attitude of mind of the ruling classes of the country towards India. It shows no outrage, however monstrous, committed against us by the agents of their Government, can arouse feelings of indignation in the hearts of those from whom our governors are chosen. The unashamed condonation of brutality expressed in their speeches and echoed in their newspapers is ugly in its frightfulness. The late events have conclusively proved that our true elevation lies in our own hands; that a nation's greatness can never find its foundation in half hearted concessions of contemptuous niggardliness.

Jawaharlal Nehru, who had collected evidence of the brutalities in Punjab, wrote:

> This cold blooded approval of that deed shocked me greatly. It seemed immoral, indecent, to use public school language. It was the height of bad form. I realised then, more vividly than I had ever done before, how brutal and immoral imperialism was, and how it had eaten into the souls of the British upper classes.

By August, Gandhi's opinion of the British had changed completely. He could no longer support the British in India. His letter to Viceroy Chelmsford on 2 August set the tone for future events:

> The punitive measures taken by General Dyer were out of all proportion to the crime of the people and amounted to wanton cruelty, and inhumanity, unparalleled in modern

---

34. 'An Unwise Voice', *Manchester Guardian*, 21 July 1920. Quoted by Derek Sayer in his paper on Jallianwala Bagh. Accessed online.

times; and your Excellency's lighthearted treatment of the official crime, your exoneration of Sir Michael O'Dwyer and Mr Montagu's dispatches, and above all, your shameful ignorance of the Punjab events and callous disregard of the feelings betrayed by the House of Lords, have filled me with greatest misgivings regarding the future of the Empire, have estranged me completely from the present government and have disabled me from tendering, as I have hitherto tendered, my loyal co-operation.

Gandhi also returned the medals he had received from the British government. The battle lines were now drawn. His hand forced by the increasing rancour between Indians and the government, King George V issued a Royal Proclamation of Amnesty on 23 December, 1919, to rule a Royal Clemency to those who had been convicted under the martial law. This meant a reduction of sentences, much to the horror of the British solicitors who had worked the trials. The clemency was strongly disapproved of by many of the British officials in India.

None of those who were guilty of the atrocities—British officers or their Indian collaborators—were punished, thanks to the Indemnity Act. And despite efforts to bridge the gap through reforms, the horror that the events in Punjab evoked would make Indians wary about trusting the British again.

Dyer withdrew from the publicity that had followed him ever since the massacre, and settled down to a reclusive life. He died on 23 July 1927. He was given a military funeral, but despite attempts by his 'well wishers' to put up a memorial in his name in India, it came to naught.

O'Dwyer was killed at Caxton Hall, on 13 March 1940, by Uddham Singh. It is believed (though not proven) that as a 16-year-old orphan, he had seen the massacre at Jallianwala Bagh and sworn revenge. Singh was hanged on 31 July 1940, at Pentonville Prison in London.

The Rowlatt Acts were never implemented. Accepting the report of the Repressive Laws Committee, the Government of India repealed the Rowlatt Acts, the Press Act, and 22 other laws in March 1922.

The deaths at Jallianwala Bagh would not go in vain. India won independence in 1947 and Gandhi, who could not forgive the British for what they had done in 1919, led the freedom struggle.

As he wrote: 'We do not want to punish Dyer. We have no desire for revenge. We want to change the system that produced Dyer.'

Appendix I
Lala Lajpat Rai on 'Imperialism Run Amuck'

The Punjab tragedy of 1919 is an event of historical importance. It is a chapter of the world's history—a bloody chapter albeit—dyed red by the high priests of Imperialism, which will retain its freshness whenever the future generations of men and women happen to read it. It has placed us in a position to visualise the barbaric possibilities of Imperialism run amuck. Modern Indians had been so inoculated with the serum of 'benevolent despotism' as to make them forget that it is easier for a leopard to change its spots than for Imperialism to alter its true nature. Benevolent Imperialism is like a caged lion. However, you may play with it so long as it is caged or under the spell of a master-tamer, the moment it gets out of control, it is bound to behave in conformity with its real nature. The atrocities perpetuated at Amritsar have proved that Imperialism run mad is more dangerous, more vindictive, more inhuman, than a frenzied uncontrollable mob. When a mob gets out of hand, it does things pretty bad and cruel; but its destructiveness is born of passion and is not deliberately planned and thought out. Imperialism on the other hand, as represented by the O'Dwyers, Dyers, O'Briens, Bosworth Smiths, Johnsons, Dovetons and others, takes revenge with a deliberate aim. It plans out with a fixed purpose, and carries out those plans in a spirit of military vindictiveness.

As to the causes of this tragedy, it should not be forgotten that the Punjab has been seething with discontent for more than twenty years. With its unique record of services in the cause of the Empire, having profusely shed its blood in the expansion and protection of British dominions all the world over, having given its best in developing British colonies and British possessions, the treatment it has received has been most cruel and bitter. In fact, that very circumstance has been the reason why the Imperial bureaucracy has considered it necessary to deny to this province the benefits of education and industrial development to the extent to which they have been fostered in other provinces. The Punjab peasantry has been deliberately kept in ignorance, because of its being the chief recruiting source of the Indian army and the military police. Its childlike faith in British justice and fair play has kept it politically backward and, in a way, inarticulate. Whatever political life was in the province was crushed by various methods of repression and corruption.

Numbers of educated young men were brought over to the Government side by rewards of lands, offices, titles and other inducements of a similar nature. Others, who proved above these temptations, were persecuted and maltreated. In this connection, I might mention in passing the unrest of 1907, the historic trial of Arya Samajists in 1909, the prosecutions for sedition of 1909-1910, the conspiracy cases of 1913-1914, and the political trials held during the war. This is neither the time nor the place to go into details; but it is obvious that these were indications of growing unrest and discontent which should have moved any wise administration to initiate measures of conciliation. Instead of that, the defiant attitude of Sir Michael O'Dwyer, his firm faith in militarism, his iron and blood policy of keeping down all agitation and stopping the free expression of public opinion, together with the contempt which he displayed towards the aspirations of the Indians for self government, only added fuel to the fire. Thus the Rowlatt Act was only the proverbial straw on the camel's back. The successful hartals of the 30th March and 6th April descended upon him and his henchmen like a bolt from the blue. The bureaucracy had all along been deluded and deceived by the false though reassuring, reports of their agents, spies and admirers; but now they found themselves suddenly disillusioned and in a fit of anger decided to embark upon a policy of unbridled retaliation and reprisals against those who had participated in the agitation against the Rowlatt Act. This short-sighted policy of the Late Lieutenant Governor and the arbitrary methods adopted to penalise those who had taken part in the agitation against the Rowlatt Act led to riots, which were followed by the declaration of martial law and all that followed it its wake.

We were brought up in an atmosphere of 'benevolent despotism' and fed on the idea of British Imperialism being something quite different from other isms of the same character. Our disillusionment began some 20 years ago; but it required an O'Dwyer and a Dyer and a Jallianwala Bagh to complete the process. Coming so soon after the Great War, which was fought ostensibly to destroy Imperialism and Militarism, the Punjab tragedy has cleared the atmosphere which enveloped the war aims of the Allies and shown the brute in its naked form. The Indians are today cursing Sir Michael O'Dwyer, General Dyer, and others; but in my humble judgement, it is the system which needs cursing, if that can give satisfaction to the aggrieved. The men are the mere tools of circumstances. They may overdo a thing, but so long as they are told that the maintenance of the system is the main thing and has to be done at any cost, their fault is only secondary. If the administration of Sir Michael O'Dwyer and the Punjab tragedy enacted by him awakens the Indians to a sense of their duty in the matter, the blood of hundreds (including children) who died at Jallianwala Bagh, Gujranwala, Lahore and other places, would not have been spilled in vain. The blood of the innocents calls not for vengeance, but the putting forth of every iota of our energy to get rid of the bureaucratic system of Government, under which we have lived for the last 70 years or so.

...A year ago, I had some kind of confidence in Mr Montagu's statesmanship; and I was under the impression that when full facts are known to him, he would not fail to heal up the wounds inflicted on the Punjab by Sir Michael O'Dwyer and his lieutenants. I had no hope in the Government of India, I had no hope in the British Cabinet; but I had some little hope in Mr Montagu, which has been completely shattered by the orders he has passed on the Hunter Committee's Report. The Government of India has failed us, as it was bound to, because it was practically a party to the whole series of oppressive measures which led to the disturbances and subsequent introduction of martial law. The Government of India being one of the guilty parties, they could not be expected to pronounce an adverse judgement on themselves. The Secretary of State has also deserted us. Our only hope lies in ourselves. The duty is two fold: first, to leave nothing undone to bring the true facts to the knowledge of the civilised world as extensively as our resources would permit; and secondly, to think out and put into practice plan of action which would impress upon the Government the fact that we are not prepared to tolerate similar outrages upon our honour and liberty. The Government must know that these methods of governing India are dead: and unless the ruling caste is ready to accept the change in the situation, the task of governing India would be extremely difficult and full of perils and pitfalls. Whether we shall inaugurate a campaign of non cooperation or passive resistance or what, I cannot say yet...But this much I might be permitted to say my educated countrymen, that the question whether they will be treated in the future as men or as beasts of burden depends in large measure on their own conduct and behaviour. It is for them to decide whether they are ready to sacrifice their individual preferments for the honour of the nation, or whether they will choose to be satisfied with the few crumbs that are thrown to them from the master's table and go to sleep again. Let us never forget that 'nations by themselves are made.'

Lahore   LAJPAT RAI
5 June, 1920

From the 'Foreword' by Lala Lajpat Rai in *An Imaginary Rebellion and How It Was Suppressed: An Account of the Punjab Disorders and the Working of Martial Law by* Pandit Pearay Mohan, published in Lahore in 1920 by Khosla Bros.

Appendix II
Rabindranath Tagore's Protest

The following letter was sent by Sir Rabindranath Tagore to his Excellency the Viceroy on 31 May 1919, asking to be 'released' of his title of Knighthood, following the atrocities in Punjab.

Your Excellency,

The enormity of the measures taken by the Government in the Punjab for quelling some local disturbances has, with a rude shock, revealed to our minds the helplessness of our position as British subjects in India. The disproportionate severity of the punishment inflicted upon the unfortunate people and the methods of carrying them out, we are convinced are without parallel in the history of civilised Governments, barring some conspicuous exceptions, recent and remote. Considering that such treatment has been meted out to a population disarmed and resourceless by a power which has the most terribly efficient organisation for destruction of human lives, we must strongly assert that it can claim no political expediency, far less moral justification. The accounts of insults and sufferings undergone by our brothers in the Punjab have trickled through the gagged silence, reaching every corner of India, and the universal agony of indignation roused in the hearts of our people has been ignored by our rulers—possibly congratulating themselves for imparting what they imagine as statutory lessons. This callousness has been praised by most of the Anglo-Indian papers, which have in some cases gone to the brutal length of making fun of our sufferings, without receiving the least check from the same authority, relentlessly careful in smothering every cry of pain and expression of judgement from the organs representing the sufferers. Knowing that our appeals have been in vain and that the passion of vengeance is blinding the noble vision of statesmanship in our Government, which could so easily afford to be magnanimous as befitting its physical strength and moral tradition, the very least that I can do for my country is to take all consequences upon myself in giving voice to the protest of the millions of my countrymen, surprised into a dumb anguish of terror. The time has come when badges of honour make our shame glaring in their incongruous context of humiliation, and I for my part wish to stand shorn of all special distinctions, by the side of those of my countrymen who, for their so called insignificance, are liable to suffer degradation not fit for human beings. And these are the reasons which have painfully compelled me to ask Your Excellency, with due deference and regret, to release me of my title of knighthood which I had the honour to accept from His Majesty the King at the hands of your predecessor, for whose nobleness of heart I still entertain great admiration.

Yours faithfully
Rabindranath Tagore

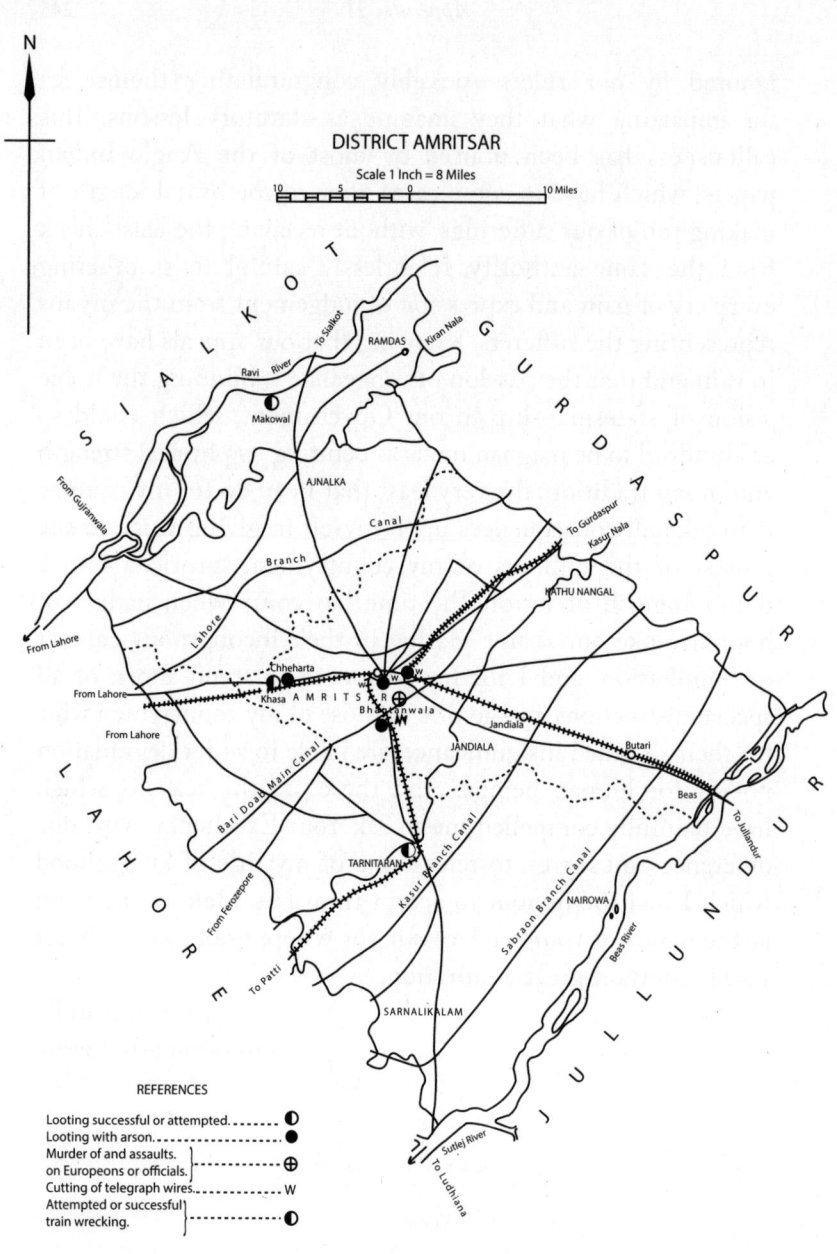

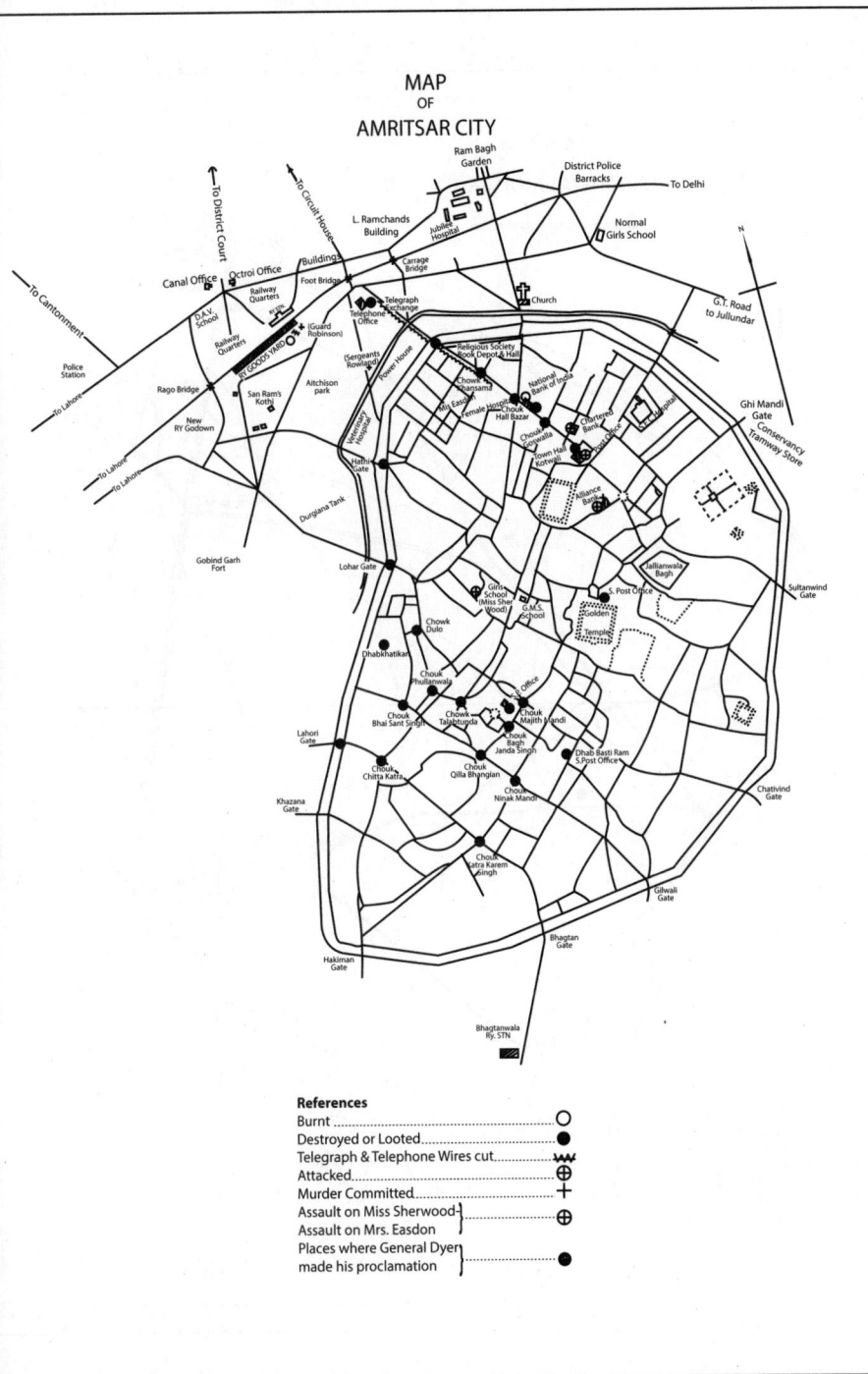

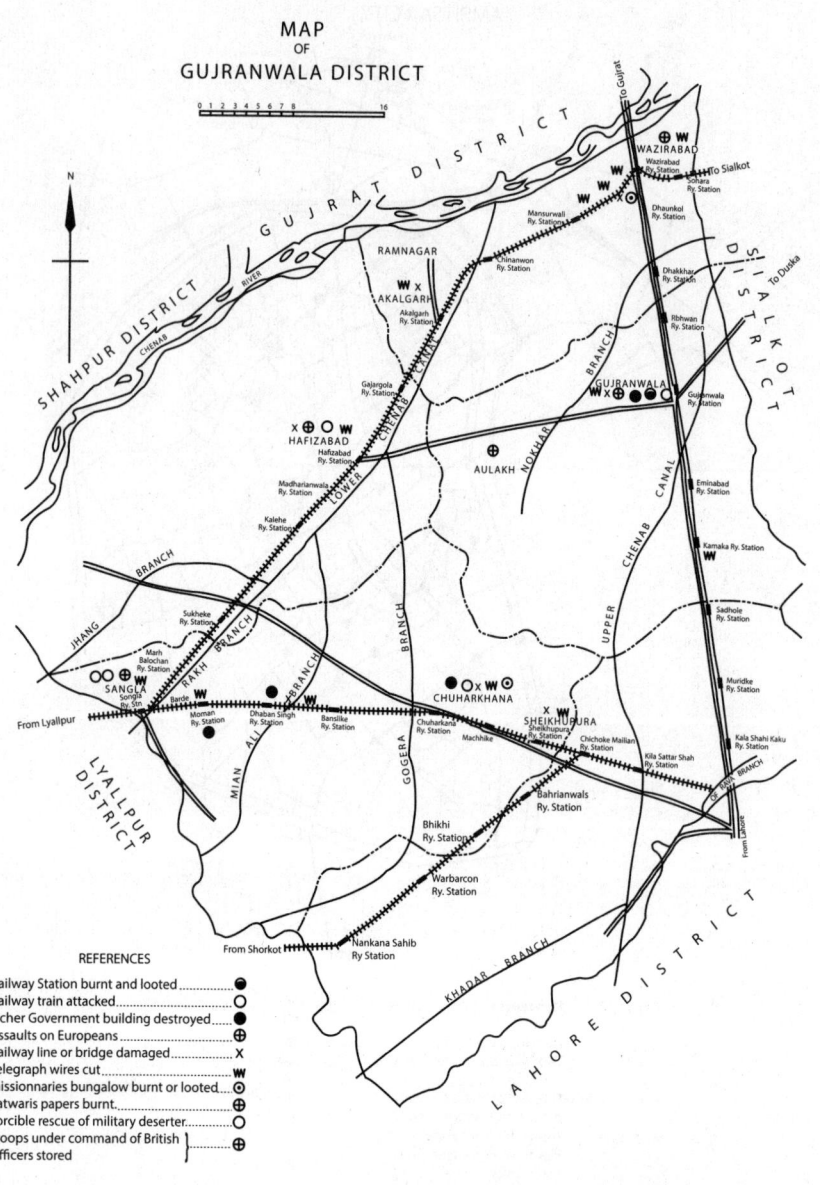

MAP
OF
GUJRANWALA
CITY AND CIVIL LINES

Report of the Committee appointed by The Government of India to investigate the disturbances in the Punjab, etc., presented to Parliament by Command of His Majesty (Published by His Majesty's Stationery Office, 1920)

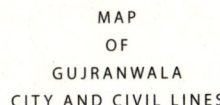

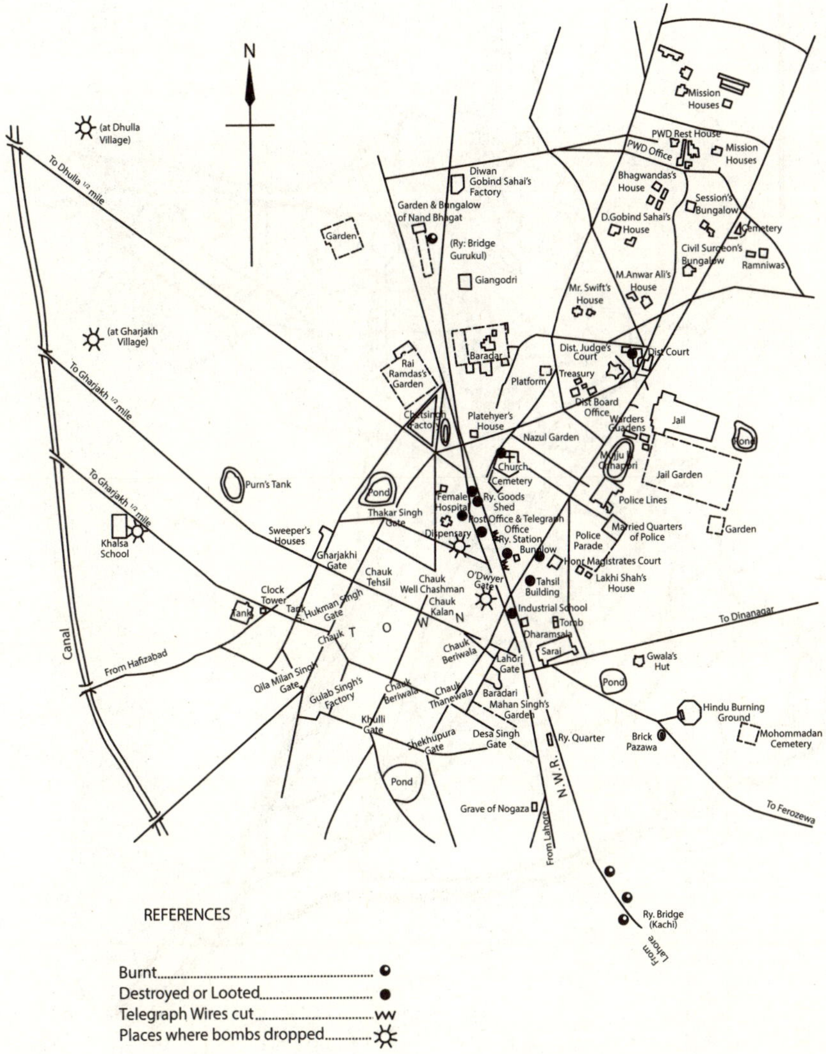

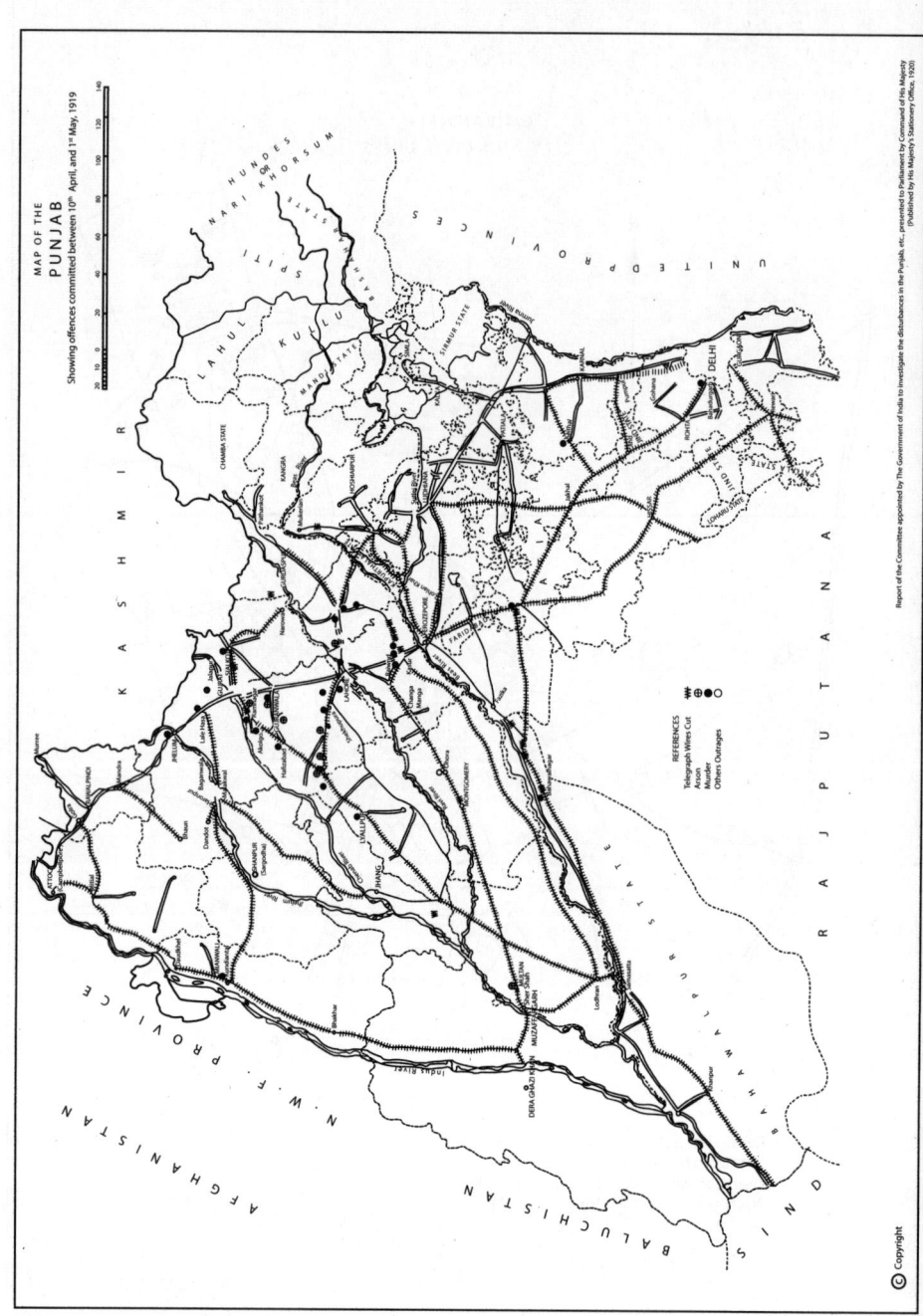

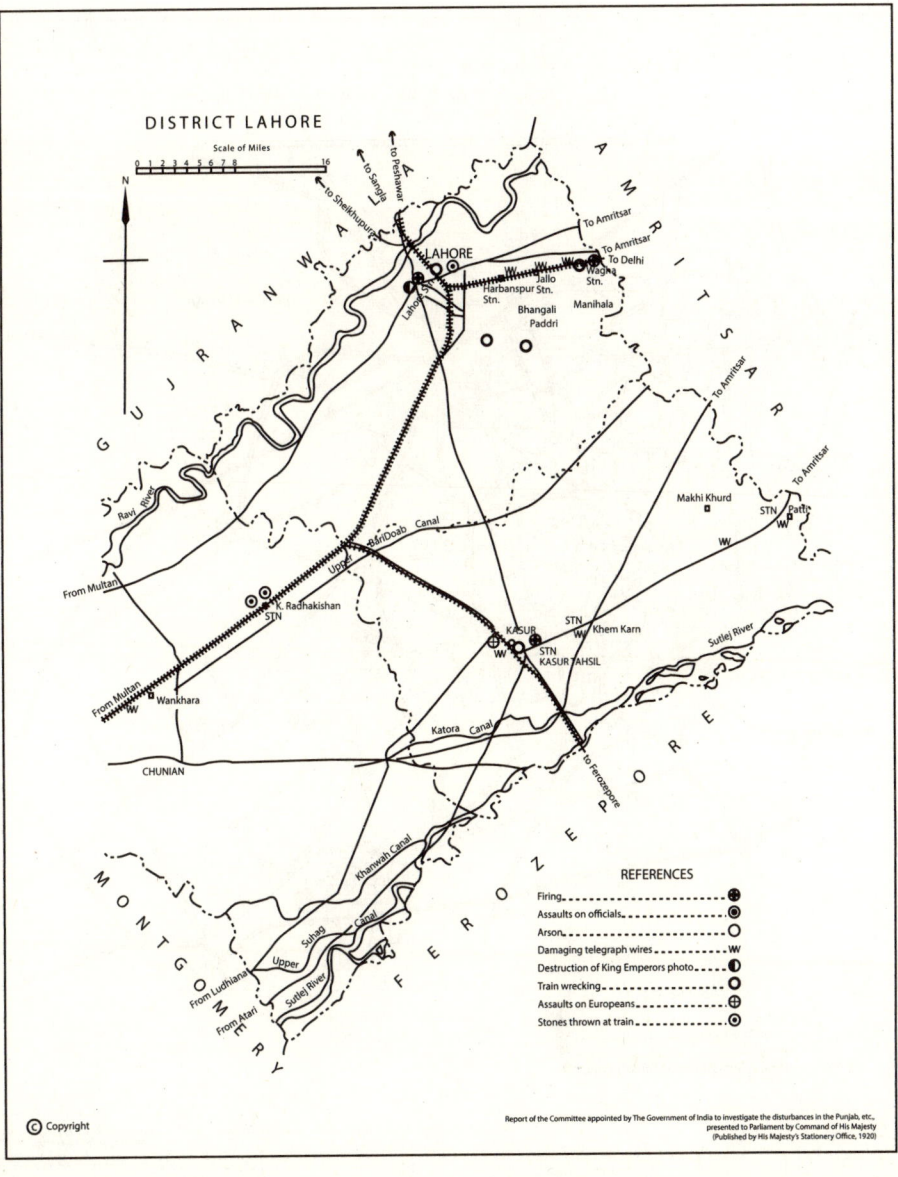

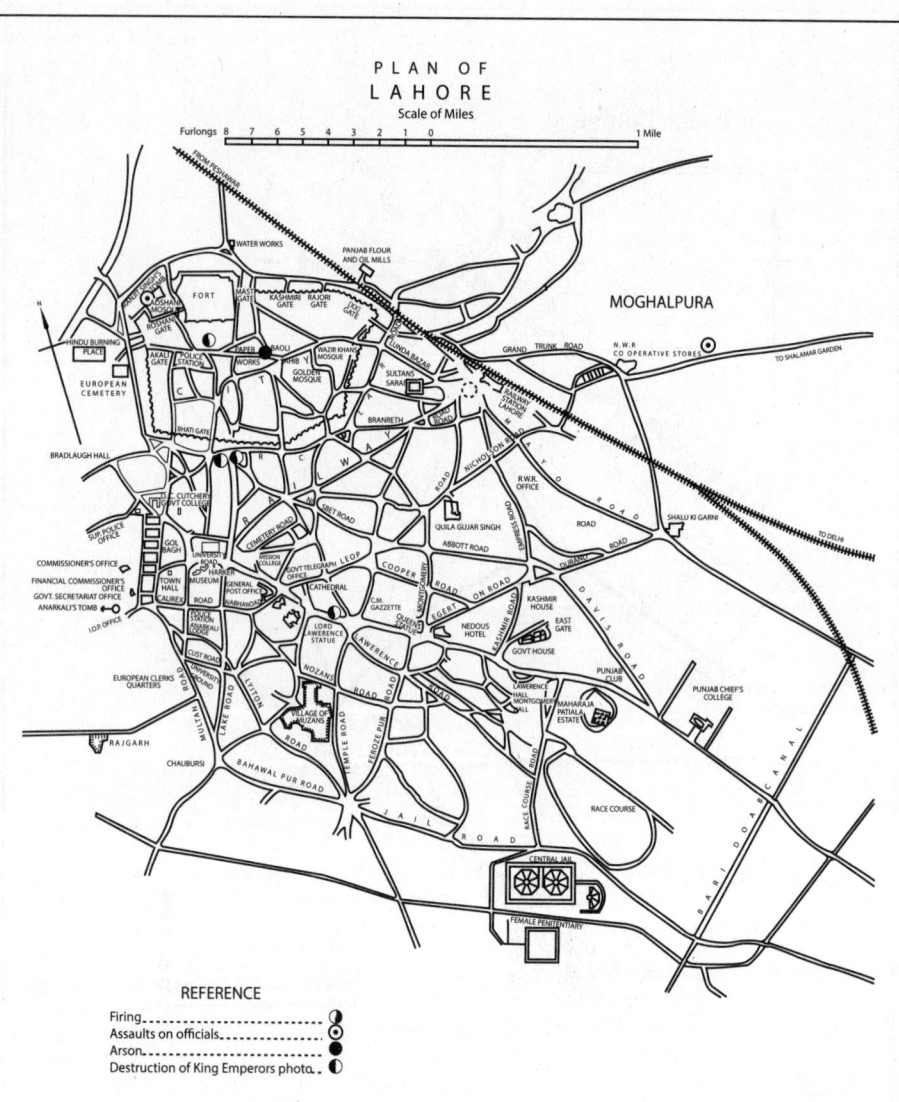

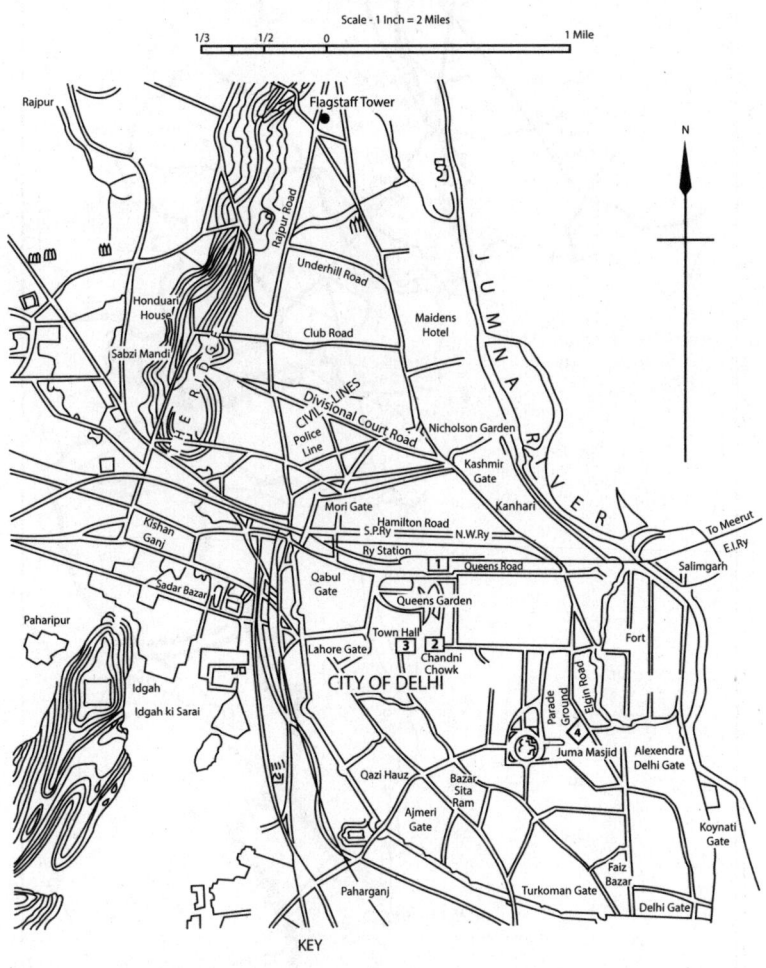

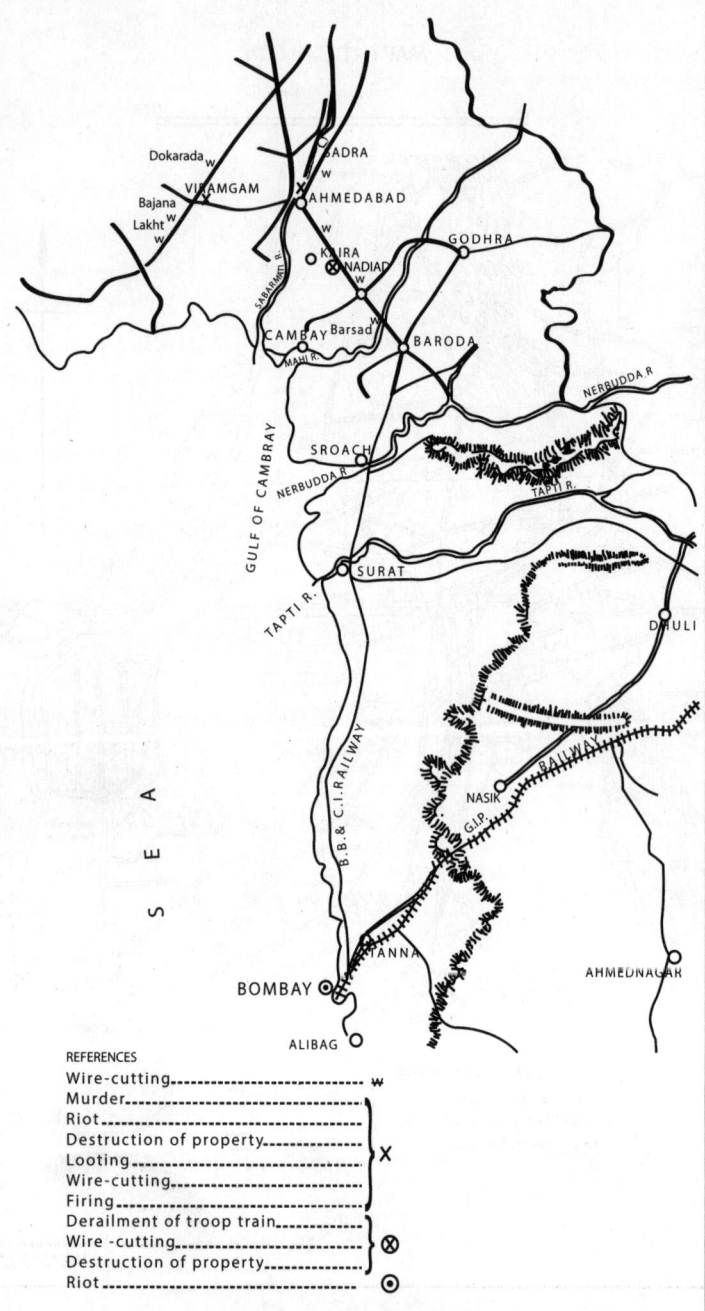

MAP OF
AHMEDABAD CITY

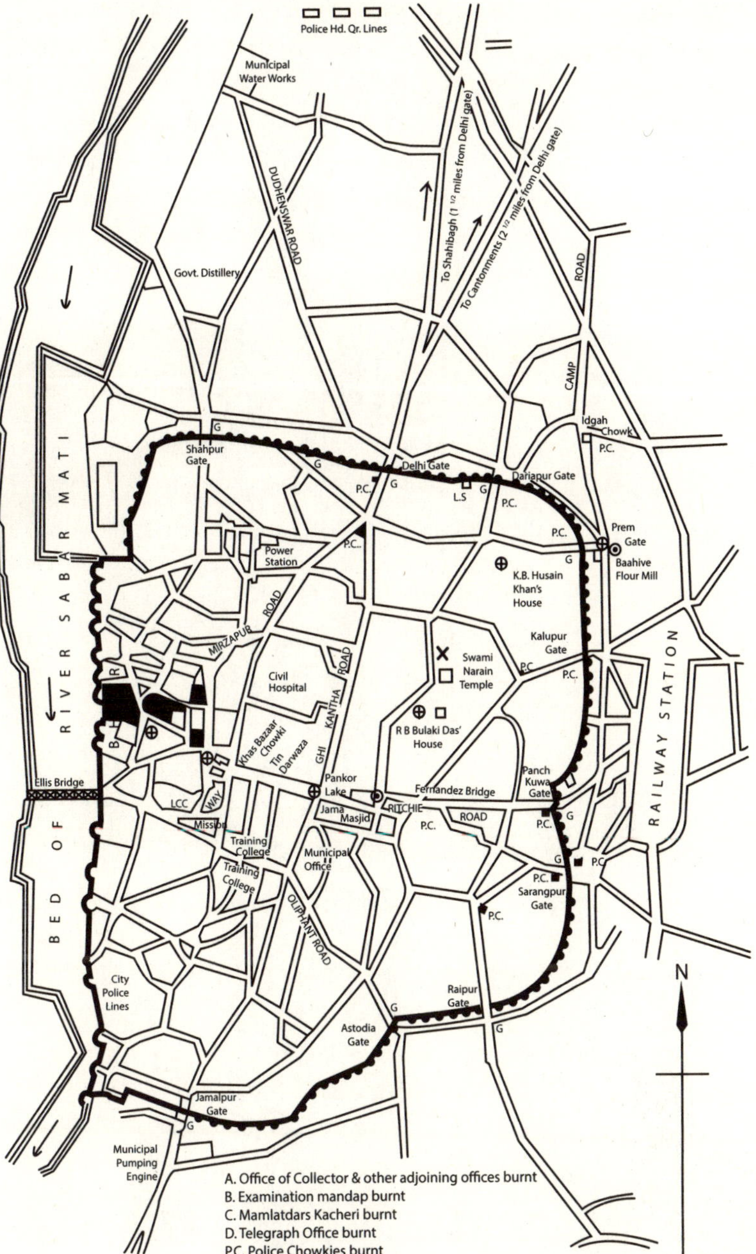

A. Office of Collector & other adjoining offices burnt
B. Examination mandap burnt
C. Mamlatdars Kacheri burnt
D. Telegraph Office burnt
P.C. Police Chowkies burnt
G. City Gates Chowkies burnt
L.S. Liquor Shops Chowkies burnt

Destruction and loot of property....... ⊕
Loot of Arms.. ✕
Murder of Sergeant Fraser.................. ●
Murder of a Police Constable............. ◉

Report of the Committee appointed by The Government of India to investigate the disturbances in the Punjab, etc., presented to Parliament by Command of His Majesty
(Published by His Majesty's Stationery Office, 1920)

Acknowledgements

My heartfelt gratitude towards the young and very hardworking team of the Partition Museum at Town Hall, Amritsar, especially Mallika Ahluwalia, Ganeev Dhillon, Tara Sami Dutt, Shivani Gandhi, and most especially Saudip Ray, who helped me with the research, as the story turned out to be much bigger than we had thought. The idea emerged when I stumbled upon some photographs which were dated '1919', while we were setting up the museum. The research led further and further, till the book got written. Meghnad Desai, loving, long-suffering and supportive as always, helped me access books and material, and I thank him for being my first reader. I also thank the UK Parliamentary Library and Archives for helping me access hundred-year-old Parliamentary debates and records.

I thank my publisher, Karthika V.K., for taking on this book on the strength of a proposal. I especially want to thank my parents, Padam and Rajini Rosha, for their patience: I have been physically present, but my mind has been completely preoccupied with the writing. I also thank my son Gaurav Ahluwalia and daughter-in-law Priyanka Kandula for bearing with my long and sudden silences.

I would also like to thank Radhika Mukherjee for her careful editing, as well as Shrutika Mathur, Janani Ganesan and Shweta Bhagat for their support and suggestions.

This has not been an easy book to write for many reasons, but it is one that completely absorbed me, and continues to do so because of those long-gone victims and survivors whose memories make up this book. I thank them for the enormous sacrifices they made in the belief that there would be a better tomorrow.

About the Author

Kishwar Desai is an award-winning author and playwright who writes both fiction and non-fiction. She worked in television as an anchor and producer for over twenty years before becoming a writer. She is the chairperson of The Arts and Cultural Heritage Trust that set up the world's first Partition Museum at Town Hall, Amritsar. She also helped to install the statue of Mahatma Gandhi outside Westminster in the UK.

Kishwar is the author of *Darlingji: The True Love Story of Nargis and Sunil Dutt* (2007). Her novel *Witness the Night* won the Costa First Novel Award in the UK, in 2010, and was followed by two others: *Origins of Love* (2012) and *Sea of Innocence* (2013). The trilogy featuring Simran Singh has since been optioned for a web series.

Kishwar's first work of political non-fiction, *Jallianwala Bagh, 1919: The Real Story* (2018), won critical acclaim and inspired exhibitions on the massacre in India, the UK and New Zealand. She also wrote a play, *Manto!*, which won the TAG Omega award for Best Play in 1999. Most recently, in 2019, her play, *Devika Rani: Goddess of the Silver Screen*, was successfully staged in venues across India.

30 Years *of*
HarperCollins *Publishers* India

At HarperCollins, we believe in telling the best stories and finding the widest possible readership for our books in every format possible. We started publishing 30 years ago; a great deal has changed since then, but what has remained constant is the passion with which our authors write their books, the love with which readers receive them, and the sheer joy and excitement that we as publishers feel in being a part of the publishing process.

Over the years, we've had the pleasure of publishing some of the finest writing from the subcontinent and around the world, and some of the biggest bestsellers in India's publishing history. Our books and authors have won a phenomenal range of awards, and we ourselves have been named Publisher of the Year the greatest number of times. But nothing has meant more to us than the fact that millions of people have read the books we published, and somewhere, a book of ours might have made a difference.

As we step into our fourth decade, we go back to that one word – a word which has been a driving force for us all these years.

Read.